Postscripts

Postscripts

Caribbean Perspectives on the British
Canon from Shakespeare to Dickens

Edited by

GISELLE RAMPAUL

and

BARBARA LALLA

THE UNIVERSITY OF THE WEST INDIES PRESS

Jamaica • Barbados • Trinidad and Tobago

The University of the West Indies Press
7A Gibraltar Hall Road, Mona
Kingston 7, Jamaica
www.uwipress.com

© 2014 by Giselle Rampaul and Barbara Lalla

All rights reserved. Published 2014

A catalogue record of this book is available from the National Library of Jamaica.

ISBN: 978-976-640-462-8 (print)
978-976-640-470-3 (Kindle)
978-976-640-478-9 (ePub)

Book and cover design by Robert Harris.
Set in Scala 10.2/14 x 27
Printed in the United States of America.

CONTENTS

INTRODUCTION
Caribbean Postscripting of the British Canon / 1
GISELLE RAMPAUL AND BARBARA LALLA

1. Dickens and Others: Metastance and Re-membering / 8
   BARBARA LALLA

2. "How Blest Am I . . . !": Colonial Desire in Selected Poetry by John Donne / 27
   GISELLE RAMPAUL

3. Recovering Nation, Recovering Woman: Shakespeare's Cressida and the Imperial Attic / 43
   GENEVIEVE RUTH PHAGOO

4. Far-off Places and the Invention of Englishness: Rereading *Robinson Crusoe* as Romance / 79
   RHONDA KAREEN HARRISON

5. Froude, Kingsley and Trollope: Wandering Eyes in a Trinidadian Landscape / 98
   JAK PEAKE

6. A Study of the Imperial Gaze: Jenkins's *Lutchmee and Dilloo: A Study of West Indian Life* / 124
   J. VIJAY MAHARAJ

7. Strange Creatures and Fantastic Worlds: The Other in Selected Nineteenth-Century Children's Texts / 154
   GISELLE RAMPAUL

   Contributors / 187

Introduction

CARIBBEAN POSTSCRIPTING OF THE BRITISH CANON

GISELLE RAMPAUL and BARBARA LALLA

> Part of mature Caribbean discourse must be the application of Caribbean experience to demystification and re-historicizing of imperial tradition and the consequent reconfiguration of Other canons. . . . The invention of a history for the colonized was a complementary (and, indeed, tributary) construction to the expansion of the colonizer's history. These constructs of our mutual pasts are interpenetrating, designed to both entrench and ratify the colonizer's own legitimacy. . . . The other side of rewriting our pasts is interrogating the colonizer's constructions of its own past, of its self-development as legitimately dominant and intrinsically designed to rule. Unravelling whatever alternative histories may underlie imperial discourse is a Caribbean imperative.[1]

WHILE IT IS ESSENTIAL TO APPROACH a literature within its own social, historical and cultural context, and to appreciate the insider's view available to critics from the same milieu, it is equally important to transcend whatever confinement of vision may attend such criticism and to apply other relevant lenses. In the same way, while it is natural and right to develop Caribbean criticism first in relation to the works of Caribbean artists, it would be both arrogant and impractical to reject scholarly interest from critics outside of the region. Similarly, for Caribbean criticism to fail in developing its own approach to other canons would amount to arrested development in one dimension of academic growth. The central thrust of this collection of Caribbean postscripts is to establish a Caribbean perspective as a crucial viewing position for Caribbean engagement with seventeenth- to nineteenth-century British canonical literary texts.

Caribbean re-visioning of British literature is well established in creative works where it expresses itself in rewriting and writing back. Further, Caribbean criticism – and, more generally, postcolonialism – has included rereadings of those imperial texts (like Shakespeare's *The Tempest*) that seem immediately applicable to the Caribbean situation. For the most part, however, critique of the British canon has been treated as irrelevant to Caribbean literary theory. There is already significant interest in implications of such works as *Jane Eyre* and *Mansfield Park* for the Caribbean, but a Caribbean approach to a range of works in the British canon is yet to be produced. Although British literature, from the medieval to the postmodern, has been the training ground of Caribbean authors, poets and critics, little has been done to integrate Caribbean approaches to British literature or any other canon into the body of Caribbean letters. At secondary and tertiary levels throughout the Caribbean, and in a wide range of countries that share our history of colonialism, the British canon continues to be taught along with a widening range of other literatures – often without reference to the viewing position of teachers and students from our own region.

And yet, according to Elleke Boehmer, "Colonial writing is important for revealing the ways in which that world system could represent the degradation of other human beings as natural, an innate part of their degenerate or barbarian state."[2] Rereading the canon from the perspective of the Caribbean is a necessary and important critical position because, as Roderick McGillis argues, "The postcolonial critic . . . has a responsibility to read works of literature for their stated and unstated assumptions about the other. To put this another way, the activity of the postcolonial critic is political."[3] Indeed, canon formation itself is also political as it is "inextricably entangled with the processes of identity formation", in the words of Michael Gluzman, and is consequently based on cultural inclusion and exclusion. Literary culture functions "as site and as tool . . . in the production of national identity by removing antithetical, oppositional voices".[4] Canonicity, therefore, not only involves self-definition, but also the definition of that which is Other to the Self. Gluzman also points out that the word *kanon*, in Greek Classical culture, referred to a measure of worth; in relation to Christian scripture, it referred to a list of texts embodying truth.[5] Furthermore, canon formation also depends on the availability of texts.[6] British canonical texts were, therefore, considered worthy of this status not so much because of their aesthetic value but, rather, because they were also widely available texts that perpetuated the "fact" of superior British culture and civilization.

The Caribbean postscript re-examines these texts that have been held up as representative of British cultural ideals to reveal their political underpinnings, their role in the imperial project and their impact on constructions of the Caribbean and other colonized places. Such a perspective is necessarily counterhegemonic. According to McGillis, the postcolonial critic "can bring a postcolonial perspective to works that themselves are not postcolonial. In other words, postcolonialism provides the opportunity for revisionary readings of canonical texts."[7] The Caribbean critic is indeed not only well-placed to unmask hypertexts of the imperial canon, but also to trace crucial operations of intertextuality in the development of that canon. As Tobias Döring argues, "By means of comparison and contrast, the familiar genres and texts can be seen to interact in new and unexpected ways. . . . Dominant discourses may . . . be seen to be connected to the other narratives against which they define themselves."[8]

Having experienced similar challenges in nation-building and identity formation, the Caribbean critic can understand and engage with the issues at the heart of British canonicity and attempts to define Britishness. The chapters in this collection examine epistemological and ontological issues related to nationhood, self-definition, freedom and confinement, and engagements with the Other – the very issues with which the Caribbean had to deal in the colonial and postcolonial eras, and in ongoing constructs and interpretations of nationhood. Rereading the British canon from a Caribbean perspective, these chapters reveal the complex insecurities and challenges associated with developing nations, with identity formation and with a background of colonization.

Barbara Lalla's chapter, "Dickens and Others: Metastance and Remembering", which opens this collection of essays, theorizes the Caribbean postscript on the British canon and argues for its importance in Caribbean criticism. Because early European writing was invested in constructing the Caribbean in certain ways even as it was attempting to articulate and consolidate its own sense of national identity, it is important to interrogate these discursive representations that came to be sacralized in the British canon. At the same time, Lalla argues that the Caribbean postscript is also instructive as it reveals useful similarities between a nation in the throes of self-definition and the Caribbean region. The physical and psychological isolation or strandedness of these texts' central characters who exist on the margins of society or who are at the mercy of power structures and discourses against which they react, the commerce in human flesh, the island sensibility, an ingrained sense of inferiority and taint are all familiar situations to the Caribbean. Adopting the concept of metastance that takes an alternative perspective, Lalla shows how literary texts by writers like Shakespeare, Austen, Brontë and Dickens can be viewed from another angle.

In chapter 2, " 'How Blest Am I . . . !': Colonial Desire in Selected Poetry by John Donne", Giselle Rampaul takes the cue from Lalla's definition of the Caribbean postscript to turn a critical and enquiring eye on canonical representations of the colonized land in seventeenth-century verse. By inverting the usual metaphor of colonized land as woman's body and exploring what it means to feminize colonized places, she uncovers the cultural anxieties that lie at the heart of the colonial project. Comparing Donne's poems "Elegy 19" and "Holy Sonnet 14" with the writings of his contemporaries about the Caribbean – especially Sir Walter Raleigh's description of Guiana – Rampaul argues that this very insecurity and anxiety were not only responsible for canonical representations of colonized places like the Caribbean, but also for the construction of British masculine identity and superiority. Writing about the Caribbean, therefore, reveals the ways in which the British also imagined themselves and exposes the complicated dynamics of power at work in the colonization process.

In chapter 3, "Recovering Nation, Recovering Woman: Shakespeare's Cressida and the Imperial Attic", Genevieve Ruth Phagoo takes a different approach to the analysis of the British canon from a Caribbean perspective by using a Caribbean text, *Wide Sargasso Sea*, through which to reread Shakespeare's seventeenth-century play *Troilus and Cressida*. Phagoo compares Renaissance England with the Caribbean by arguing that Shakespeare's England was a space in the process of forming its national identity and dealing with the challenges of defining a cultural consciousness. In this chapter, the juxtaposition and comparison of these two female characters and their contexts becomes a useful way of understanding Renaissance England. Phagoo argues that a comparison with Rhys's Antoinette reveals the complexity of Shakespeare's Cressida as a doubly marginalized subject, as both writers attempt to revision canonical meta-texts and to uncover the aftereffects of colonization on the bodies of their female characters. The reconsideration of the dominant discourses responsible for the cultural indoctrination of a developing nation – particularly in the representation of the "Other" woman – shows how the writer negotiates with anxieties associated with the cultural collision arising from colonial encounters.

Chapter 4, "Far-off Places and the Invention of Englishness: Rereading Defoe's *Robinson Crusoe* as Romance" by Rhonda Kareen Harrison, examines the first English novel's establishment of national identity. Harrison explores the ways in which the romance genre influenced Defoe's novel and contributed to the construction of Englishness in the eighteenth century, showing how encounters with Otherness perpetuated and consolidated ideas about what it meant to be English. Significantly, the setting of the first English novel is the Caribbean, which came to be defined in contrast to Britain, with its associations of cultural superiority. However, the Caribbean also came to absorb some of the themes of the romance, such as treasure, adventure and quest, as well as some of the ideological aspects, such as utopia and identity. An early construction of the Caribbean based on realism and fantasy was, therefore, important to national myth-making. By examining the placement of the English Crusoe in a situation outside of England, Harrison shows how Defoe is able to construct and impose a sense of Englishness on the Caribbean landscape and peoples (in the figure of Friday) through the creation of a utopia. The Caribbean, featured in many early colonial writings, was therefore important to reinvigorating national consciousness and indispensable to the fabrication of English nationhood and identity.

In chapter 5, "Froude, Kingsley and Trollope: Wandering Eyes in a Trinidadian Landscape", Jak Peake investigates how envisioning the Trinidadian landscape was crucial to Froude's, Kingsley's and Trollope's travel writing in the latter half of the nineteenth century. In each case, their accounts of travels on and around the island reveal a dual purpose: to present the island to the naked "eye" or "I" of the European, and ultimately British, subject; and, furthermore, to aid the imperialist project throughout the British West Indies. Peake's discussion delineates how the picturesque, art, nature, utility, gardening, landscapes and, indeed, *landscaping* were closely bound up with particular ways of *seeing* and *knowing*. In considering how the picturesque was a strategic device deployed by all three writers, Peake highlights the fallacy of the innocent "eye/I" in the Trinidadian landscape. The point at which the observer turns actor – and how this affects the narration – is a key to understanding how the sensual and experiential were vital to these Victorian travelogues on Trinidad. In using particular visual and sensual experiences, each writer sought to reclaim the heroic for the Victorian era and to revitalize an island in which the futures of residents hung in the balance.

Addressing the issue of selectivity in the British canon in chapter 6, "A Study of the Imperial Gaze: Jenkins's *Lutchmee and Dilloo*", J. Vijay Maharaj examines a neglected text written by John Edwards Jenkins, who was involved in the abolitionist movement in the Caribbean. By placing the text within the framework of the Warwick project to expand the Caribbean canon, which results, unwittingly, in expanding the British canon as well, Maharaj draws attention to the importance of scrutinizing the imperial gaze cast on indentured labourers in the Caribbean. Because this group was largely underrepresented in literary texts before the mid-twentieth century, Jenkins's text provides crucial information about how coolies were represented in British texts during the indentureship period and helps to contextualize contemporary attitudes to and by descendants of this group. Maharaj takes the cue from, but also interrogates, Amar Wahab's frame of West Indian Orientalism to uncover the contradictory and essentializing ways in which Indians and Indian indentured labourers were constructed by the imperial gaze.

The final chapter of the collection, chapter 7, "Strange Creatures and Fantastic Worlds: The Other in Selected Nineteenth-Century Children's Texts" by Giselle Rampaul, turns the critical gaze on the "Golden Age" of British children's literature. Beginning with *Robinson Crusoe*'s crossover from adult to children's literature, and its influence on subsequent canonical children's books, Rampaul shows how Defoe's representation of the Caribbean and its native inhabitants constructed and perpetuated ideas about the Other and furthered the colonial imperative by establishing a fantasy of the Caribbean. This chapter also traces the evolution of the primitivist fantasy of colonized people as *tabulae rasae*, as noble savages and as "child-like" beings, and examines the ways in which this affected construction of black characters in nineteenth-century children's literary texts. Canonical books like *Treasure Island, Peter Pan or The Boy Who Would Not Grow Up* and *Alice in Wonderland*, read by millions of British and non-British children, were not culturally or politically innocent. Therefore, Rampaul argues that it is important to read their settings and characters in the context of colonization, and to recognize their potential for spreading ideas about British superiority.

This collection of essays thus re-examines British canonical texts to reveal their underlying (often erroneous) assumptions about, and constructions of, spaces like the Caribbean that were used to justify British political and cultural domination and to consolidate and validate British national identity. By offering Caribbean rereadings of these texts that were produced and disseminated at the height of British imperialism, these essays offer scholars new critical perspectives on the process and meaning of canon formation, and on early representations of the Caribbean in the British literary tradition.

NOTES

1. Barbara Lalla, *Postcolonialisms: Caribbean Rereading of Medieval English Discourse* (Kingston: University of the West Indies Press, 2008), 33.
2. Elleke Boehmer, *Colonial and Postcolonial Literature* (New York: Oxford University Press, 1995), 21.
3. Roderick McGillis, introduction to *Voices of the Other: Children's Literature and the Postcolonial Context* (New York: Routledge, 2000), xxvii, xxviii.
4. Michael Gluzman, *The Politics of Canonicity: Lines of Resistance in Modernist Hebrew Poetry* (Stanford: Stanford University Press, 2003), 1.
5. Ibid., 2.
6. Nick Turner, *Post-War British Women Novelists and the Canon* (London: Continuum, 2010), 16.
7. McGillis, introduction, xxvii, xxviii.
8. Tobias Döring, *Caribbean-English Passages: Intertextuality in a Postcolonial Tradition* (London: Routledge, 2002), 13.

Chapter 1

DICKENS AND OTHERS
Metastance and Re-membering

BARBARA LALLA

IN FABRICATING DISTANT LANDS AND INSCRIBING histories, European writing early built on accounts and perceptions that entrenched the value systems of its own societies, thus legitimizing and perpetuating inequitable distributions of power. This essay theorizes the Caribbean postscript on the British canon as a crucial dimension of Caribbean criticism. In re-appraising treatments of the Caribbean (or similar sites) in British texts, the chapter applies a lens peculiarly sensitive to multiplicity, ambivalence, contradiction and diversity, but it also interprets canonical texts on the basis of Caribbean values that have regional, national and transnational dimensions. To facilitate such postscripting, this study proposes metastance for refocusing on well-known texts of the British canon; in so doing, it adopts a perspectival adjustment that enables us to opt out of fixed ways of viewing so as to see the familiar from anOther angle.

A crucial concern of writers in our plural pasts was the making of that Atlantic space that we have inhabited and journeyed beyond. Our memories are ineluctably entangled with the colonizers' projects even as we re-member ourselves in our own terms. Even in theorizing a Caribbean discourse we must extend it to a critical discourse that takes note (in British canonical literature) of the dystopic island, castle or manor; that throws our own light on orphanage, imprisonment, inequity, homelessness and exploitation. We need to assess the significance of these in contexts that included awareness of the West Indies, contexts in which the canon was evolving in what was or had been itself a developing nation.

In according special significance to cultural collision, displacement and forced resettlement, what I term a *postscript* brings new sensitivity to canonical works that explore unfamiliar landscape, location between worlds and stifling or unfree circumstances. In particular, postscripting focuses on convergence and interface of routes, on reformulations by writers in the still-evolving British canon that take account of ambivalence and slippage between cultures and of transgression or at least testing of borders. Thus, for example, I have found it enlightening to reread English medieval literary discourse through the lens of a Caribbean sensibility, in terms of colonizing force leading to culture collision (Germanic, Celtic, Latin, French); hyphenated existences (such as Anglo-Norman French); seizure of power and property, and remapping; marginalization of the disempowered; rewriting of history to legitimize the rule of the colonizer; psychic fracture; and the linguistic consequences of contact between governing and submerged languages.[1] Thus, in early English verse, I have traced areas of postcolonial resistance through physical struggle; evolution of a contact language and a multilingual/multivocal discourse situation, with the rise of a vernacular literature; operation of an oral-scribal continuum; counter-discourse and rewriting; and the development of such themes as dislocation, otherness, journey, inequity, liberation struggle, exile, identity and nationhood.

The Caribbean postscript looks back at matters long regarded as already settled, at material now regarded as privileged beyond question, so as to detect and inscribe something more and, probably, something other than established readings. Caribbean rereading applies a view from the periphery of the British canon, for scrutinizing ideological positions that maintain reverential attitudes to text. In so doing, the postscript relates to the canonical text through an unavoidable reorientation in the spatial and temporal relationships between these texts and their rereadings, so that *direction* and *distance* themselves are interrogated.

DIRECTION AND DISTANCE

In the analysis of postcolonial discourse, much is yet to be done on how the positioning of a postcolonial consciousness may be encoded. This essay, however, considers how the positioning (or, I would say, posture) of a *reader's* postcolonial consciousness enables alternative decodings of privileged texts from the colonizer's canon.

Narratologists have long described point of view, or perspective, in terms of the angle of viewing from which a narrator regards the events recounted and situations described. Narrative theory distinguishes perceptual from conceptual point of view, distinguishes spatio-temporal from psychological and ideological points of view. Quite apart from the angle of viewing, however, narrators establish distances (small or great) between them and their subjects. The position of the narrator in relation to the narrated not only depends on direction or angle of viewing but on distance.[2]

In nineteenth-century fiction in the British canon, such as that of Charles Dickens, reference to the West Indies often serves as a mechanism for establishing distance between persons and situations narrated. I choose Dickens here not in spite of, but because of, his lack of direct experience of the colonies, as opposed to, for example, Rudyard Kipling. Dickens's reactions (misguided or not) are not worked out on the basis of experience so much as loosely acquired, and expressed at times in explosive reactions to specific incidents such as the Indian Mutiny. In this sense, I suspect that Dickens better reflects general home-bred perceptions, but, more to the point, he draws on the West Indies not as a topic but, rather, as a narrative device.

In *Oliver Twist*, the West Indies is the place to which Mr Brownlow (whom Oliver depends on seeing again) has unaccountably departed, and the separation comes as a crushing blow to Oliver. In chapter 32, the West Indies provides a means of separating Oliver from stability and security with the man who turns out to be his one link to his father. The following brief extract demonstrates how this gulf is implicated through identifiable elements of the discourse: "She presently returned, and said that Mr. Brownlow had sold off his goods, and gone to the West Indies six weeks before. Oliver clasped his hands."[3]

- *returned* – The informant had to actually absent herself in order to find information about this departure.
- *sold off* – Dislocation is not only spatial but social, a financial uprooting and a severing from the familiar.
- *gone* – Distancing in time as well as in space, reinforced by *six weeks before*, and the separation between Brownlow and those who knew of him is increased by the circumstance of the departure itself having been unknown. He has been swallowed up in an information void.
- *clasped his hands* – The departure destabilizes others, has emotional, almost spiritual dimensions.

This example, little more than one sentence in length, demonstrates how the West Indies is referenced in canonical British fiction through distal elements.

How, then, does the Caribbean reader treat with these texts? A Caribbean postscript requires us to transcend the spatial orientation of others, to adopt a posture independent of them – a posture I associate with *metastance*.

In defining *metastance*, James P. Driscoll's 1980s application of the term to Prospero's position in *The Tempest* is a useful place to begin: "Prospero speaks from the metastance of one who has transcended both tragedy and its denial to attain a vision of wholeness."[4] In reviewing Driscoll's approach, John T. Shawcross underscores that "metastance is the vantage a character gains as he or she steps back to observe the self and its initial stances. It distances while maintaining a range of validity for the stance observed."[5]

Writing in nineteenth-century British literature reveals a stance on the West Indies from which the term itself, *West Indies*, could be employed to connote distance, and this equating of the West Indies with the ends of the earth is a cognitive process that West Indians may wish to interrogate. Metastance involves a relational orientation to human engagement that is not physically or conceptually fixed. So it is a term we can also use for a situation that unlocks the viewer from rigid attachment to an inflexible identity, that enables the viewer to see identity in a wider context; it facilitates transcendence. The definitional issue is one to which this discussion will return again and again precisely because this first chapter seeks to articulate frames of thought and conceptual positions for Caribbean rereading of canonical works. To start with, it may be enough to suggest that metastance allows the viewer to embrace conceptual and attitudinal choices instead of remaining bound by choiceless adherence to convention. It is in view of this refusal of fixity that it perhaps constitutes not so much a position as a posture.

Returning to *The Tempest*, we might note that Prospero's posture is overviewed by Shakespeare, Shakespeare's by his rewriters in such works as Elizabeth Nunez's *Prospero's Daughter*, and the rewriters' by rereaders who critique these intertextually related works.[6] I would, therefore, also characterize metastance as a stance for regarding stances – both those stances traditionally entrenched and those stances that may have been taken up in resistance and become politically correct. Moreover, metastance adopted in Caribbean rereading must accommodate contending views, must eschew inertia and monolithic positioning, and accommodate incompatibility and accept paradox. Adopting a metastance for rereading European literature such as the British canon therefore requires a renegotiation of spatio-temporal orientation as we adopt a somewhat complex we-perspective.

So who is *we*? In postscripting the canon *we* may be not only a plural voice but a widely inclusive one.

REREADING

Readers operate through anticipation, through prediction based on connections in the text, and Noel Carroll points out that where these are not as expected there may be a sense of indeterminacy.[7] These operations of anticipation and prediction are greatly intensified in the rereader's engagement with canonical texts, because such writing is repeatedly read, and often, even before reading, known in advance through references, synopses and quotations. Such writing comes to us consecrated as *text meant to be reread, text already evaluated, text on hand for wider application,* or *text available for intertextual allusion.*

To detach oneself from the readymade position through which we meet the canonical text requires more than just an engagement in reader response, in an imparting of one's own meaning or in interpreting on the basis of personal interest and experience rather than with regard to the writer. Rereading resites content in relation to the reader's context, rather than primarily in relation to the writer's. (I do not accept that it necessarily involves rejecting the expansion of one's own experience by another's – what Chris Lang terms a privatization of meaning.)[8] Metastance, in addition, enables not just a replacement or contrast of contexts but also an interface and negotiation between contexts. This makes it possible to scrutinize the ideological positioning that underlies a reverential attitude to text.

This does not mean that metastance renders spatial and temporal dimensions irrelevant; for it requires a peripheral vision in all senses (a view from what has been the periphery, a view that refocuses periphery to centre, a view that includes the edges). It also requires a retroactive assessment in interacting with the text. José Angel García Landa notes the significance of retroactive assessment through rereading in approaching both cognitive form and cultural significance of a text: "New forms of complexity, new relationships, are continually being discovered in apparently simple or well-known texts, on which apparently everything had been told, once they are recontextualized within a new critical frame or paradigm."⁹ To assess eighteenth- and nineteenth-century British literature that equates the West Indies with the ends of the earth, the Caribbean critic may adopt a posture in relation to space and time that resists fixed orientation and interrogates both distance and direction as encoded in the text.

One way to such interrogation is the analysis of metaphor, not only in cognitive but in critical terms. In understanding one idea in terms of another idea, in organizing a concept on the basis of some human experience along the lines of cognitive linguists like George Lakoff and Mark Johnson, it is possible to connect perceptual organizations to neural mappings, to ascribe universality to the analogies at work. But if the connection between directionality and quality (for example, up is good, white is virtuous and high) is neural (versus political), some of us are in deep trouble. A Critical Discourse Analysis approach to metaphor, on the other hand, relates perceptual organizations of reality to culture and to sociocultural experience and political agendas. In enabling us to interrogate issues of power distribution installed in discourse regarding the West Indies, Critical Discourse Analysis may be employed to assist in a rereading of Dickens.¹⁰

For the West Indies is not only *physically* distant in Dickens. In *Barnaby Rudge* (1841), Edward leaves home for the West Indies, which is conceived of as more than spatially or even socially distant:

> In the mind's eye of Mr. Willet the West Indies, and indeed all foreign countries, were inhabited by savage nations, who were perpetually burying pipes of peace, flourishing tomahawks and puncturing strange patterns in their bodies. He no sooner heard this announcement, therefore, but he leaned back in his chair, took his pipe from his lips, and stared at his son with as much dismay as if he already beheld him tied to a stake, and tortured for the entertainment of a lively population.¹¹

The West Indies is distanced lexically: it is *foreign* and, being foreign, an unhomely space occupied by Others, or *inhabited*. It is *savage* and, also, backward in that it *perpetually* suggests fixity in behaviour, lack of progress or advancement in a people hopeless of improvement. The West Indies is also distanced syntactically by past tense and by a stripping of agency through passivization: *were inhabited* distinguishes the inhabitants of the West Indies by denying their agency.

The West Indies is further distanced through discursive strategies such as metaphor, which relegates the West Indies to the imaginary, and establishes it as a mental construction by decent stay-at-home British citizens; such as metonymy, which imbues it with violence through association with tomahawks and other devices (while maintaining ineffectuality through lexical selections like *flourishing*); such as simile, which makes explicit the analogy between imaginary and real; and such as oxymoron, which unites the incompatible (torture and entertainment) to infer incomprehensible behaviours and ways of thought. The conceptual operations are extremely complex because all the associations above are operating within an encompassing metaphor in which the British thinker is spectator and evaluator, before whose gaze all is played out: *mind's eye, stared, beheld, entertainment*. We must bear in mind that the placing of Mr Willet's vision in his "mind's eye" distinguishes it (at least officially) from Dickens's vision, but Dickens is not in a position to supply any alternative, corrective vision of the West Indies. Moreover, this torture for entertainment is for *a lively population*, reinforcing a semantic opposition between civilized (rational, sedentary and fixed) and uncivilized (irrational and frenetic). Selection of the West Indies as Edward's destination thus adds not only physical but social, moral and spiritual distance to the emotional distance looming between father and son.

Physical distancing to such a dangerous space is the (punitive) answer to those who fail to observe social distance in *Dombey and Son*, where the West Indies is early established as that unhealthy place where an "elder brother died of Yellow Jack".[12] A father, Dombey, offended with a young man (Gay) who has been in correspondence with Dombey's daughter, stares at Gay fiercely, sends him out of the room, then says: "You want somebody to send to the West Indies? . . . Send young Gay." When Dombey sends Gay to the West Indies to get him out of the way, Gay is stunned by a sense of loss based on perception of distance – out of sight of mentors, beyond the glance of Florence, relegated to the unfathomable: "Walter could hardly believe that he was under orders for the West Indies." Quite apart from the threat of fever and a sense of unreality, the mention of the West Indies carries with it a sense of overpowering heat: "I am frightfully faint and sensitive this morning, and you smell of the sun. You are absolutely tropical", remarks a character whose addressee reflects on experiencing the hothouse heat of the West Indies. The West Indies is distanced not only as a hostile environment associated with disease (*fever*), but as an unbelievable destination, an environment so exotic as to be unreal, almost artificial (*hothouse*).

Oppressive associations accompany even glancing references such as those in *David Copperfield*, where the West Indian connection is invoked in accounting for and describing child labour and exploitation in the seamiest circumstances. At ten years old, labouring in the service of Murdstone and Grinby, David Copperfield (in "the dirt and rottenness of the place" and amid "the squeaking and scuffling of old grey rats") affixes corks and labels on bottles of wine or spirits for trade by ships. This purpose of maritime trade is hedged by uncertainty: "I forget now where they chiefly went but I think there were some among them that made voyages both to the East and West Indies."[13]

The West and East Indies are swept together vaguely. Indeed, any unhealthy clime offers potential basis for comparison. In *Little Dorrit*, Mrs Sparkler refers to Edward's "bout" of malaria and her husband compares it to the case of "some of our other fellows in the West Indies with Yellow Jack", at which "Mrs Sparkler closed her eyes again, and refused to have any consciousness of our fellows of the West Indies, or of Yellow Jack".[14]

In a way of thought in which "they all seem the same", it becomes easy to draw analogies wildly between quite unlike circumstances. Charles Dickens and Wilkie Collins allegorize the Indian Mutiny through a narrative set on a fictional West Indian island, "The Perils of Certain English Prisoners", narrated by one of the English soldiers protecting the island from pirates. The "native Sambo" whom the English employ and who treacherously serves the pirates takes part in a murderous attack on women and children. The English subsequently kill this servant and leave him hanging, "all alone, with the sun making a kind of sunset on his black face".[15] In a more than metonymic finale, the dangers of hot lands and dark skins hang together – Dickens's statement on the Indian Mutiny.

It is obvious enough that a Caribbean postscript on such writing relocates the text in a new framework for evaluation, and that metastance constitutes a viable posture for postscripting. At the same time, I would argue that metastance also enables some degree of independence not only from imperial frameworks of evaluation but (to some extent) from postcolonial frameworks as well.

UNFIXING CARIBBEANNESS

In a sense, Caribbean political correctness responds to British canonical distancing of the West Indies with a shrug, a reciprocal distancing of the canonical European text, for example by rejection or by replacement through rewriting. I would argue that Caribbean criticism must reread Europe not merely to lay bare European constructions of the West Indies but to re-view European self-constructions. Approaching the British canonical text requires engagement with other elements of discourse besides the distal.

Cultural Studies treats proximity as a political force through which some speakers may distance others or through which readers may reduce this distance through textual analysis especially with regard to spatial organization, through which the remote can be made close and immediate. The distance between subjects can be reduced to that point where they stop repelling each other or absorbing each other and simply remain distinct – what some term "critical proximity".[16] To benefit from the astronomical overtones of the term there is interrelationship, even an attraction, a gathering and holding together, a coherence in progress but not a falling into each other – an equilibrium threshold.[17]

I suggest that a detachment is required not only from imperial but from postcolonial frameworks, because our rereading and commentary demands a balance between distance and engagement, equivalent to *critical proximity*. In the balance, for wholeness of vision, critical proximity is as crucial a requirement as detachment, for Caribbean rereading of Europe.

The potential ambiguity of the term *metastance* is perhaps useful here because of varied understandings of the prefix *meta-*. On the one hand, the term might reasonably be taken as implying a pre-established and governing position; yet, on the other, it may be understood as a position about a position or (better) a posture adopted in relation to fixed positions. In this way, the term conveys a rejection of fixity that enables angles of viewing hitherto unknown – the sense usually intended in this chapter – though with the understanding that any angle of viewing (however new or flexible) must be from some position – in this case a Caribbean locus. A Caribbean point of view, then, is not the same as a Caribbean fixation. Temporally and spatially unfixed from traditional perspectives on the colonizer's canon as this may be, the Caribbean angle of viewing is unavoidably framed by our own mindset. And why shouldn't it be – once we remain *aware* of our mindset.

While our angle of viewing is deflected from that way of seeing governed by colonially prescribed lenses (the traditional established stance), it is crucial, in approaching canonical British literature, that we ensure our vision also remains ungoverned by positions adopted in resistance to the colonial that may have hardened into political correctness. Metastance thus constitutes a flexible posture to enable multidimensional viewing.

Spatial and temporal complexity of Caribbean experience demands a conceptual location in relation to the rest of the world that is non-linear and multidimensional, and that reorients relationships from hierarchy to continuum. The metastance adopted for Caribbean postscripting embraces heterogeneity rather than homogeneity and reaffirms contradictory or negated identities. The (re)reader who assumes this posture also recognizes both hybridity, on the one hand, and, on the other, a plurality in which uncreolized cultures and ways of being may remain distinct. Not that a Creole perspective needs to confer fixity of position. Indeed, it should be expected to facilitate alternative decodings of the canon. In this context, creolization is not only a process (rather than a fixed condition) but a conditioning, discursive operation that resites home, remaps space and reinterprets time. Crichlow argues for an understanding of creolization as dislodged from a "specifically plantation fulcrum" that is bound to geography and time period and is therefore unable to "address *creolization processes*, not to mention present post-Creole imaginations".[18] In Caribbean discourse, creolization enables new and independent discourses well suited to metadiscourse (in the sense of a discourse about discourse). Creolization offers a faultline, an area of slippage in space and time where past and present interrogate each other and the colonial gaze may be reversed or met and engaged.

The texture of Caribbean experience is not smooth but woven from threads entangled in or severed from a fabric folded, multi-faceted, disintegrating at borders and disrupted by crisis. In this flexible fabric, the Caribbean is troubled by ambivalence regarding its Westernness/non-Westernness, its unhomeliness, its self-contradiction.

If Caribbean development has indeed involved "fleeing the plantation", then metastance takes us to a space distinct from plantation orientation, one in which agency is possible.[19] In this space, dialectical relationships persist and Caribbean critique *must* address inequity in these relationships, whether they invoke the Caribbean or not. The Caribbean critic is well-placed to evaluate ideological projects of generating identity (however incoherent) as crucial to community construction, as propelling nation-building beyond welfarism, as deeply involved not only in improving, de-territorializing and re-territorializing but in creating new territory.

So the unfixity achieved through metastance is not merely spatial. Just as the concept of *habitus* goes beyond spatial location to a durable system of practices, governed by schemes of perception that are entrenched but transposable, metastance enables us to operate diasporically even as, say, creolization processes enable new contours of belonging, of being enfolded in space and time and of rearticulating power relationships.[20] Creolization processes in the Caribbean have enabled metastance in destabilizing earlier accepted systems of thought regarding universalism and cultural convergence and in projecting the Caribbean as neither margin (periphery dependent on centre) nor enclave but as frontier zone.[21]

Metastance is distinct from liminality in the sense that the latter is a condition while the former may be more usefully regarded as a posture. More importantly, metastance does not actually locate itself in spatial or cultural inbetweenity but, rather, renders borders irrelevant. In rising above fixed positions rather than inhabiting the spaces in between, metastance facilitates an overarching view.

Caribbean literary discourse is imaginary in the sense that all texts are inscribed with voices from their writers' territories rather than from any overarching regional form of speech. Yet the Caribbeanness of the discourse is real to the extent that it comprises a composite and interactive discourse, polyvalent, transgressive and transnational. The transcendence enabled by metastance both facilitates and urges our rereading of English canonical discourse. However, anglophone Caribbean literary discourse remains linked with British discourse not only through the literary heritage passed to us by the colonizer but by the implications of the West Indies for British self-conceptualization. Not only is the British canon part of our baggage, but we are part of theirs – and we have arrived at that point at which we must not only define ourselves independently of British experience, and define for ourselves our experience of British intervention, but define British self-construction as influenced by our presence. Metastance enables such a relational literary history, a dual vision of creolization in which not only the colonized but the colonizer is changed. From such a posture as metastance, a sort of rogue criticism might theorize world discourse from a Caribbean way of knowing, rejecting a geography in which the Caribbean is outposted on the edge, struggling with subalternism or hemmed in by tunnel-visioned concepts of "relevance".

Caribbean artists and scholars have noted that Caribbean criticism has contributed heavily to the articulation of postcolonial theory and that such theorizing has (at least in part) operated in resistance to Caribbean literature being swallowed up in imperial European literatures.[22] Long recognized (for example, by Wilson Harris) as at the crossroads, the Caribbean not only discards romanticization of the savage, but has moved beyond replacing the icon of the savage with that of the peasant and, subsequently, that of the *rude bwai*.[23] The posture of metastance is one which detaches itself not only from stereotype but from a quarrel in which attention to traditional British texts is somehow not the concern of enlightened Caribbean scholars. Such a quarrel is not far removed from a frame of thought in which there are true West Indians – those who stayed, versus those in the diaspora. It is a quarrel built on fixity in the sense that real Caribbean intellectual inquiry is somehow defined by exclusively regional focus, a frame of thought that accepts that space for intellectual attention may be demarcated.

In other words, the critic may adopt metastance as a posture from which the Caribbean thinker can evaluate a European sense of physical, social and moral distance installed through deixis, lexical choice, metaphor or other discursive devices; or as a posture from which to reread and postscript canonical works even when they make no reference to the West Indies.

Take, for example, Dickens's curious character Tattycorum in *Little Dorrit*. Tattycorum is a young woman from a foundling hospital, who is renamed by the family who take her in to attend their daughter. She is renamed from Harriet Beadle to Hattie and then to Tatty, following which her surname is replaced by that of the philanthropic founder of the hospital, so that her identity is subsumed under his. She is continuously advised on governing her temper by her adopted father, told to count to five-and-twenty at each sign of rebellious rage. She asserts herself by running away, but throws herself into the power of a different benefactor, the mysterious Miss Wade, who is associated with a violent criminal and who apparently exploits the girl in a lesbian relationship. Within the ideology of the time, Tattycorum can only reject this life in the end. The Caribbean critic, however, is well-placed to apply postcolonial criticism to the paternalism underlying this embedded narrative of orphaning and of identity loss and construction. Drawn parallel to a picture of smothering benevolence that denies independence are views of homelessness and dislocation, of recategorization through renaming, and of silencing when the young woman voices dissatisfaction with such well-intentioned rule.

In this way, even as metastance enables defamiliarizing of the canonized text, it permits familiarization through recognition of shared attributes. Those who are not flung to the outer margins of the earth (sent to the West Indies, for example) may be locked in securely and deeply in their British setting. Not only do *Bleak House* and *Little Dorrit* present a range of those carceral experiences that haunted Dickens, but Thornfield Manor, Wuthering Heights and the Grange, Macbeth's castle and other sites of containment comprise carceral situations that madden and even demonize those *inhabitants* who diverge from mainline British English civility. From V.S. Naipaul's Hanuman House or Tiphanie Yanique's leper colony, to the prison planet of Nalo Hopkinson's *Midnight Robber*, Caribbean locations for alienation and confinement provide points for comparison with settings in British texts that have been constructed in the period of expansion and colonization.[24]

As Caribbeanness extends beyond the postcolonial, incorporating the post-Creole, and as the Caribbean reconceives itself as a frontier with a pioneering thrust, rather than as a margin, Caribbean errantry may take its own stance on European stances. In these circumstances the postscript functions not simply as an afterword, but also as a continued engagement with a script, an ongoing rereading that extends beyond interrogating an established meaning and beyond postcolonial writing back to inscribe new meaning. The postcolonial reinterpretation that I describe as *postscript* not only unmasks hypertexts of the imperial canon but reconsiders revisions of these by our own developing canon. The postscript interrogates monolithic discourse in drawing alongside traditional canonized literature our own multiple, often conflicting discourses – sometimes revealing in the past of the developing canon ambivalence or polyphony similar to our own but not immediately detectable to the metropolitan eye. Thus *Barnaby Rudge* ironically plays out its murder mystery against a background of revolution in England, even as it invokes the West Indies as socially and morally distant.

The Caribbean critic is particularly able to adopt a posture from which to read the island in estate and castle, to recognize a commerce in flesh, a mindset imposed by oppressive pedagogical practice, an ingrained sense of taint or fragmentation of self, a psyche of unfreedom, a stigma of unreason, a compulsion to transgress borders. In Shakespeare's Miranda and Austen's Fanny Price, on the one hand, and in Shakespeare's Lady Macbeth and

Brontë's Bertha, on the other, we are in a position to discern two faces of Jean Rhys's Antoinette. We may reassess writers such as Shakespeare, Austen and Brontë, who were subsequently embraced by their canon. But we should bear in mind that they were (in their own time) at least in some respects (re)writing their own island's history or interrogating their own society's values through identity constructions against or through which they not only perpetuated but negotiated or even challenged constructs of a developing English national identity.

The Caribbean critic takes note, for example, of how in Dickens's *Bleak House* the mysterious character Nemo (translated, "No One") connects the others. He is Esther's father, Lady Deadlock's lover, General George's friend, the owner of crucial letters (hoarded by Crook, negotiated for by Guppy, demanded by Tulkinghorn and written by Lady Deadlock, who dreads their exposure); he is the mystery Tulkinghorn is resolved to decipher in order to control others. How has Nemo, the well-kept secret, remained elusive, unreachable? He has been in the West Indies and (perhaps, or perhaps not) died on his return. But quite apart from this actual reference, the major events of *Bleak House* play out against themes on which Caribbean readers are sensitive: themes of orphanage, of illegitimacy, of identity loss and construction, of civilizing projects (Africa and inner-city London), of entrapment in systems and institutions (interminable court cases, grinding poverty, social strictures), of exploitation and blackmail, of abduction. Metastance facilitates such resonance. It also enables alternative decodings of the canon.

For example, Skimpole's ethereal vision of slaves in the Americas as delicate contributions to landscape and to a sense of poetry in his conceptualizing of this distant space is not merely a construction of the West Indies; Skimpole is Dickens's construction of a mind occupied in refining ways of exploiting Others. The West Indies operates here not only as a narrative strategy for conveying distance but as part of a context in which Others are contemplated, evaluated, debated. Esther, similarly romanticized by Skimpole, becomes not an orphan but a child of the universe – within a romantic sensibility that privileges the child, even as Skimpole legitimizes his irresponsibility by identifying himself as a mere child in all matters practical. His own absenteeism from his family, his exploitation of Rick and his abduction of a suffering child for his own gain are inscribed in a socio-historical context in which we share. We cannot afford to miss this complexity of Dickens's vision, the nuance alongside the stereotype.

In the same spirit, Dickens savagely goes after Romantic admiration for the noble savage, concluding as follows:

> To conclude as I began. My position is, that if we have anything to learn from the Noble Savage, it is what to avoid. His virtues are a fable; his happiness is a delusion; his nobility, nonsense. We have no greater justification for being cruel to the miserable object than for being cruel to a William Shakespeare or an Isaac Newton; but he passes away before an immeasurably better and higher power than ever ran wild in any earthly woods, and the world will be all the better when his place knows him no more.[25]

There can be no mistaking Dickens's association of the Other with all that is un-English – the immoral, the joyless, the low, the uncivil, the unknown and, set up on the other side of the equation, void, untruth, unreality, foolishness and extinction. But the same writer locates shallow toleration of slavery in the character of Skimpole, and Skimpole is Dickens's negative construction of a mind that constructs others to suit himself. For this is the same Dickens who inscribes his loathing of slavery in *American Notes* (chapter 17) and was outspoken enough on the subject to offend his hosts in America on that topic in 1842, the same Dickens whose deep concern for public health, the conditions of the poor, and exploitation of the helpless fired novel after novel.[26]

Earlier, Keats describes poetical character as having no self, as relishing both dark and bright sides of things "because they both end in speculation", and this *camelion poet*, to use Keats's term, continually invests his subjects with their own fixed identities, but "the poet has none; no identity", says Keats.[27] This *non-identity*, which Bertonèche terms *meta-identity*, combines personalities, genres, positions, facilitating ambiguity and transgression, but also "gets actively caught up in its own game", says Keats. The artist in this sense lives in a mist, possesses a *negative capability* – which Keats compares to Shakespeare's: "when a man is capable of being in uncertainties, Mysteries, doubts, without any irritable reaching after fact & reason".[28] Descriptions of how poets like Keats, Shakespeare and Sidney, through a kind of distancing, arrive at "coherence in that irrational playfulness" need not surprise anyone in the world of Caribbean letters, where the artist is often critic, sliding between levels of viewing (a shift comparable to that which narratologists call *metalepsis*). The detachment from a specific spatio-temporal, attitudinal or ideological position is not only a possible critical approach but is practised by artists of the canon even while these artists project and perpetuate entrenched traditional positions.

Choices are open to the Caribbean critic – choices of adherence to or detachment from positions. Caribbeanness is not necessarily, indeed *cannot be*, a monolithic position. The Caribbean is not simply postcolonial and post-Creole, but is engaged in an ongoing creolization process that is not static and complete but dynamic, ongoing, continually refreshed. Caribbean discourse is not only in progress but as abstract as it is concrete, as imaginary as it is real. In dreaming the Caribbean, the transformative nature of creolization involves continued entanglement of scripts and ongoing reinterpretation. Metastance engages memory and anticipation, intervenes in a given way of knowing, fills gaps from the reader's own knowledge and resists naturalization of knowledge.

Metastance enables detachment from conventional and politically correct positions, as well as proximity through which to decode European canons – on the basis of Caribbean value systems and ways of knowing, but also in spite of Caribbean grudges. Even as Dickens's references to the West Indies imply distance, metastance enables a critical proximity that draws Caribbean sensitivities alongside Dickens's concerns regarding the unparented, the imprisoned and the unhomely. Skimpole's vision constitutes a failed Romantic text, providing Dickens with a mechanism for interrogating stereotypical visions of Others. However stereotypical some of Dickens's own visions might be, he includes alongside these evidence of a deeply sensitive and nuanced critique of stereotyping – multiple, often contradictory, texts embedded in his fiction, to be discerned as we reread Dickens against the readings of traditional critics.[29] Useful applications for postscripting, for example, might include constructions of national identity and representations of the developing nation by Shakespeare; representations of exploration and the penetration of new lands through seventeenth-century erotic imagery; connections between divine right and images of ravishment in seventeenth-century religious verse; specific fictional circumstances like absentee ownership of Mansfield Park; such interrogations of incarceration and orphaning as those of Dickens; and many more.

Rereading through a dialectic of detachment and engagement, we hold and return a gaze like Jane Austen's when she raises that famous unanswered question in *Mansfield Park* regarding the West Indies and its central concerns.

"Did you not hear me ask him about the slave trade last night?" Fanny

Price refers to an exchange with her uncle, proprietor of Mansfield Park (with all his experience of the Antigua plantations), even as this deeply introspective central consciousness experiences the pale, *pale* reflection of plantation existence in Mansfield Park.[30]

The unending interception of one text by another sets up a pattern of recursive intertextuality and, in situations such as Caribbean rereading of the British canon, produces an infinite web of relationships such that the canonical text can only be read through detachment, and remains, ultimately perhaps, illegible – unresolvable. The existence of the West Indies in nineteenth-century British discourse tampered with the development of a moral framework for British fiction, a framework within which Englishness itself was defined. A productive posture for rereading facilitates engagement even with the unanswerability of some questions raised about the West Indies.

> "Did you not hear me ask him about the slave trade last night?"
> "I did – and was in hopes the question would be followed up by others. It would have pleased your uncle to have been enquired of farther."
> "And I longed to do it – but there was such a dead silence!"

Austen's text neither reports nor proposes an answer to Fanny's question and we cannot categorically verify an established *position*; but it is clear that in the mind and conscience of the author – hovering – something is *alive*.

NOTES

1. Barbara Lalla, *Postcolonialisms: Caribbean Rereading of Medieval English Discourse* (Kingston: University of the West Indies Press, 2008).
2. Gerald Prince, *Dictionary of Narratology* (Lincoln: University of Nebraska Press, 1987), 22.
3. Charles Dickens, *Oliver Twist* (London, 1838), ch. 32, http://www.literaturecollection.com/a/dickens/oliver-twist/32/.
4. James P. Driscoll, "The Shakespearean Metastance: The Perspective of *The Tempest*", in *Shakespeare: Contemporary Critical Approaches*, ed. Harry R. Garvin and Michael Payne (East Brunswick, NJ: Associated University Presses, 1980), 158.
5. John T. Shawcross, review of *Identity in Shakespearean Drama* by James P.

Driscoll (Lewisburg, PA: Bucknell University Press; London and Toronto: Associated University Presses, 1983).
6. Elizabeth Nunez, *Prospero's Daughter* (New York: Ballantine, 2006).
7. Noel Carroll, "On the Narrative Connection", in *New Perspectives in Narrative Perspective*, ed. Willie van Peer and Seymour Chatman (Albany: State University of New York Press, 2001), 39.
8. Chris Lang, "The Reader-Response Theory of Stanley Fish", in "A Brief History of Literary Theory III", http://www.xenos.org/essays/litthry4.htm.
9. José Angel García Landa, "Rereading(,) Narrative(,) Identity(,) and Interaction" (2006), http://www.unizar.es/departamentos/filologia_inglesa/garciala/publicaciones/commintern.html, para. 15.
10. See, for example, Terrell Carver and Jernej Pikalo, *Political Language and Metaphor: Interpreting and Changing the World* (London: Routledge, 2008), and Andrew Goatly, *Washing the Brain: Metaphor and Hidden Ideology* (Amsterdam: John Benjamins, 2007).
11. Charles Dickens, *Barnaby Rudge* (London, 1841), chap. 78, http://www.online-literature.com/dickens/barnabyrudge/79/.
12. Charles Dickens, *Dombey and Son* (London, 1848), ch. 10, http://www.dickens-literature.com/Dombey_And_Son/10.html. Subsequent references are taken from this edition.
13. Charles Dickens, *David Copperfield* (New York: Barnes and Noble Classics, 2003), 139.
14. Charles Dickens, *Little Dorrit* (London: Chapman and Hall, 1907), chap. 24.
15. Charles Dickens and Wilkie Collins, "The Perils of Certain English Prisoners", *Household Words*, 7 December 1857, http://www.readbookonline.net/readOnLine/2542/.
16. See Jane Simon's discussion "Critical Proximity", in *Cultural Studies Review* 16, no. 2 (2010): 4–23.
17. R. Buckminster Fuller, *Synergetics: Explorations in the Geometry of Thinking* (New York: Macmillan, 1975), www.rwgrayprojects.com/synergetics/s05/p1500.html, 518.
18. Michaeline A. Crichlow, *Globalization and the Post-Creole Imagination: Notes on Fleeing the Plantation* (Durham: Duke University Press, 2009), 177, 182.
19. Ibid., xiv.
20. Compare ibid., 33.
21. Michaeline A. Crichlow, note 1:98, refers usefully to Saskia Sassen, "Spatialities and Temporalities of the Global: Elements for Theorization", *Public Culture* 12, no. 1 (2000): 219, 221.

22. Jennifer Rahim comprehensively discusses this "aesthetic wrangling" in "Issues and Developments in Caribbean Literary Theory and Criticism", in *Methods in Caribbean Research: Literature, Discourse, Culture*, ed. Barbara Lalla, Nicole Roberts, Elizabeth Walcott-Hackshaw and Valerie Youssef (Kingston: University of the West Indies Press, 2013), 15–40. See especially 18–27.
23. Wilson Harris, "Creoleness: The Crossroads of a Civilization", in *Wilson Harris: The Unfinished Genesis of the Imagination*, ed. Andrew Bundy (London: Routledge, 1999), 227–36.
24. V.S. Naipaul, *A House for Mr Biswas* (London: André Deutsch, 1961); Tiphanie Yanique, *How to Escape from a Leper Colony* (Minneapolis: Greywolf Press, 2010); Nalo Hopkinson, *Midnight Robber* (New York: Warner, 2000).
25. Charles Dickens, "The Noble Savage", *Household Words* 7, no. 168 (11 June 1853), 3.
26. Charles Dickens, *American Notes* (London: New Oxford Illustrated Dickens, 1957).
27. John Keats, letter to Richard Woodhouse, 27 October 1818, in *The Keats Circle: Letters and Papers 1816–78*, ed. Hyder Edward Rollings (Cambridge, MA: Harvard University Press, 1948), 1:366–87, quoted in Caroline Bertonèche, " 'Negative Capability' as a 'Gift for Invention': On the Positive Contradictions of John Keats' Poetic Theory", *GRAAT OnLine* 8 (August 2010): 78–89, http://www.graat.fr/bertoneche.pdf.
28. John Keats, letter to his brothers George and Tom Keats, 22 December 1817, in *The Letters of John Keats*, ed. Hyder Edward Rollings, 1:193.
29. Charles Dickens, *Bleak House* (London, 1853), http://www.online-literature.com/dickens/bleakhouse/.
30. Jane Austen, *Mansfield Park*, in *The Works of Jane Austen* (Feltham, Middlesex: Hamlyn, 1968), 474.

Chapter 2

"HOW BLEST AM I . . . !"
Colonial Desire in Selected Poetry by John Donne

GISELLE RAMPAUL

IN EXAMINING MEDIEVAL ENGLISH VERSE FROM a Caribbean perspective in her 2008 publication *Postcolonialisms: Caribbean Rereading of Medieval English Discourse*, Barbara Lalla paved the way for Caribbean scholars to analyse British canonical texts from Other, if not also new, perspectives.[1] In chapter 1 of this collection, Lalla defines the Caribbean postscript thus: "The Caribbean postscript looks back at matters long regarded as already settled, at material now regarded as privileged beyond question, so as to detect and inscribe something more and, probably, something other than established readings. Caribbean rereading applies a view from the periphery of the British canon, for scrutinizing ideological positions that maintain reverential attitudes to text."[2] The words "privileged", "established" and "reverential" are important to the idea of canonicity against which Lalla is implicitly reacting. Donne, arguing in his poem "The Canonization" for the religious canonization of the narrator, his lover and the love they share, simultaneously achieves the feat by preserving all three for posterity through the immortality of his verse. But Donne's poems, as well as many other British canonical texts, preserved far more enduring ideas about colonized places and colonized people. The question of canonicity in this project is, therefore, relevant to the colonial and contemporary Caribbean as certain perceptions about and constructions of the Caribbean (and other colonized regions) were disseminated not only among British traveller- and settler-writers, but also among stay-at-home British writers who, in turn, constructed the region in certain ways. For example,

Lalla shows how Charles Dickens wrote about the West Indies in some of his novels, including the well-known *Oliver Twist* and *David Copperfield*, without ever having any direct experience of that part of the world. Jane Austen, similarly, alludes to the slave trade in *Mansfield Park*, and Charlotte Brontë writes about the mad West Indian Bertha in *Jane Eyre*. British representations of the Caribbean have had enduring consequences as our contemporary Caribbean writers, through various counter-discursive strategies, still react to these constructions.

However, "the historic encounter between the Old World and the New . . . revolutionized the world outlook of the European mind", so early representations of the Caribbean also seemed to influence the ways in which British writers came to understand, represent and construct their *own* societies, identities and personal relationships.[3] According to Mary Louise Pratt, "empires create in the imperial center of power an obsessive need to present and re-present its peripheries and its others continually to itself. It becomes dependent on its others to know itself. Travel writing, among other institutions, is heavily organized in the service of that need."[4] The Caribbean, therefore, had a direct bearing on how the British imagined *themselves*. Donne himself was not a stay-at-home British writer. He was closely associated with the Virginia Company and "contemplated a more active involvement in the colonization of America than merely writing about it".[5] He travelled (though not specifically to the Caribbean) and his vast knowledge of all aspects of the contemporary colonial enterprise is reflected in the themes, imagery and symbolism of his poetry.[6] Most times, however, he was writing about life at home in England or about travelling from England to other parts of the world. But, in the latter case, England is still his point of departure. And yet an examination of his poetry reveals that writings about the Caribbean might have influenced his own work and, more significantly to me, his constructions of the British. In this chapter, I would therefore like to examine the ways in which colonial representations of the Caribbean construct the British colonizer and colonial desire.

To do this, I would like to examine "Elegy 19: Going to Bed" and "Holy Sonnet 14: Batter My Heart". Although Donne does not specifically write about the Caribbean, I am interested in the way in which his construction of colonial desire compares with that of contemporary and later writings about the Caribbean. Donne's use of the colonization motif is informed by related ideas of cartography and the new formulations and appreciations of space that the discovery of new lands necessitated (and I am aware that to refer to the "discovery" of these places is to adopt a certain perspective), but he also specifically compares the male lover colonizing the female body with the colonizer colonizing the land, in his love poetry especially. When Donne's narrator takes the position of the woman/land in the religious poem "Holy Sonnet 14", the writer's construction of God, represented as a lover and colonizer, makes an important comparison with the colonizer/lover of the love poetry that reveals cultural anxieties in relation to both the woman and the colonized lands. This insecurity, I am arguing, lies at the heart of canonical representations of the Caribbean and the constructions of British masculine and imperial identity and supremacy.

O MY AMERICA! MY *TERRA INCOGNITA!*

In "Elegy 19: Going to Bed", in which the narrator describes his beloved undressing as they get ready for bed, there is a direct comparison between newly discovered lands and a woman's body:

> O my America! my new-found-land,
> My kingdom, safeliest when with one man manned,
> My mine of precious stones, my empery,
> How blest am I in this discovering thee![7]

I take "America" to be a synecdochical reference to the whole region – to the Americas, including the Caribbean region.[8] In fact, some critics argue that these lines refer specifically to Sir Walter Raleigh's discovery of Guiana and his attempt to persuade Queen Elizabeth to give her permission (or "seal" or "license") to seize the coveted El Dorado from the Spanish in his own account, entitled *The Discoverie of the Large, Rich and Beautiful Empire of Guiana*.[9] Tom Cain also cites Donne's epigram "Cales and Guiana", and a verse letter, "To Mr R.W.", in which he approves of Raleigh's expedition.[10]

Now, in relation to the conceit above, many critics have examined the characterization of the woman as colonized land in their exploration of the gender politics in the poem.[11] However, according to David Punter in his book *Metaphor*, "The question of what to compare with what is . . . in no sense a universal or natural one, but one that is guided by strict lines of power."[12] In my analysis of the conceit, I wish to, in Punter's words, swing the metaphor around "like a coin revealing its obverse side" by making the land the tenor and the woman, the vehicle.[13] In other words, I want to examine the significance of the gendering, and specifically feminizing, of the *colonized land* in the poem, and how this contributes to the construction of the British colonizer and colonial desire.

Postcolonial critics like Kadiatu Kanneh point out that "the feminising of colonized territory is, of course, a trope in colonial thought", and Anne McClintock also argues that "uncertain continents – Africa, the Americas, Asia – were figured in European lore as libidinously eroticised" and had become "what can be called a porno-tropics for the European imagination"; "the world is feminised and spatially spread for male exploration".[14] Much analysis has also been done on Jan van der Straet's drawing entitled *America* (ca. 1598) in this regard.[15] Writing centring specifically on the Caribbean also characterizes the region in terms of a "pornutopia" and focuses on the gendering of the landscape. According to Elizabeth DeLoughrey et al., "Since Columbus's early journals, Europeans marvelled at the 'variety and newness' of the islands' flora and fauna, their 'eternal greenness'. . . . This in turn led to hyperbolic misinterpretation of tropical fecundity . . . [and the] [g]endering [of] the soil as a receptive woman's body that 'rejoices' at the insertion of male seed."[16] Raleigh, for example, referred to Guiana as "a Countrey that yet hath her Maydenhead" when he landed there, arguing that this made it an especially attractive potential British acquisition.[17]

According to Punter, "Metaphor is a crucial way in which we can apprehend the quality of the uncanny, considered as the process which establishes the inseparability of the familiar and the unfamiliar . . . something is recapitulated into recognisable terms."[18] The construction of the colonized lands as receptive female body might have been a way of familiarizing the unfamiliar, but it is also important to note that the relationship between the colonizer and the land was being expressed in terms of another unequal relationship (between the lover and the woman). Bill Ashcroft et al. argue that "women . . . have been relegated to the position of 'Other', 'colonized' by various forms of patriarchal domination" – and the narrator does refer to the male dominant missionary position both in the extract ("with one man manned") and more overtly at the end of the poem when he asks the woman, "What needst thou have more covering than a man?"[19] And, as Evelyn O'Callaghan argues, "colonialism was generally imaged as a 'masculine' project" and imperialism was "as much about constructing a *masculine* British identity as constructing a national identity *per se*".²⁰ The feminizing of the landscape, therefore, not only reflects an unequal power relationship between the colonizer and the colonized (whether the colonized is figured as the woman or as the land), but it also reveals a patriarchy and desire for dominance at the heart of the colonial project.

According to John R. Gillis, "the first things Europeans did when they arrived at any new place was . . . name it and mark off boundaries. . . . The vast extension of space had the unanticipated effect of increasing the felt need for knowable, bounded places."²¹ This naming and marking of boundaries is done to the woman's body through a curious use of the Petrarchan blazon in the poem. The inventory of the articles of her clothing as he imagines them "going off" (line 13) *conjures* visual images of the woman's body parts, having the same effect as the blazon of making the woman's body, piece by piece, the centre of male attention, enquiry and investigation. Franz Fanon, though speaking specifically about the colonizer's relationship with the colonized woman, also equates "unveiling" with "revealing . . . baring . . . breaking her resistance . . . making her available".²² Indeed, Donne's lover refuses to leave an inch of the beloved unexplored by his "roving hands" (line 27) that will go "Before, behind, between, above, below" (line 28).

Looking at the map-making of early colonists in his essay "Isla Incognita", Derek Walcott discusses the ways in which explorers sought to place boundaries around and, therefore, assert authority over places they discovered. Walcott writes: "The weird, raggedly inaccurate, infantile maps of the old explorers . . . were more fearful than comic. The wrongly real outlines were perhaps more terrifying than their blank confession, 'Terra Incognita'" because they gave a false sense of knowing.²³ According to McClintock:

> Map-making became the servant of colonial plunder, for the knowledge constituted by the map both preceded and legitimized the conquest of territory. The map is a technology of knowledge that professes to capture the truth about a place in pure, scientific form, operating under the guise of scientific exactitude and promising to retrieve and reproduce nature exactly as it is. As such, it is also a technology of possession, promising that those with the capacity to make such perfect representations must also have the right of territorial control.²⁴

At the same time, she recognizes that maps also belie the "contradictions of colonial discourse" in that "the edges and blank spaces of colonial maps are typically marked with vivid reminders of failure of knowledge and hence the tenuousness of possession".[25] But map-making might have been a way of dealing with the "epistemological difficulties that destabilise[d] meaning and certainty" that accompanied *terra incognita*, belying a "desire for mastery".[26] To name the fear is the beginning of overcoming it, a way of transforming *terra incognita* into *terra cognita*, and the colonists attempted to do this in a number of ways.

For example, the colonizer/lover repeatedly "names" the land in the four lines quoted above. In the first line, the narrator names the land twice ("America" and "new-found-land"). The proper name, "America", gives the land an identity, bestowed upon it by he who defines it: "To name a foreign land, to make of that land and its ways a textual artefact, was to exercise mastery."[27] The second descriptive name the colonizer/narrator gives the land is "new-found-land", significantly almost the opposite of *"terra incognita"*. The announcement of its discovery – the fact that it is "found" (and, better yet, *newly* so) – gives the colonizer/lover the authority of *knowledge* (albeit inaccurate and subjective) over it. The repetition of the possessive "my" in these lines – he uses the word five times in four lines – is another way of asserting authority over the landscape. And the hyperbolic reference to the "mine of precious stones" reminds us of the acquisitiveness, the avarice that was at the heart of the colonial enterprise and, therefore, at the heart of claiming the land.[28] In fact, Albert C. Labriola points out the twofold significance of the lover's "roving hands", as "roving" meant not only wandering, but also robbing.[29]

Further analysis of this conceit of woman as colonized land, and specifically of the ground between the tenor and vehicle in the metaphor, sheds light on how the colonizer and colonial desire are characterized. Glenn Hooper argues: "Sometimes arrogantly, at other times nervously, the landscape is remodelled by colonists, not just because it needs to be contained . . . but because it is also regarded as a very visible marker of ownership and authority."[30] Arrogance and nervousness also characterize the male lover's approach to and description of his female lover in Donne scholarship. In fact, Donne has been outrightly lambasted for what some critics see as misogyny, whereas other critics, like Benet, have adopted a more nuanced approach to his poetry, recognizing "a profound interest compounded of fear, hostility, admiration and desire" in relation to the woman.[31] Shankar Raman argues that the "rhetorical parcelling of [the body]" only belies the "frustration at never being able fully to master the female body".[32] Although she might be characterized as desirable and pursued, the woman is also figured "as a treacherous object", the unknowable, undefinable "Other".[33]

So, despite all of the strategies used in the poem to make the woman "knowable" to the lover/narrator, he is still aware that only through the granting of her permission would he be allowed the pleasure of exploring her sexually. He must ask her to "license" and "let" his hands explore her body (line 25); he suggests the signing of a legal contract that he hopes will allow him the pleasure of her body; he describes himself as "blest" (line 30) in being allowed to explore her body; and he acknowledges that only those "whom their imputed grace will dignify" (line 42) would see women "revealed" (line 43). There is thus the sense that the woman has the power to deny him as a lover. Although the poem is phrased like a series of commands, it is still generally regarded wooing and, therefore, asking – if not begging. The "cultural anxieties" about women also extend to the colonized lands, as they are part of the grounds on which the metaphor is working.[34] So, according to McClintock, "If, at first glance, the feminising of the land appears to be no more than a familiar symptom of male megalomania, it also betrays acute paranoia and a profound, if not pathological, sense of male anxiety and boundary loss."[35] In the words of Jackson Lears, "American bounty was enticing, but also emasculating, perhaps worse."[36]

FROM FLOWERY MEADS TO MAHOMET'S PARADISE

This anxiety about newly discovered places is also revealed in two other comparisons that Donne employs to describe the woman in the poem. The first is a simile in which the woman's body is described in terms of the English landscape: "Your gown's going off such beauteous state reveals, / As when from flowery meads th' hill's shadow steals" (lines 13–14). The second is the comparison of the pleasures of her body to "Mahomet's Paradise" (line 21). Although, at this point, the woman is not yet directly compared to the colonized land in the poem, it is significant that both comparisons are consistent with the ways in which colonized lands were described by other writers in the colonial period – "as paradisal and pastoral, images that [were] perpetuated in colonial discourse".[37]

The simile of the "flowery meads" is part of the hyperbolic flattery employed in the poem, but the comparison also helps to familiarize the unknowable female body by comparing it to the ideal English countryside with which the lover is, presumably, familiar. The use of the direct article before the word "hill's" as well as the lack of further clarification of this comparison suggest that the lover and the implied reader share the knowledge of this particular landscape. It is, therefore, an effective tool in making the woman's body seem more controllable and manageable to the leery lover. This very technique was used in face of the unfamiliar Caribbean landscape: "Moving through unfamiliar country, travellers adapted the familiar concepts of hill, meadow, brook, and so on to give shape to their experience."[38] To deal with the fear and anxiety associated with *terra incognita*, colonizers often tried to make connections between the lands they encountered and the lands from which they came. According to Gillis, "For centuries, Europeans would try to assimilate what they found in the Americas . . . to what they were familiar with back home. . . . Importing old world landscapes had a similar effect of domesticating a world that initially defied description. At every step of the way, exploration and colonization depended on fictions, or an illusory familiarity."[39] Similarly, O'Callaghan, writing about female travel writing in the nineteenth century, points out one description of Jamaica, for example, as "a hot place, belonging to Us". She observes that while the island is characterized as exotic and strange ("a hot place" – and the indefinite article contributes to its strangeness), the phrase "belonging to Us" "counterbalances this strangeness by translating it in terms of familiar prescriptions, making it safe because [it is] ultimately framed within the categories of European knowledge-building . . . and European rule".[40] The need for these "familiar prescriptions" and "illusory fictions", however, only belies psychological anxieties about the unknown.[41]

The description and conception of the discovered lands as Paradise are also well established in colonial expression and thought. According to Steve Nicholls, "the very first European visitors to the New World . . . frequently described what they found as Paradise".[42] Gillis, importantly, points out that although "Paradise has been located in all kinds of times and places . . . all have one thing in common: inaccessibility".[43] This relates to the contradictory way in which the woman is described in the poem. Although she is described in terms of the recognizable and knowable in the comparison to the English landscape, she is, just a few lines later, described in terms of the unfamiliar and the unattainable.[44] There is another paradox here. The word "Paradise" "derives from the Persian *pairi-daeza*, meaning a walled enclosure", so the woman is, on the one hand, described in terms of the bounty and limitlessness of a familiar landscape (the "flowery meads"); and, then, on the other, she is described in terms of an unattainable, inaccessible landscape defined by its boundaries.[45] Through the comparison, the colonized land is also characterized in terms of its attractiveness and its inaccessibility, and it elicits similar feelings of frustrated desire in the colonizer/lover.

As Elleke Boehmer argues, "A country was 'mapped' or spatially conceived using figures which harked back to home ground. . . . Classifications and codes imported from Europe were matched to peoples, cultures, and topographies that were entirely un-European."[46] However, "the effort to graft on to the colonized environment [the colonizers'] own hermeneutic structures constantly met with difficulty. There was no necessary consonance between colonial imported metaphors and the colonized land. No assurance was available to the European that his transference of tropes would produce a perfect fit."[47] DeLoughrey et al.'s argument that "European reports rendered the landscape in a binary between the similarity to the writer's homeland and its radical differentness" is thus apparent in the complex and contradictory ways in which the lover/colonizer attempted to make *terra incognita* into *terra cognita*, and emphasizes the "colonial anxiety" at the heart of these descriptions.[48]

"HOW BLEST AM I . . . !"

In "Elegy 19", the colonizer, in the face of these fears and anxieties, admits that he feels "blest" to dis-cover the woman's body and to discover the colonized lands, and to enjoy a wealth of riches because of it. The exclamation "How blest am I . . . !" might also suggest a feeling of being undeserving, related to the insecurities discussed earlier, especially when compared to the characterization of beatitude in "Holy Sonnet 14". This inconvenient feeling of unworthiness as it relates to the colonizer seems to be addressed by the religious sonnet that constructs the colonized as "blest" as well – in fact, *far more* "blest" than the colonizer of "Elegy 19". The colonized is constructed as "wanting it and wanting it bad" so the colonizer in that poem becomes *deserving* and, therefore, need not feel hesitant about invasion or insecure in the face of *terra incognita*.

The same conflation of the woman and the colonized land that we see in "Elegy 19" occurs in "Holy Sonnet 14", although in the latter poem, the narrator seems to exchange his role of pursuer in the love poetry for that of the woman, the object of his wooing – and, by extension, his role of colonizer for the colonized. In asking God to "Batter my heart" , "heart" also being Elizabethan slang for "vagina", the narrator assumes the persona – or at least the position – of "a woman urging her suitor to take her by force rather than by courtship", conjuring startling images of a divine rape.[49] The feminizing of colonized land is not as apparent in this poem, but references are made to colonization, as in the "viceroy" metaphor (line 7) and in the war imagery, specifically in relation to fighting over territory. Moreover, if the narrator is assuming the position of the woman and compares him- or herself to "a usurpt town" (line 5), the comparison between woman and territory is maintained. The suggestion that the colonized body is an isolated and contained territory that will be broken into, possessed and ravished by right of the colonizer/God, further constructs the colonized body as an island. Perhaps "no man is an island", but every woman is.[50]

M. NourbeSe Philip characterizes rape as "the most efficient management tool" of the female body that "always presents a subversive threat", and the poem's treatment of rape is indeed significant to the construction of colonial desire and the power politics involved in the colonization of the woman and of the land.[51] Rape, it seems, is redefined in this poem to remove its associations with victimization, although it still involves violent invasion of the body. Here, however, it seems to be intimately linked with salvation and beatitude; "images of physical penetration and humiliation shatter the body in the interest of renewal or salvation".[52] John Stachniewski points out that this "solicitation of divine aggression and rape" was "widely used to characterize Calvin's conception of conversion".[53] God's possession of the narrator's body and soul is, therefore, welcome – in fact, the narrator desperately and ardently pleads to God to descend upon him with immense and intense violent love and to utterly "ravish" (line 14) him such that he might be, paradoxically, "free" (line 13) and "chaste" (line 14). If "God's ravishment" is constructed as an "ideal" that is "worthy of emulation", according to Craig Payne, then colonization of the woman and the colonized lands is regarded not only as desirable and benedictional, but also as the will of God.[54] After all, in "Elegy 18: Love's Progress", again linking the woman with the colonized lands, he describes the woman's lips as "Islands *Fortunate*" (line 51; emphasis mine), simply because they are being kissed by her lover – a kiss that is the prelude to possession of her body as he moves across her "Atlantic navel" (line 66) to find her "India" (line 65).

All of this is hardly surprising given that the colonizing nations were not only fighting for land, but were also competing for religious dominion over different parts of the world. According to Donne's contemporary Ben Jonson, "The strength of empire is in religion."[55] So let us look at the rest of what Raleigh says to Queen Elizabeth in his idealized description of Guiana: "Guiana is a Countrey that yet hath her Maydenhead. . . . It hath neuer beene entred by any armie of strength, and neuer conquered or possessed by any Christian Prince."[56] In his attempt to persuade her to seize Guiana from Spanish "tyrannie and oppression", he points out that the territory is an ideal candidate for conquest, possession and, especially, Protestant dominion. According to Silvio Torres-Saillant:

> Raleigh wrote in 1595 to Queen Elizabeth I to request authorization for the conquest of Guyana, emphatically urging her to see herself in the mirror that the King of Spain presented. The Spanish monarch, he argued, went from being a nobody to parading himself as the greatest prince of Europe simply because he had wisely taken advantage of the riches of these Indies. Such opportunities, Raleigh insisted, now presented themselves to her majesty the Queen.[57]

One wonders, then, at the identity of the "enemie" to whom the narrator is "betrothed" in Donne's poem. Certainly, there was a lot of propaganda against the Spanish, who were conceived as occupying the "spiritually vital role of *super*natural enemy", perpetrating unforgivable atrocities in the New World which made "the English response seem – to most Protestant imaginations at least – spiritually righteous", according to Christopher Hodgkins, who also makes a comparison with Milton's Satan and the Spanish conquistador from whom the British had to protect and save the Edenic New World.[58] Almost two centuries later, Daniel Defoe also wrote *Robinson Crusoe*, which embodied the same sort of colonial fantasy or wish fulfilment constructed in Donne's poem. Hodgkins continues: "The British were able to transmute their own daunting imperial liabilities into ideological advantages and virtues, and even their anti-imperialist impulses into a divine mandate for a reforming empire."[59] God (or Jesus) the colonizer in the sonnet is very much comparable to the Christian Prince of Raleigh's *Discoverie*, who can "save" the land from the clutches of the Spanish Devil. And the virginal woman/land, in turn, "Labour[s] to admit [God]", reminding us that he or she *wants* to be ravished by the colonizer, that it is a salvation and a blessing to be invaded, possessed, dominated and overcome by the colonizer's "love". The colonizer in the poem, therefore, becomes a hero, and anxieties and insecurities are argued away.

The mapping of the psychological complexity not only in the relationship between the male lover and the woman, but also in the relationship between the colonizer and the land, effectively reveals the complicated dynamics of desire. Comparing "Elegy 19" and "Holy Sonnet 14" is, therefore, useful to an examination of how both the colonized and the colonizer were constructed in the British imagination. Taken together, the two poems consider the complexity of colonial desire and its attendant anxieties, but also address the complicated politics of power involved in the colonization of both body and land.

NOTES

1. Barbara Lalla, *Postcolonialisms: Caribbean Rereading of English Medieval Discourse* (Kingston: University of the West Indies Press, 2008).
2. Barbara Lalla, chapter 1 in this collection: "Dickens and Others: Metastance and Re-membering".
3. Gordon K. Lewis, *Main Currents in Caribbean Thought: The Historical Evolution of Caribbean Society in Its Ideological Aspects, 1492–1900* (Baltimore: Johns Hopkins University Press, 1983), 29.
4. Mary Louise Pratt, *Imperial Eyes: Travel Writing and Transculturation* (London: Routledge, 2007), 3.
5. Tom Cain, "John Donne and the Ideology of Colonization", *English Literary Renaissance* 31, no. 3 (2001): 441.
6. See Lisa Gorton, "John Donne's Use of Space", *Early Modern Literary Studies* 4, no. 2, Special Issue 3 (September 1998): 9.
7. John Donne, "Elegy 19: Going to Bed", *The Norton Anthology of English Literature*, 4th ed., ed. M.H. Abrams et al. (New York: W.W. Norton, 1979), 1:1093–94, lines 27–30. Subsequent references appear parenthetically in the text and are taken from this edition.
8. Jak Peake, in his chapter in this collection, also shows how theorists like Édouard Glissant and Antonio Benítez-Rojo connect the Caribbean to the American continent in their descriptions of it.

9. See, for example, R.V. Young, "Love, Poetry and John Donne in the Love Poetry of John Donne", *Renascence: Essays on Values in Literature* 52, no. 4 (Summer 2000), http://www.luminarium.org/sevenlit/donne/donnessays.htm; and Lemuel A. Johnson, "The Inventions of Paradise: The Caribbean and the Utopian Bent", *Poetics Today* 15, no. 4 (Winter 1994): 685–724.
10. Cain, "John Donne and the Ideology of Colonization", 441, 442.
11. See, for example, Diana Treviño Benet, "Sexual Transgression in Donne's Elegies", *Modern Philology* 92, no. 1 (August 1994): 14–35; Sandy Feinstein, "Donne's 'Elegy 19': The Busk between a Pair of Bodies", *Studies in English Literature* 34, no. 1 (Winter 1994): 61–77; Roma Gill, "Musa Iocosa Mea: Thoughts on the Elegies", in *John Donne: Essays in Celebration*, ed. A.J. Smith (London: Methuen, 1972); Shankar Raman, "Can't Buy Me Love: Money, Gender, and Colonialism in Donne's Erotic Verse", *Criticism* 43, no. 2 (Spring 2001): 135–69; and R.V. Young, "'O My America, My New-Found-Land': Pornography and Imperial Politics in Donne's 'Elegies'", *South Central Review* 4, no. 2 (Summer 1987): 35–48.
12. David Punter, *Metaphor* (Abingdon: Routledge, 2007), 113.
13. Ibid., 123. See I.A. Richards, *The Philosophy of Rhetoric* (Oxford: Oxford University Press, 1936), for definitions of *tenor* and *vehicle*.
14. Kadiatu Kanneh, "Feminism and the Colonial Body", in *The Post-Colonial Studies Reader*, ed. Bill Ashcroft, Gareth Griffiths and Helen Tiffin (London: Routledge, 1995), 364; Anne McClintock, *Imperial Leather: Race, Gender and Sexuality in the Colonial Contest* (New York: Routledge, 1995), 22, 23.
15. See Peter Hulme, "Polytropic Man: Tropes of Sexuality and Mobility in Early Colonial Discourse", in *Europe and Its Others*, ed. Francis Barker et al. (Essex: University of Essex, 1984); Peter Hulme, *Colonial Encounters: Europe and the Native Caribbean, 1492–1797* (London: Methuen, 1986); McClintock, *Imperial Leather*; and Louis Montrose, "The Work of Gender in the Discourse of Discovery", in *New World Encounters*, ed. Stephen Greenblatt (Berkeley: University of California Press, 1993), 177–217.
16. Elizabeth DeLoughrey, Renée K. Gosson and George B. Handley, introduction to *Caribbean Literature and the Environment: Between Nature and Culture* (Charlottesville: University of Virginia Press, 2005), 6.
17. Andrew Sinclair, *Sir Walter Raleigh and the Age of Discovery* (Harmondsworth: Penguin, 1984), 59.
18. Punter, *Metaphor*, 87.
19. Ashcroft et al., *The Post-Colonial Studies Reader*, 245. According to Merry E. Wiesner, the male-dominant missionary position was considered "the proper

sexual order", in *Women and Gender in Early Modern Europe: New Approaches to European History* (Cambridge: Cambridge University Press, 2000), 58. And, as Achsah Guibbory argues, "The act of sex confirms what is seen as the legitimate, rightful mastery of man", in "'Oh, Let Mee Not Serve So': The Politics of Love in Donne's Elegies", *ELH: English Literary History* 57, no. 4 (Winter 1990): 822.

20. Evelyn O'Callaghan, "'A Hot Place, Belonging to Us': The West Indies in Nineteenth-Century Travel Writing by Women", in *Landscape and Empire, 1770–2000*, ed. Glenn Hooper (Aldershot: Ashgate, 2005), 94.
21. John Gillis, *Islands of the Mind: How the Human Imagination Created the Atlantic World* (New York: Palgrave Macmillan, 2004), 61, 62.
22. Franz Fanon, *A Dying Colonialism* (New York: Grove Press, 1970), 43.
23. Derek Walcott, "Isla Incognita", in DeLoughrey et al., *Caribbean Literature and the Environment*, 51.
24. McClintock, *Imperial Leather*, 27.
25. Ibid., 27–28.
26. Glenn Hooper, introduction to *Landscape and Empire*, 3; Kofi Campbell, "Maps of Desire", *Postcolonial Text* 2, no. 2 (2006), http://postcolonial.org/index.php/pct/article/view/391/207.
27. Elleke Boehmer, *Colonial and Postcolonial Literature: Migrant Metaphors* (Oxford: Oxford University Press, 2005), 19.
28. The mine image suggests that the "treasures" of the woman lie hidden somewhere within her body and it is the male narrator's desire to discover them. This might be related to the tendency of early modern physicians and anatomists to regard female sex organs as more mysterious than male organs because they were hidden. "Anatomical guidebooks use[d] illustrations of autopsies on women's lower bodies as symbols of modern science uncovering the unknown" (Wiesner, *Women and Gender*, 56).
29. Albert C. Labriola, "Painting and Poetry of the Cult of Elizabeth I: The Ditchley Portrait and Donne's 'Elegie: Going to Bed'", *Studies in Philology* 93 (1996): 42.
30. Hooper, introduction, 1, 2.
31. See, for example, Kenneth Muir, ed., *Collected Poems of Sir Thomas Wyatt* (Cambridge, MA: Harvard University Press, 1949); Gill, "Musa Iocosa Mea"; John Carey, *John Donne: Life, Mind and Art* (New York: Oxford University Press, 1981); Patrick Crutwell, "The Love Poetry of John Donne: Pedantique Weedes or Fresh Invention?", in *Metaphysical Poetry*, ed. David Palmer and Malcolm Bradbury (Bloomington: Indiana University Press, 1971); Benet, "Sexual Transgression", 35.

32. Raman, "Can't Buy Me Love".
33. Walter S.H. Lim, "'Let Us Possess One World': John Donne, Rationalizing Theology, and the Discourse of Virginia", in *The Arts of Empire: The Poetics of Colonialism from Raleigh to Milton* (Newark, DE: University of Delaware Press, 1998), 69.
34. Ibid.
35. McClintock, *Imperial Leather*, 24. See also Feinstein, "Donne's 'Elegy 19'". In this essay, the author also shows how presumptions about desire are undercut through an analysis of the symbolism of the busk, which at once represents male power and impotence.
36. T.J. Jackson Lears, *Fables of Abundance: A Cultural History of Advertising in America* (New York: Basic Books, 1994), 28–29.
37. Melanie A. Murray, *Island Paradise: The Myth: An Examination of Contemporary Caribbean and Sri Lankan Writing* (Amsterdam: Rodopi, 2009), ix.
38. Boehmer, *Colonial and Postcolonial Literature*, 87.
39. Gillis, *Islands of the Mind*, 46, 61.
40. O'Callaghan, "A Hot Place", 93.
41. See also Boehmer, *Colonial and Postcolonial Literature*.
42. Steve Nicholls, *Paradise Found: Nature in America at the Time of Discovery* (Chicago: University of Chicago Press, 2009), 7. See also Mimi Sheller, *Consuming the Caribbean: From Arawaks to Zombies* (London: Routledge, 2003).
43. Gillis, *Islands of the Mind*, 67.
44. The lover also refers specifically to Mahomet's Paradise, a place of sensual delight and erotic pleasure, not the Christian Paradise with which the Englishman would have been more familiar.
45. Gillis, *Islands of the Mind*, 67.
46. Boehmer, *Colonial and Postcolonial Literature*, 17.
47. Ibid., 87.
48. DeLoughrey et al., introduction, 6; Hulme, *Colonial Encounters*, 2.
49. John Donne, "Holy Sonnet 14", *The Norton Anthology of English Literature*, 4th ed., ed. M.H. Abrams et al. (New York: W.W. Norton, 1979), 1:1101–2, line 1. Subsequent references appear parenthetically in the text and are taken from this edition. The soul was regarded as feminine in Elizabethan thought. Craig Payne, "Donne's Holy Sonnet XIV", *Explicator* 54 (1996): 211; John E. Parish, "No. 14 of Donne's Holy Sonnets", *College English* 24, no. 4 (January 1963): 300.
50. John Donne, "Meditation 17".
51. M. NourbeSe Philip, "Dis Place: The Space Between", in *A Genealogy of Resistance and Other Essays* (Toronto: Mercury, 1997), 75.

52. Nancy Selleck, "Donne's Body", *Studies in English Literature* 41, no. 1 (Winter 2001): 164.
53. John Stachniewski, "John Donne: The Despair of the 'Holy Sonnets'", *ELH: English Literary History* 48, no. 4 (Winter 1981): 689.
54. Payne, "Donne's Holy Sonnet 14", 211.
55. Quoted in Christopher Hodgkins, *Reforming Empire: Protestant Colonialism and Conscience in British Literature* (Columbia: University of Missouri Press, 2002), 137.
56. Ibid., 63.
57. Silvio Torres-Saillant, *An Intellectual History of the Caribbean* (New York: Palgrave Macmillan, 2006), 22.
58. Hodgkins, *Reforming Empire*, 57.
59. Ibid., 56.

Chapter 3

RECOVERING NATION, RECOVERING WOMAN
Shakespeare's Cressida and the Imperial Attic

GENEVIEVE RUTH PHAGOO

THE STRUGGLE FACED BY THE CARIBBEAN to heal the wound of colonialism and establish a national identity parallels that with which sixteenth-century England was wrestling when Shakespeare presented his own re-creation of history in *Troilus and Cressida*. Sixteenth-century Cressida could be almost a mirror image of Jean Rhys's Antoinette, re-created by Rhys to give Charlotte Brontë's Bertha, whom Brontë calls a "clothed hyena ... [with] a pigmy intellect", a history, voice and context.[1] Cressida and Antoinette/Bertha are two of English literature's most incarcerated women.

In *Troilus and Cressida*, Shakespeare conspicuously engages with issues that concern England as a developing nation, and the complications inherent in identity and national consciousness that permeate the established structures of a developing people, in somewhat comparable ways to many contemporary Caribbean writers. A comparison of these situations of evolving nationhood may be conducted through analysis of the female subject and their corresponding contexts in Shakespeare's *Troilus and Cressida*, as it can in Jean Rhys's *Wide Sargasso Sea*. That is, the complexity of Shakespeare's Cressida may be better understood with reference to Jean Rhys's Antoinette, as Shakespeare, like Rhys, attempts a re-visioning of canonical metatexts in an effort to trace the scars engraved into the bodies of their women, and effect some measure of healing.

Interest in postcolonial studies has heightened scholarly response to Shakespearean drama showing the playwright's negotiation of the anxieties that exist in colonial encounters.[2] In some of Shakespeare's most noted works, such as *The Merchant of Venice*, *Othello* and *The Tempest*, there are obvious cultural, racial and religious tensions when Others encounter the dominant, white, male and Christian centre. And in *Troilus and Cressida*, Shakespeare devastates the overarching foundation of English society's cultural and political norms in his vicious critique of the Trojan and Arthurian myths and his rousing social commentary. Holding up his society as the supposed mirror image of Trojan society and Arthurian chivalric behaviour, he finds his world ideologically incapable of sustaining the perfection that the myths advocate, and the perfection that his Elizabethan world thinks it possesses. Shakespeare's attempt to reconsider dominant intellectual traditions, through his decentring of the postcolonial subject, resembles Caribbean literary engagements involving the similar issues of a developing national identity. Using Rhys's *Wide Sargasso Sea* as a lens for rereading *Troilus and Cressida* uncovers similar negotiations with models of authority as they pertain to nation-building, gender dynamics, concepts of home and belonging, and recovery of the exploited female.

Renaissance England, though colonized almost five centuries earlier, was still an emerging nation, wrestling with issues of nationhood and identity bequeathed by its colonial past. The brutal Norman invasion, subsequent conquest, and colonization of England from 1066 to 1154 redefined the political, cultural and social borders of England in bringing it and its people, the Anglo-Saxons, under French imperial control. In the immense social, cultural and political upheaval that marked the Renaissance, medieval issues and institutions were remembered and revisited as that era was also engaged in a collective restructuring of received authority as it related to "Englishness". Culturally, medieval England had experienced colonization in a way familiar to Caribbean peoples, where the interests of the dominant class were promoted over those of the conquered, and native knowledge and power were undermined and restructured to consolidate the legitimacy of conquest. The extensive social and political upheaval that resulted from colonization brought with it many of the same postcolonial preoccupations with history, cultural convergence, resistance and identity that have characterized postcolonial discourse and ensuing concepts of nation in the Caribbean.

Shakespeare's engagement with *translatio imperii* in *Troilus and Cressida* critically investigates what constitutes English national politics and the legitimacy of the highly privileged Trojan tradition as he unglues and resets the idea of his England. Benedict Anderson remarks that every nation requires a "national history" where the community, as an entity, is given ideological credibility; not only does history create nations, but nations also create their own histories.[3] By Shakespeare's time, centuries after the postcolonial medieval era, economically and politically, England's developing status as a burgeoning imperial superpower mitigated its earlier subordinate position as a colony.[4] So established were the Trojan and Arthurian foundation myths in the English psyche that Elizabethan England was an imperial force which promised success in the quest to conquer and claim "lesser" territories, some of which today comprise Caribbean territories. This region is still in the throes of renegotiating a destructive colonial past – a situation today which mirrors England's own past of dispossession, trauma and brutality of the colonial experience that the English suffered at the hands of the French, leaving them with a situation similar to what Derek Walcott describes as our own region's "wounded sensibilities".[5]

Elizabethan England, as a developing society, continued the medieval tradition of strengthening national identity through the use of the Trojan and Arthurian foundation myths. Deliberately anglicizing the Trojan myth and the Celtic Arthur, medieval nationalist poets had transmitted the mythic grandeur that these sovereign bodies represented to a conquered people needing national healing in the aftermath of a colonization process that was particularly brutal. George Huppert offers reasons why emergent nations, such as those of medieval and sixteenth-century England, found it prudent to make ancestral links with Troy. Having a Trojan background was akin to being royalty, its antiquity making national pedigree infallible. Troy was also the seat of chivalry. Politically, the *translatio imperii* from Troy to Rome "established one's blood relationship with the Romans . . . justif[ying] one's title to the possession of parts of the Roman Empire".[6] This noble, though constructed, ancestral link offered developing nations a much desired imperial historical context to aid in expansions of empire.

In the same way that Rhys used England as the model for social, political, religious and cultural constructs, medieval authors had used the Trojan and Arthurian myths to express their own ideal visions of social structure, culture, military strategy, kingship, chivalry and history. These foundation myths were a form of *translatio imperii*, as they set the framework against which contemporary religious, social, cultural and political models were established. These mythographic constructs imbued the Trojan and Arthurian histories with nuances of national identity which made them culturally powerful in any political or dynastic endeavour. Medieval historiographers, Geoffrey of Monmouth in particular, relied on the potent ideological and cultural potential of establishing ancestral links with Troy and Camelot. The *Historia* traces the journey of Brutus (Aeneas's grandson) from Rome to England and ends with Brutus's founding of *Troia Nova*, also known as London. Geoffrey establishes a monarchical regime for the English, rooted in Troy, perpetuated through King Arthur and culminating in the Tudor and Stuart reign of sixteenth- and seventeenth-century England.[7]

Imagining Anglo-Norman victory in the face of invasion by the Saracens, a group that retains cultural significance as the marker of racial Otherness, the intent of Geoffrey's *Historia Regum Brittaniae* (ca. 1136) was to "buttress Anglo-Norman claims to superiority and difference".[8] This enhanced existing power dynamics in favour of the Anglo-Normans, and aided greatly to perceptually legitimize, for the Anglo-Normans, their conquests of Wales, Scotland and Ireland, uniting the British Isles under a single, governing body. Robert M. Stein examines the racial poetics of medieval narratives like Geoffrey's, which, he argues, must be read neither as fantasies nor as simple historiography but as "practical social policy". This was because, at this time, elites "began to conceive of secular society as homogenous" and therefore implemented "systematic marginalization, persecution, expulsion, and ultimately extermination of groups imagined as alien".[9] Anglo-Norman dominance in constructions of Otherness was concretized with the genealogical links to ancient imperial centres – Camelot especially – as the main purpose of Arthur's knights seemed to be to rid the land of marginalized, border-dwelling trouble makers. So pervasive were Geoffrey's fictions, and others like it, that they became embedded in popular history.

Similar to the way in which the myths were used in the Middle Ages as a reinforcement or legitimizing of power, sixteenth-century England's appropriation of the Trojan and Arthurian metanarratives was a shrewd political tactic. In sixteenth-century England, interest in the Trojan and Arthurian foundation myths was resuscitated in the developing nation's investigation of history as it related to concepts of nation and tools of nation-building. Spurred by the Elizabethan ambition to translate imperial ideology to the Tudor and Stuart court with the claim that Elizabeth was King Arthur reincarnate and that the Tudor line was directly descended from Arthur, the Trojan and Arthurian myths of origin, powerfully functioning as medieval tools of national stability and nation formation, were reviewed to fortify

Elizabeth's position on the throne.[10] With their masculine ideals, the myths operated as a class discourse to perpetuate the patriarchal values and ideology of the aristocracy, with Elizabeth, Arthur's supposed reincarnation, as its sovereign. While culturally potent, both the Trojan and Arthurian models of authority reinforced existing social divides, as conceptualizing the nation involved establishing boundaries, ideological and otherwise. Although this created a sense of national belonging, it offered mechanisms for exclusion in constructions of the norm and Other, similar to the way they operated in Anglo-Norman England. And within these models of belonging, there existed hierarchies of power geared towards male dominance and female subordination intricately interwoven into how the nation was constructed.

Also, the Elizabethan return to the myths helped with social stabilization. Seeking to fortify a dwindling sense of faith in the corrupt reality of their political existence, England returned to history. Reminders of ancestral links to successful, elite communities, displaying noble warrior qualities, infinitely capable of defending their own, provided historical continuity and operated like national balm. Renaissance writers thus began to revision time. Anderson, in discussing the role of time in the emergence of national consciousness, draws attention to the way historical perception informs national consciousness. He argues that the concept of time undergoes a radical shift from the medieval "simultaneity of past and future in an instantaneous present" to "'homogenous empty time', in which simultaneity is, as it were, transverse, cross-time, marked not by prefiguration and fulfilment, but by temporal coincidence, and measured by clock and calendar".[11] It is between these two concepts of time, the linear and the typological, that English nationhood resides, especially when one considers Homi Bhabha's assessment of Anderson's concept of "homogenous empty time" as contrasting with the inscrutability of modern temporality: the "repetitive time of the alienating anterior . . . the alienating and iterative time of the sign". Bhabha observes that modern concepts of time, which are so crucial to nation formation, have the potential to create a dislocation between present and past, in that while the present engages some elements of the "repetitive" from the past, the past emerges "as an anteriority that continually introduces an otherness or alterity within the present".[12] Renaissance writers faced a temporal disconnect in historical continuity since Catholicism, the temporally unifying force between past and present, was discredited. Universal truth, as presented by Catholicism, was no longer relevant. Elizabethans, faced with decaying manuscripts and certain Hell within that concept of God that they had forsaken, therefore had to resort to earlier mechanisms of nation-building, such as the foundation myths, to enable social progress. This historical uncertainty proved discouraging to Renaissance writers who were searching for "an ideal of community, that is, by definition, either proleptic or passing, ever just beyond reach".[13]

Additionally, with sixteenth-century England's emerging imperial character, there was the need to be genealogically anchored to historically elite imperial bodies to demonstrate inherited cultural prestige as justification for English dominance in current and future colonization endeavours. The political authority that is inscribed into the Trojan and Arthurian myths of origin possessed the transcultural and transhistorical potential to seamlessly bridge the divide between the medieval and Renaissance eras, and those beyond. These "imaginary homelands" that the myths represent lurk in literary shadows to be invoked by Chaucer, Spenser, Mallory, Shakespeare and Walcott, among others, to either legitimize or ironize ideological concepts centred around constructions of nation.[14] Unlike other encomiastic versions of the Troy legend, Shakespeare, along with others of his time – like Polydore Vergil and John Selden, for example – engages the cultural legacy of the Trojan and Arthurian foundation myths with a very critical eye. Heather James argues that, to Shakespeare, "the Troy legend amounts to the syphilitic diseases that accompany the degeneration of exemplars into social tropes, pandars, Cressids, a Hector or Achilles".[15]

The chivalric code, popular in medieval England, was resurrected alongside renewed interest in the Arthurian myth during Elizabeth's reign. So pervasive was this revival that it was tantamount to obsession. Eric S. Mallin notes that "the chivalric premise lay behind virtually every late Tudor court formality: progresses, pageant entertainments, anniversary celebrations, diplomatic embassies, conferrals of dignities".[16] Superficial accolades, such as those celebrating sovereign glory and loyalty, the ideal of the chivalric code that Elizabethan England inherited and revered, were intrinsically contradictory. Under the chivalric code, the knightly ethos of the Middle Ages, masculine aggression was celebrated in the name of honour, *gentilesse* and the pursuit of the unattainable woman. This had the adverse effect of legitimizing unmerited violence masked as bravery, to the point that "the line between chivalry and criminality was frighteningly thin".[17] The Elizabethan court was rife with rivalries and feuds, dissolute in the semblance of upholding chivalric honour. Rampant noble squabbling and sovereign disagreement led the queen to lament, "Now the wit of the fox is everywhere on foot, so as hardly a faithful or virtuous man may be found."[18] This sentiment finds blatant representation in *Troilus and Cressida*, whose world comprises such ignoble examples of nobility who persistently reduce human worth in whatever chivalric game they think is afoot. Pandarus's crass "How go maidenheads?" puts a price on deflowering virgins; the traditional seat of a woman's worth has a going rate to the highest bidder.[19] In short, the Elizabethan court, already marked by administrative divisiveness, attempting to mask its baseness in the historically ideal code of conduct, only highlights its corruption and its failure to produce a socially cohesive nation, which in no way assures the English of future unity and stability.

It is worth delving into the historical point at which England conceptualized the nation, since modernists like John Breuilly, Ernest Gellner, E.J. Hobsbawm and others argue that nation and nationalism are relatively new concepts, theoretically centring their relevance to western political thinking in the nineteenth century, as an outcome of modernization.[20] They argue that the period of the French Revolution marked the historical moment when nationalism entered world history. It was during this time that citizens agitated for Enlightenment principles of citizenship, nationalism and inalienable rights in the quest for equality, fraternity and liberty as a signifier of cultural homogeneity to create self-determining nations. Hence, nations as well as nationalism are purely modern phenomena, without roots in the past.[21]

However, in England, nation and nationalism were conceptualized long before the nineteenth century, as medievalists have argued. As Keith Stringer says, "medievalists and modernists have more to learn from each other than has often been thought" in relation to "the thorny problem of nationalism", as it constitutes quite "a current crisis of historiography".[22] While nationalism may have been theoretically defined as a modern concept, it existed and operated quite powerfully long before its modern parameters of meaning, in eras before the period of Enlightenment. Adrian Hastings argues for a medieval origin to both nation and nationalism, citing biblical religion and the development of vernacular literatures as mechanisms for fostering a sense of national identity. He concludes:

> England presents the prototype of both a nation and a nation-state in the fullest sense, that its national development, while not wholly uncomparable with that of other Atlantic coastal societies, does precede every other – both in the date at

which it can fairly be detected and in the roundness that it achieved centuries before the eighteenth. It most clearly manifests, in the pre-Enlightenment era, almost every appropriate "national" characteristic. Indeed it does more than "manifest" the nature of a nation, it establishes it.[23]

Medieval concepts of nation, as Kathy Lavezzo discusses, were "pre-Enlightenment structures of communal thinking that strikingly correlate with the forms of modern nationhood".[24] Therefore, medieval England had a sense of nation, augmented, ironically, by the Norman conquest. As Hastings argues, the Normans "were really good at conquering people . . . and very brutally. As they fused with the English, they turned the latter into potential imperialists, and English nationalism would ever after have an imperialist tone to it, as it did not have before."[25] Therefore, constructing ancestral links to the highly masculinized worlds of Troy and Camelot, which valued knightly acquisition and conquest of lands and women in the name of love, honour and masculine prowess, gave the English a powerful base upon which to structure future expansions of empire.

In the medieval context of cultural upheaval and power struggles, we find English writers, whose works incidentally now comprise the English canon, negotiating postcolonial issues of gender, identity, resistance and power. Such issues lingered in the medieval consciousness and, subsequently, in England's sixteenth-century Renaissance, the still-developing nation went on to investigate more thoroughly what its postcolonial past had entailed for national identity. Shakespeare appropriates national myths of origin as an act of self-constituted agency; and by demystifying authority in *Troilus and Cressida*, he attempts to reconstruct English thought. Anthony Smith asserts that "the concept of a nation . . . cannot be sustained without a suitable past. . . . In order to create a convincing representation of the 'nation', a worthy and distinctive past must be rediscovered and appropriated. Only then can the nation aspire to a glorious destiny."[26] Shakespeare questions the suitability of the Trojan and Arthurian foundation myths as models for the paradoxical reality that is Elizabethan society, highlighting the dissonance between the perceived ideal and reality. His interrogation of national identity engages issues of Otherness in the operation of these myths because, as Linda Colley argues, the English "came to define themselves as a single people not because of any political or cultural consensus at home, but rather in reaction to the Other beyond their shores".[27] Otherness, for Shakespeare, came in the dynamics of gender and legitimacy, both issues lingering in the emergent consciousness of Elizabethan England, as in the Caribbean. The tension between England's external status as an imperial force and the internal social divisions found in a still-developing society is evidenced in Shakespeare's engagement with the authority of English origins as established by the Trojan and Arthurian foundation myths.

The concept of "nation" in sixteenth-century England became more complex than the "communal thinking" of the Middle Ages. According to Krishan Kumar, it was the Victorians who first associated the Tudor Age with the birth of the nation.[28] By the sixteenth century, England was making huge strides in the world market by expanding her economic borders "to seek new worlds for gold, for praise, for glory".[29] Yet, within her own national boundaries, England was still struggling with establishing a cohesive national identity other than the "imagined community" of England as part of the Trojan diaspora, which had been perpetuated for almost five centuries.[30] Renaissance England was "yearning for a collective identity. . . . The dream of a nation was one of the strongest and most suggestive constituents of the powerful web of the Renaissance desire for self-fashioning."[31] Catalysts for the formation of the English nation were major social developments – the formation of the Protestant church, the colonization of the New World, the defeat of the Spanish Armada – and powerful governance from Henry VIII and Elizabeth I. According to Richard Helgerson, the generation of writers who "engendered . . . a cultural national formation" also contributed to national development.[32]

However, the sixteenth century was also a period of great social and political divisiveness. Contributing in large measure to this was Henry VIII's break from the Catholic Church to the Church of England, which resulted in a number of religiously motivated and brutal massacres that fuelled pervasive national unease. In addition, frequent clashes with the Irish and rumours of a Spanish invasion created a populace so preoccupied with the threat of war that the law required that every householder have "in a readiness, such armes as is appointed by the Commissioners . . . at least a bill, sword or dagger".[33] Socially, national progress was stultified, as national energies were concentrated on defensive, protective measures, a situation not unlike that found in the aftermath of conquest.[34] Fear and suspicion permeated sixteenth-century England.[35]

Politically, Elizabethan England was fraught with conflict where "the over-riding political issue of the time was the question of sovereignty and the legitimacy of the monarch", as Andrew Hadfield notes.[36] There were other legitimate claims to the English throne, and the Catholic Church declared Elizabeth a heretic and a usurper because of Henry VIII's break from Catholicism.[37] There was, therefore, considerable local and regional opposition to her reign. Also, Elizabeth's court was corrupt. Decision-making entailed furthering the interests of a chosen few, advisors and royal councils, in whose hands the core of political power lay.[38] Court interest focused on securing powerful political positions such as Lord Admiral of the Fleet.[39] It could be said, therefore, that political life in Elizabethan England comprised office holding rather than political representation.[40] Added to all this were the political factions and groupings that created a divisive court. The chief threats to the political unity of Elizabeth's court were the Cecil and Essex factions, which sought "control of the Queen's purse and person".[41] It was only after Essex's attempt to depose Elizabeth, prompted by his failure to gain reward and court support which he demanded as his right, that the court factions became more systematic.[42] As Mallin argues, "Factionalism, like the national military posture and Cressida's misunderstood sexuality, was essentially defensive; it was a strategy to control and redirect hostility."[43] The diseased Elizabeth body politic engendered an unstable body natural. Andrew Hadfield notes that "English intellectuals saw their nation in danger of dissolving or self-destructing" because of social fear and a weak and divided administrative body.[44] The corruption of Elizabeth's court would forever prevent the Elizabethans from achieving their aspirations of being another Troy or Camelot, whose ideal civilizations were created from and sustained by sovereign strength and unified administrations.

The temporal location of Trojan and Arthurian worlds in eras of social conflict, much like those of medieval and Renaissance England, also contributed to the popularity of myths in Elizabethan England. Perceptions of the behaviour and codes of conduct of the ancient Britons in battle – be it social, military, religious or cultural conflict – contributed to their glory and immortalized them as heroes worthy of emulation and possessing enormous appeal for both the aristocrat and the peasant alike. This made the myths easy to manipulate by the powerful few who sought to maintain or create mechanisms of controlling and perpetuating existing power structures.

Władysław Witalisz argues that Trojan and Arthurian "history" provided the "model[s] for chivalric institutions and aristocratic identity placed against a myth of national origins", which was a potent ideological unification tool in building a nation, albeit one that solidified patriarchal positions of authority by perpetuating the uneven distributions of power in the rigid social hierarchy.[45] These myths provided internal pacification, a key condition of nation formation. Norbert Elias identifies such pacification as a "civilizing process".[46] It involved the centralizing of the aristocracy as an absolute power seeking to perpetuate their own ideals that, for them, constituted civility and prestige, fortified by rigid religious orders advocating disciplined comportment. Therefore, through the appeal to Trojan and Arthurian authority, the monopolization of the mechanisms of domination by the patriarchal elite ensured an obedient populace and a stable status quo.

Some of these values were already being interrogated in medieval England by authors such as Chaucer, whose Wife of Bath launched a scathing attack on patriarchal medieval authorities for their inflexible structures of control and subordination. By the sixteenth century, in parodying Elizabeth's court, Shakespeare's treatment of the myths in *Troilus and Cressida* was so brutal in its unravelling of exemplarity that it could well have provoked a crisis. Textually eviscerating national icons, which are at the foundation of national identity, potentially jeopardized the prestige that England enjoyed through its inherited ancestry. Shakespeare presents his Trojan heroes onstage with the assumption that his audience is aware of their multiple textual personalities, derived from their historically different narrative versions. Therefore, discerning the motivation behind the acts of these textually fragmented heroes might not always be clear. For example, the reason for Achilles's refusal to fight in the Trojan War could be attributed to his wish to preserve his honour, or to clandestinely offer for Polyxena's hand. The point is that we do not know if Achilles is Ovid's character, Homer's character or even the medieval chroniclers' character. *Troilus and Cressida* effectively sums up the literary dilemma of appearance versus reality, where the characters have the heroic context, but very little else to acquaint them with their historical version.

In *Troilus and Cressida*, Shakespeare upsets the notion of self-evident identity, as the characters themselves are veiled by their narrative histories. This literary destabilization also applies to the transmission of the Troy legend as Shakespeare presents such scurrilous representations of traditionally valorized heroes and their corresponding value systems, which strike at the heart of the nation that produced them. Written after Tudor propaganda had canonized these myths, Shakespeare's *Troilus and Cressida* queries the integrity of the cultural currency of these myths as received authority. This had dangerous social potential, as Shakespeare overtly demonstrates to the English audience the gross inconsistency between his Trojan buffoons and the great reverence with which the Trojan legend and Arthurian values were held in royal and civic pageantry. His contamination of these myths of origin also had the power to destabilize the ground on which the Tudor dynasty was built, drawing the public eye closer to the deeply entrenched debauchery, corruption and, indeed, hypocrisy which Elizabeth's court embodied.

Shakespeare mocks contemporary political figures, such as Essex, who was regarded by many as having the heroic qualities of history's greatest warrior, Achilles. In *Troilus and Cressida*, Shakespeare engages the ongoing Essex conflict, replicating the political and social drama of the Elizabethan court, through his debasement of Achilles. In 1598, a few years before *Troilus and Cressida* was written, George Chapman created a translation of the *Iliad*, dedicating it to the Earl of Essex, conferring on him heroic, demigod qualities by comparing him to Achilles in his dedication: "To the Most Honored now living Instance of the Achilleian vertues eternized by divine Homere, the Earl of Essex."[47] However, Shakespeare's Achilles is a reductionist representation of Chapman's virtuous hero, and of Ovid's and Homer's heroes. In *Troilus and Cressida*, Achilles is imaged as the bearer of the fearsome and highly contagious plague, which would invoke audience anxiety considering England's traumatic history with infectious plagues. Ulysses characterizes him as "so plaguy proud that the death-tokens of it / Cry 'no recovery'" (2.3.178–79).[48] Achilles's masculinity is devalued with the implication of a homosexual liaison with Patroclus. Contempt is demonstrated in Thersites's accusation that Patroclus is Achilles's "masculine whore", his "male varlet" (5.1.15–17). In the ancient warrior society where masculine values and desires are highly esteemed, Achilles's transgressive sexuality could weaken the value system traditionally associated with the heroes of Homeric legend. However, Elizabethan society was a patriarchal one, and, as Bruce Smith suggests, Achilles was "too important to patriarchal polity to be ostracized as a sodomite".[49] Therefore, we see Achilles's devotion to Polyxena and Patroclus's sexual interest in women as an effort to deflect the suggestion of homosexuality. Achilles's historical prestige is the subject of ridicule from Ulysses, who mocks the send-up that Patroclus gives the Achilles faction (1.3.151–84). Shakespeare's treatment of Achilles/Essex could be part retaliation for Essex's use of the theatre as a subversive force to further his nefarious agenda to rout Elizabeth. On the eve of his revolt, Essex commissioned Shakespeare's company to perform *Richard II* to incite public opinion in his favour against the queen, an act with treasonable implications. Both Essex and Achilles are embodiments of epidemic, spreading "an envious fever" that makes everyone "sick / Of his superior" (1.3.132–33), corrupted by a desire for power above his station that contravenes the very concept of "degree", which would destabilize a politically beneficial status quo.

Ajax, as well, is so undone by a surfeit of heroic associations that his representation upsets the Aristotelian balance, and becomes a mismatch of all the heroic parts that comprise his traditional identity. He

> hath robbed many beasts of their particular additions. He is as valiant as the lion, churlish as the bear, slow as the elephant: a man into whom nature hath so crowded humours that his valour is crushed into folly, his folly sauced with discretion. There is no man hath a virtue that he hath not a glimpse of, nor any man an attaint but he carries some stain of it. He is melancholy without cause, and merry against the hair; he hath the joints of everything, but everything so out of joint that he is a gouty Briareus, many hands and no use, or purblind Argus, all eyes and no sight. (1.2.19–30)

Shakespeare seems to systematically scrutinize the literary tradition associated with the Trojan war, single out traditionally celebrated heroes and elaborately amplify their more unsavoury characteristics.

The ideal worlds of Trojan and Arthurian myths rely on conformity to patriarchal codes of behaviour to maintain their insular perfection. Unfortunately, within these worlds, the significance of women rests in their roles as objects of the chivalric game, other to the norm of the dominant, aggressive and highly masculine knight. So in conceptualizations of the norm in the masculine worlds of Troy and Camelot, gender is a principal factor in the construction of otherness. Governing systems of behaviour inherent in nation, gender and sexuality were intricately intertwined as patriarchal social and cultural constructs, and definitions of all three are integral to conceptualizations of power in the categorizing of "norm" and "other". Anne McClintock identifies one of the main principles of Western imperialism as "the imperial command of commodity capital", which basically refers to women as commodified entities.[50] In medieval England, prescribed codes of behaviour which maintained the oppressive gender hierarchy, with females at the lowest rung, permeated every aspect of daily life, dominating ecclesiastical writing, letters, sermons, theological tracts, discussions and compilations of canon law; scientific works, as part of biological, gynecological and medical knowledge; and philosophy.[51] As Mosse argues, "women [are] sedate rather than dynamic . . . they [stand] for immutability rather than progress, providing the backdrop against which men determine[d] the fate of the nation".[52] Thus, codes of behaviour, informed by patriarchy, influenced constructs of nation where "nation" was synonymous with the female figure and was, therefore, needing conquering, owning, keeping and "taming". Therefore, "*nation* remains, like other feminized entities – emphatically, historically and globally – the property of men".[53] The politics of possession, found in colonial contact, demonstrates how territory is equated with the female body: both are the *tabula rasa* on which male imperial power and discourse exploratively penetrate the interiors with their need to inscribe and map their journeys in their quest for possession. Similarly, in *Wide Sargasso Sea*, the interchangeability of Antoinette and the island in the husband's derogatory comments, observations and feelings reflects the ways in which the nation is feminized by imperial eyes.

McClintock argues that "knowledge of the unknown world was mapped as a metaphysics of gender violence . . . the world is feminized and spatially spread for male exploration, then reassembled and deployed in the interests of massive imperial power".[54] This ideology figures into what Evelyn Stevens terms the "cult of virility" for the private individual whose masculinity is measured by the number of women he "explores", which has wider implications for imperial machismo, assessed by the number of territories acquired, since men were direct agents of empire.[55] Therefore, the brutality inherent in conquest parallels brutal ownership of women over the centuries, linking concepts of female and nation. Hence, feminizing the land is symptomatic not only of masculine megalomania, but also of male anxiety in the face of possible loss of both nation and female to another, more aggressive imperial/masculine entity. Such masculine paranoia to protect that which is owned results in often violent means of containment, even after conquest, and rigid mechanisms of control to sustain female submission and enforce masculine dominance. This is clearly demonstrated in *Wide Sargasso Sea* when Antoinette's husband likens her to an orchid, and then proceeds to crush the flower under his heel.[56] Similarly, in *Troilus and Cressida*, a war is started to re-establish Menelaus's control over Helen's body.

So because "nation" and "feminine" are intricately interwoven, the qualities associated with femininity, such as vulnerability, weakness, chastity and purity, are transferred to the nation. Guarding the sanctity of the woman and the nation was seen as a primary masculine function, justifying masculine rule of both. The early literary performances of gender demonstrate this, showing the damsel in distress waiting to be rescued in tales of Arthurian knightly adventure. The knight was the manly hero who saved the woman and the kingdom from the monsterized Other, thus ensuring the possible continuity of his lineage and the promise of future imperial power. The image of the ideal hero is also mythologized, canonizing the male not only as warrior, but also as protector of the virtue of woman and, by extension, nation. Any threat to the masculine makes the nation vulnerable. By this reasoning, a deviant woman (characterized by her resistance of patriarchal control) poses a direct threat to the nation. Therefore, gender is inexorably relevant to postcolonial ideas of nation, national identity and nationalism, as gender relations are at the "heart of cultural constructions of social identities and collectivities as well as in most cultural conflicts and contestations".[57] The power plays involved in territorial conquest are thus re-enacted in the domestic space, where women form part of commodity acquisition. Even in the ideal world of Troy and in the perfection of Arthurian chivalric behaviour, women's worth is measured in capital power to further a male agenda, as is seen in Cressida's barter as a wartime pawn, and Helen's abduction to inflate masculine prestige gained from owning the face that launched a thousand ships. Also, the sexual banter between Troilus and Cressida is framed in the legal terminology of property transactions, showing further how sex is seen as a right of property.

Because female and nation are traditionally inextricably linked, a female on the throne complicated patriarchal notions of masculine authority and, hence, masculine efforts of nation-building. Ultimate power resided in the hands of a female. While chivalry in Elizabethan England was used to "secure the allegiance of the nobility and the knightly classes . . . to the sovereign", a major strut of the chivalric code that undermined Elizabeth's potency by bringing her femininity to the fore was the Elizabethan version of the essence of knighthood: "service to a lady".[58] Despite her own powerful political influence, evidenced in her capability of evoking military might to defeat the Spanish Armada, a female on the throne did pose a threat to masculine security. The eroticization of the body of the queen as head of the nation problematized negotiations of the body politic. Especially in Elizabeth's later years, there were some shocking public acts of male insubordination in which physical beauty, the marker of the ideal courtly woman, was used as a weapon.[59] Elizabeth's own contradictory and inappropriate tendency to officially have her courtiers maintain the appearance of sexual fidelity to her while keeping her own virginity inviolable, and her insistence on absolute power over her courtiers' private affairs, exacerbated her own objectification.[60] The sexually chaste woman, patriarchy's ideal, held powerful political sway over her male courtiers. This provoked masculine anxiety and hostility towards a woman to whom they swore total obeisance, and frustrated male hegemonic traditions. Louis Adrian Montrose argues that "the political nation – which was wholly a nation of men – sometimes found it annoying or perturbing to serve a prince who was also a woman, a woman who was unsubjected to a man".[61] The masculine desire to possess the female and claim the nation remains unfulfilled and, as the French Ambassador de Maisse noted, "if by chance [Elizabeth] should die, it is certain that the English would never again submit to the rule of a woman".[62] While this statement could be read through a sixteenth-century French patriarchal lens, it nevertheless reflected existing court tensions stemming from masculine anxieties towards female authority. In Troy and Camelot, no woman holds any real power; respect for the female is dependent on the respect given to the male to whom she belongs.

A nation's foundation myths culturally authorize social and psychological control of its citizenry by a chosen few, and determine self-representation to other nations, to establish, on some level at least, national pride and loyalty, which could facilitate confidence in national projects. Foundation myths determine socially acceptable ideology and pre-programme psychological expectations of life. "Myth", as Stefan Berger says, "was often perceived by nation-builders as being far more powerful in mobilizing people than history".[63] Perpetuation of myths depends on memory which, as Huyssen argues, "shapes our links to the past, and the ways we remember define us in the present . . . and nurture [our] vision of the future".[64] Memory fosters an alternative view of the past, reconstructing a historical identity free from colonial degradation and negation. Indeed, the past, present and future power and survival of the nation rest on its foundation myths because "the longer the continuity that could be constructed in the name of nation, the more ancient and the more valuable – that is, the higher standing – the nation was".[65] This is why England claimed kin with Troy.

Claiming to be part of the Trojan diaspora, being part of the model of the past, had been, from the fourteenth century on, a legacy of "postcolonial nostalgia" for the English. It was a way for them to make use of the "twilight zone" between history and memory to cohesively renegotiate their fractured colonial identity, which would facilitate rebuilding and rebirth.[66] And because of the colonial cultural legacy passed to the Caribbean, we find ourselves negotiating comparable conflicts between inherited "truth" and historical reality in the way that sixteenth-century writers did. Walcott's *Omeros*, for example, situates St Lucia within the ancient Trojan framework as Shakespeare did in *Troilus and Cressida*. In doing this, Walcott ironizes the Trojan myth and suggests the revisioning of Caribbean identity and, by extension, Caribbean nation, by the people themselves. He demonstrates that Caribbean identity resides within the individual psyche and should resist external cultural models to define the Caribbean sensibility, as identity belongs with actual history and actual ancestors. When the Caribbean is able to negotiate its own identity on its own terms, only then will its true potential be realized. Walcott's ironized treatment of the classical Trojan myth enables a reading of Shakespeare as an emergent sensibility, interrogating a myth reflective of imperial cultural norms. Shakespeare demonstrates the worthlessness of basing local identity on an imperial model that is inherently flawed, as this makes individual and national aspirations futile. This conflict is succinctly postulated by Wilson Harris: "One may with hindsight glimmeringly perceive that vehicles of genesis, that human cultures tend to symbolize into absolute structuralism, may possess ironic textures to mirror apparently non-existent life in subordination to ruling unconsciousness across aeons of matter and space that are the geologic equivalent to blind cultural habit by which we are governed."[67]

Jean Rhys's *Wide Sargasso Sea* enables a rereading of Shakespeare's *Troilus and Cressida* because both authors excavate the concealed stories of the female that reside in national histories. The authors interrogate their characters' respective worlds, concepts of home and belonging (for the woman), female desire and female representation, and the psychic fragmentation that occurs when the female tries to negotiate a world which denies her very existence. Both Rhys and Shakespeare re-vision their developing societies by showing that, because concepts of nation and woman are inextricably bound, constructive national progress requires recuperation of the female. This aesthetic of metamorphosis and renascence is one not unfamiliar to us in the Caribbean.

Our writers have long been re-examining and revisioning the literary traditions and the memory of Empire in the process of reconstructing our shared histories and mythologies in the hope of envisioning a change in the way we negotiate our world.

To begin rewriting feminine space and place, Shakespeare, like Rhys, engages in the counter-discursive practice of what Salman Rushdie coined "writing back to the centre".[68] This involves strategies that would theoretically enhance the subjectivities of the marginalized and empower their discourse, while examining closely the inherited socio-cultural values disguised as universal truth. Shakespeare engages history through canonical counter-discourse and dismantles assumptions of canonical metanarratives by creating a counter-text, *Troilus and Cressida*, which preserves many of the identifying signifiers of the original, but alters its power structures so as to reconsider traditional authority or authenticity. Along with writing back to the centre, Shakespeare, like Rhys, participated in what Edward Said describes as a *contrapuntal* reading of an authoritative text, taking into account the processes of imperialism and resistances to it.[69] Reading colonial history contrapuntally exposes the plurality of histories as they intertwine and overlap. The text itself, *Troilus and Cressida*, is a *contrapuntal* reading of the Trojan myth, even as *Wide Sargasso Sea* is of *Jane Eyre*, as they expose the structural ironies of intertextuality and parallel histories that exist alongside a metanarrative. It is important to note, however, that *Wide Sargasso Sea* is a "prequel" to *Jane Eyre*, while *Troilus and Cressida* inserts alternative material into an already established authority.

Wide Sargasso Sea interrogates the cultural legacy of imperialism through the counter-discursive practice of rewriting. Rhys releases the imperial frozen representation of the colonized female, and offers opportunities for her liberation. As Michael Thorpe avers, Rhys's undertaking is "an act of moral restitution to the stereotyped lunatic heiress in Rochester's attic".[70] While Rhys's "prequel" re-perceptualizes the individual female figure of Antoinette, Shakespeare's negotiation of the Trojan metanarrative complicates the notion of what constitutes a national ideal, considering the disparity between ideal Troy and the corrupt Elizabethan court. *Troilus and Cressida* decimates history's supposed Trojan heroes and the codes of behaviour inherent in chivalry, established as Arthurian legacy, on which the playwright's society's concept of national identity is based. Shakespeare's *Troilus and Cressida* exposes the tainted ideal and unmasks the brutish individuals who occupy the chivalric space, posing as heroes. By ridiculing the Elizabethan claims to Trojan ancestry, Shakespeare engages in an anti-mythmaking enterprise as he paradoxically inflates and deflates received foundational history. As Douglas Cole suggests, "On the one hand, he intensifies the rhetorical, intellectual, and ethical dimensions of the Greek and Trojan conflict, particularly in the parallel council scenes early in the play. On the other hand, devices of deflation serve to ridicule, contradict, and befoul the issues and persons treated so earnestly and ceremoniously elsewhere."[71] He revisions historically celebrated figures and events, revealing them to be base and deluded; the traditional values that his society fawns upon are cynically revealed to be moral failures. Shakespeare's complicating of the textual authorities raises the central question of *Troilus and Cressida*: "What's aught but as 'tis valu'd?" (2.2.52).

According to Thersites, the world of *Troilus and Cressida* is one of "lechery, lechery, still wars and lechery, nothing else holds fashion" (5.2.194–5); antiquity's most legendary war was started simply because of "a whore and a cuckold" (2.3.72–73); and two of English literature's most noteworthy characters, Menelaus and Paris, are reduced to "the cuckold and cuckold-maker" (5.7.9). Indeed, the political depravity of Elizabethan England, forced into an ill-fitting Trojan model in the world of the play, promises national collapse should ineffective leadership continue. Ulysses's speech on "degree" encapsulates this topical issue quite precisely:

> Troy yet upon his bases had been down
> And the great Hector's sword had lack'd a master
> But for these instances.
> The specialty of rule hath been neglected;
> And look, how many Grecian tents do stand
> Hollow upon this plain, so many hollow factions.
> (1.3.75–80)

Shakespeare's cultural reinterpretation of the Trojan and Arthurian foundation myths questions the sense of the ideal. He shows the hypocritical "ideals" held by the Elizabethan court as perpetuating national disorder. The historically perfect world of Troy, as Elizabethan England, is marked by chaos. The concept of universal order, found in Shakespeare's other plays, is lacking in *Troilus and Cressida*, and ideological concepts and correlating behaviours seem arbitrary. Shakespeare's Troy seems haphazardly arranged, lacking a multi-dimensionality that results in a marked absence of the character complexity that has made other Shakespearean personae such as Hamlet, Viola, Lear and Othello intriguingly immortal. A world steeped in such chaos can never bring forth resolution or restitution for any of the characters. All that could be produced is a social cacophony of what John Dryden calls "a confusion of drums and trumpets, excursions and alarms", relevant only to the Elizabethan world, as Shakespeare does not aspire to create yet another aggrandizing version of the Troy story.[72] As Robert Kimbrough remarks on the "experimental principle of discontinuity" found in *Troilus and Cressida*: "There is no handling of the Troy legend before Shakespeare's which does not try to point the story with some kind of moral or ethical observation. The sources may be responsible for the facts that make up the ending of *Troilus*, but the same sources emphasize that Shakespeare made no attempt to shape his material so that it would carry thematic reverberations outside the play."[73] At the end of the play, there is nothing to be restored.

The challenge facing Shakespeare to articulate citizenship and nationality impacts as greatly on Cressida's concepts of home and belonging as on Antoinette's. Both women are Othered and alienated by their own people, primarily because of their gender but, more importantly, because they fall into the shadowy hybrid space of in-betweenness, with no real sense of belonging, no sense of home anywhere. The concept of home conjures the images of shelter, protection, comfort and nurturing, usually a stable space of rootedness. Rosemary Marangoly George argues that

> the basic organizing principle around which the notion of the "home" is built is a pattern of select inclusions and exclusions. Home is a way of establishing difference.... [It] acts as an ideological determinant of the subject. The term "home-country" in itself expresses a complex yoking of ideological apparatuses considered necessary for the existence of subjects: the notion of belonging, of having a home, and a place of one's own.[74]

Discussions regarding hybridity and inbetweenity in the developing nation can throw light on Shakespeare's rewriting of the Trojan myth in *Troilus and Cressida*. Both Antoinette and Cressida conform to the status of hybrid, persons who, as described by John McLeod, live " 'border lives' on the margins of different nations, in-between contrary homelands", which provokes, in Bhabha's words, "a mental ambivalence that evolves from the instability of dislocation".[75] Indeed, *Troilus and Cressida* itself reflects a hybrid character, neither tragedy nor comedy, composed of ill-fitting parts of a long and varied tradition, coupled with the fragmentary political and economic context of an emergent Elizabethan society that values exploitation and conquest.

For dominant mainstream groups or cultures, people who are in between two or more identities or nations have to renegotiate the world. In doing so, they pose a threat to dominance because, in the process of finding a fixed and stable home and identity, and finding a new way of viewing the world, they could destabilize those with a "pure" identity and, by extension, destabilize the nation, for they are "the people of the diaspora, exiles and migrants who are at once here and elsewhere and whose presence disrupts received definitions of the nation".[76] Excluding the Other secures dominant identity. As Richard Kearney remarks: "Ever since early . . . thought equated the Good with notions of self-identity and sameness, the experience of evil has often been linked with notions of exteriority. Almost invariably, otherness was considered in terms of an estrangement which contaminates the pure unity of the soul."[77]

Like Antoinette, the "white nigger", Cressida, neither Trojan nor Greek, occupies a space which Sanford Sternlicht describes as "trapped between two disdainful cultures".[78] She faces cruel ostracism, which unanchors her and makes her easy prey for masculine attempts to claim her. As Gayatri Spivak argues, "Rhys suggests that so intimate a thing as personal and human identity might be determined by the politics of imperialism."[79] This is demonstrated in *Troilus and Cressida*, where patriarchy digests women and throws them up as "the fragments, scraps, the bits and greasy relics" (5.2.159). Though feelings of home and belonging in the Caribbean situation can be racially contextualized, Cressida's precarious social position stems from instability in national belonging. Initially, she is Trojan, but her national identity is rooted in her father's nationality. When Calchas defects to the Greek camp and renounces his Trojan loyalties, he destabilizes his daughter's nationality and her own sense of social security. He effectively leaves Cressida floating homeless in wartime, when patriotism is of paramount importance. As Carolyn Asp remarks, she "is a pawn in the male game of war, has been deprived of a secure place in the social hierarchy by her father's treachery".[80] Indeed, Shakespeare introduces Cressida as a defensive figure, expecting attack from any quarter, and responsible for her own protection: "Upon my back, to defend my belly; upon my wit, to defend my wiles; upon my secrecy, to defend mine honesty; my mask, to defend my beauty; and you, to defend all these: and at all these wards I lie, at a thousand watches" (1.2.260–64).

Cressida's paradoxical words, demonstrating how vulnerable she truly is, take on military as well as sexual resonance, which is quite befitting the current war that started because of female abduction. Cressida's words also recall Helen's forced passivity as a female captive to augment her captor's worth in the masculine chivalric game of conquering women. Also noticeable is Cressida's pun in "lie", as even her own words reflect that what she says is unreliable and unstable.

Because of Calchas's actions, Cressida is unwillingly split in two: neither Trojan nor Greek, neither exclusively Troilus's nor Diomedes's lover; she is both. Cressida's role as a member of a national community will change depending on the community in which she lives and in relation to the men to whom she "belongs". And this is also true of Helen, who is in limbo, neither Trojan nor Greek, not knowing if or when she will be returned to Greece, displaced from a national identity. On the Trojan side, Cressida belongs to Troilus and Pandarus, the body and blood tie, respectively; and on the Greek side, the exact situation exists with Diomedes and Calchas. She is split right down the middle, with equal loyalties to both Trojans and Greeks. And neither group wants her because, for the Trojans, she is the daughter of a traitor and she betrayed their king's son; and the Greeks see her as a Trojan whore whose father's national loyalties are easily compromised.

With the inherent masculine anxiety attached to a woman's ability to be faithful when she is faced with numerous suitors in the courtly love tradition, Trojan and Greek perceptions of Cressida's sexual constancy are influenced by her state of non-belonging, her rootlessness. With no real home to establish roots, and no male protector, she is marked as inconstant; nowhere is this more evident than in the way she is treated the moment she enters the Greek camp, passed from man to man to kiss, in "a mock-chivalric ritual strongly evocative of a group rape".[81] Ulysses's response when she avoids his kiss lays bare the hatred and paranoia that underpin the elevated sense of female worth in the chivalric tradition, once the game of pursuit has ended. He regards Cressida as the "sluttish spoils of opportunity", a "daughte[r] of the game" (4.5.62–63). Ulysses's vicious reaction is largely due to the fact that the "whore" humiliated him in front of his men. To his male ego, Cressida's kiss represents her bestowal of her favour on the men according to the chivalric code of courtly love. As Mallin observes, this exploitation of Cressida brings to mind the larger scale of the war where the woman is the canvas to showcase male desire and male posturing before other men: "Helen is not the goal of the war, she is its local excuse."[82] Troilus gives this weight in his reduction of Helen, describing her as a "theme of honour and renown, / A spur to valiant and magnanimous deeds" (2.2.200–201). Similarly, in *Wide Sargasso Sea*, Antoinette's husband views their courtship as military strategy where her body, owned through marriage, is the prize: "So it was all over, the advance and retreat, the doubts and hesitations. Everything finished, for better or worse" (39). Although Helen's own husband, Menelaus, has been fighting for ten long years to reclaim her, he says to Hector, who assures him that she is well: "Name her not now, sir, she's a deadly theme" (4.5.180). He effectively deems her irrelevant in this masculine power play of lucrative war making.

The prime reason behind England's expansionism of the sixteenth century was economic power, as imperial wealth is measured by the accumulation of foreign territories. As native histories are rewritten in the commercial terms of the imperial ledger, native inhabitants of colonized lands are commodified as an effect of the commercial context of the imperial agenda. Within the people themselves, the power structures implicit in invasion and conquest are rooted and are reflected socially in the superior/inferior, powerful/subordinate divide where patriarchal control determines the side on which power rests. The woman, like the territory for which imperial and patriarchal powers compete, is held up as either the reward for greater might, or as a bargaining tool in the masculine game of war.

Cressida, like Antoinette, constitutes a colonized product, a commodified object to be bartered. As Montrose observes, "the female body is a supreme form of property and a locus for the contestation of authority".[83] In *Wide Sargasso Sea*, Antoinette's husband adopts a strategy for owning her that assumes the form of military tactics – the game of love is likened to war where he barters for her body (39). In *Troilus and Cressida*, the war and power struggles are more literal, but Cressida's body, like Antoinette's, is bartered. The strategies of war and sex are intertwined; because the body of woman is linked to nation, the siege of Troy is an attack on the female. Conquest of the female validates the masculine duty to protect his nation because, as Coppélia Kahn argues, "the Greeks and the Trojans fight over the possession of a woman because for each of them, masculinity depends on retaining exclusive property in women".[84] As Carol Cook contends, both Helen and Cressida are "objects of exchange mediating the relations among men. . . . The play consistently reveals the operations by which women . . . are produced as objects" by an "economy of masculine desire ... reveal[ing] a deeply problematic relation between desire and representation".[85]

Troilus compares Cressida to "a pearl" (1.1.100), Pandarus to a ship (103) and himself to "the merchant" (103), deliberately commodifying the woman he claims to love. Pandarus is the tool to acquire Cressida. Troilus's actions and words are at odds with each other. While Troilus can wax poetic about how tantalizing Cressida is and how she "enchants [his] sense" (3.2.20), his "ruder powers" (25) dictate that all he wants to do with this love is "wallow" in Cressida's "lily beds" (12). He therefore actively participates in the baseness of his world, despite his claims of purity and true love. Likewise, Troilus uses the same imagery of commodification as he did with Cressida to describe Helen to the Trojan council. To Troilus, Helen is "a pearl" that "turn'd crown'd kings to merchants". It is not Helen's face that launched a thousand ships but her "price" (2.2.81–83). Helen is to be bargained for, sold to the highest bidder. The play of economics, in which the play itself is entangled, is a relation which is revealed particularly in the problematic status of women as objects of desire. As René Girard remarks, "The intensity and durability of a man's desire for a woman will prove inversely proportional to her willingness to satisfy it."[86] A woman's desire is contextualized as reciprocal, as a reaction to a man's desire for her. Very early, we see that Cressida recognizes the misogynistic chivalric principle that the woman remains desirable only as the object of pursuit:

> Yet hold I off. Women are angels, wooing:
> Things won are done; joy's soul lies in the doing.
> That she belov'd knows naught that knows not this:
> Men prize the thing ungain'd more than it is.
>   (1.2.291–94)

A woman who actively desires is seen as disobedient. This notion is supported in Sonnet 129 ("Enjoy'd no sooner but despised straight"), and echoed by Cressida when she asks Troilus to stay awhile after the first night they slept together:

> Prithee, tarry.
> You men will never tarry.
> O foolish Cressid! I might have still held off,
> And then you would have tarried.
>   (4.2.15–18)

Once Cressida succumbs to Troilus's will, he, like Antoinette's husband once he acquires her inheritance, no longer wants her. In the aubade scene, Troilus shares a laugh with Pandarus at Cressida's expense, "ha ha", and hurries to leave once he has eaten the "cake" for which he has "tarried". So thoroughly discarded is she that Troilus, the man who single-handedly convinced the entire Trojan council to keep Helen, does not utter a single word in Cressida's defence. He complacently allows her to be sacrificed to the war effort, acknowledging that possession of the female by one male implies a collective ownership by the group, powerful to do with her as they choose. Afterward, when he attempts to wrap base intentions in linguistic finery, he effectively couches their love in the words of barter: "We two, that with so many thousand sighs / Did buy each other, must poorly sell ourselves / With the rude brevity and discharge of one" (4.4.40–42). He then proceeds to issue a series of imperatives which implicitly assumes continuing control of her female desire, although he has effectively given her away. In ten lines, he repeats no fewer than four times, "Be thou true" (4.4.60–70), showing that his only concern is her fidelity to him, even though he has betrayed her in the interests of masculine dominance among competing males on the stage of war. Betrayed by her father, her uncle, her lover and her nation, Cressida now has to rely on those virtues – her wit, her wiles, her beauty – that she defensively guarded, and perhaps subconsciously knew she needed in the fickle world of masculine desire, to protect herself.

Both Antoinette and Cressida are subjected to the violence that comes from being treated as an object. Although not limited to sexual abuse, their mistreatment is most commonly in that area, as sex is the vehicle through which power is exercised over the most intricate aspects of women's lives. Power relations and arguments of authority are inscribed on the female body, leaving it deeply and permanently wounded. G.R. Quaife has remarked that in Renaissance England, "violence was very much part of the sexual scene. . . . Any woman of the same or lower social order was seen as a legitimate object of a man's sexual desires."[87] The cat and mouse pursuit then takes on the resonance of a war, emulating the imperial politics of invasion and conquest. Sexual contact is imagined as colonial possession. In Shakespeare's plays, we find desirable women being regarded as colonial spaces, regarded in mercantile terms. Cressida's "bed is India" for whose "pearl" Troilus must dive (1.1.100). His desire for her is expressed in the colonial vocabulary of male conquest and violent possession. Ironically, the violence that is enacted on both Cressida and Antoinette is contained within the sphere that is traditionally regarded as safe, the home, and is actualized by those traditionally regarded as protectors, the closest male relative or the male lover/husband. Pandarus, who is supposed to traditionally assume the role of protector to Cressida in the absence of her father and husband, blithely orchestrates Troilus's possession of her, setting in motion events that would textually crucify her. Like Troilus, he also stands aside and lets the Trojan council do with Cressida as they would.

As with Antoinette, Cressida's hopelessness stems from her occupying an undefined space. Ambivalence permeates every aspect of their condition. Bob Hodge and Vijay Mishra's definition of an ambivalent hybrid as "dispossessed, schizophrenic, exilic, often profoundly unhappy and exploited under capitalism", could be applicable to both these women.[88] The continuous social exclusion and rejection faced by the hybrid slowly undermines her psychological stability. External prejudices are internalized into the body, and expressed as psychic fracture. As David Cooper says, "one does not go mad; one is driven mad".[89] Just as Antoinette's social and emotional status and background render isolation and disintegration inevitable, Antoinette's treatment by her husband pushes her over the edge of sanity. At the end of the play, Shakespeare's Cressida starts to display symptoms of psychic confusion. This perhaps self-consciously recalls the fate of Henryson's Cresseid, doomed to wander the earth, diseased with leprositic boils as penance for being unfaithful to Troilus.[90] Despite their efforts to create a space for themselves, the machinations of patriarchy drive both women mad. The forced passivity that patriarchy and their social conditions impose on them contribute to their psychic disintegration.

While Antoinette is driven to psychic fragmentation by her husband's deliberate oppression, Cressida is psychically wounded by her own desires, which directly conflict with patriarchy's will. Her fractured Self is equally divided between Trojan and Greek loyalties. In Troy, Cressida's Trojan Self is conflicted between dictates of the mind and body when confronted with the dilemma of being with Troilus: her mind cautions prudence and her body desires. She is aware of this when she remarks to Troilus: "I have a kind of self resides with you, / But an unkind self that itself will leave / To be another's fool" (3.2.138–40). Cressida severs her blood ties to her father, and remakes her identity around that of Troilus, joining the community to which he belongs: "I have forgot my father; / I know no touch of consanguinity; / No kin, no love, no blood, no soul so near me / As the sweet Troilus" (4.2.94–97). When Calchas initiates the trade of Antenor for Cressida, and Troilus complacently allows the Council to make the trade, both her father and her lover, around whom her identity revolved at different times, participate actively in unravelling Cressida's identity. She moves from "my Cressid" (3.2.116) for Troilus to "Diomed's Cressida" (5.2.137). She physically resides in the Greek camp now, her father and new lover are on the Greek side, while her heart remains in Troy.

This fragmentation of Cressida, precipitated by situations out of her control, creates in her a psychic schizophrenia: "Troilus, farewell! One eye yet looks on thee, / But with my heart the other eye doth see" (5.2.105–6). Both identities residing within Cressida are warring with each other, creating a psychological rupturing of Self, a confusion of mind that makes her seem whimsical and flighty, eventually a whore for betraying Troilus. She is unsure where her loyalties lie. Because of her psychic fragmentation, her interactions with Diomedes seem a little disconnected: she gives Troilus's sleeve to Diomedes and then takes it back; she makes an appointment with Diomedes, announces that she will not keep it, and then coaxes him back. Cressida's psychic split also creates a divide in Troilus, who says: "Within my soul there doth conduce a fight / Of this strange nature, that a thing inseparate / Divides more wider than the sky and earth" (5.2.145–47). So psychologically disturbed is Cressida that she becomes mentally malleable. Diomedes, recognizing Cressida's fear of further abandonment, easily manipulates her. Each time she hesitates in fulfilling his demands, he pretends to leave. While Cressida should reject his advances, her recognition of her vulnerable position in the enemy camp makes it impossible for her to alienate her only protector. In a paradoxical twist, her agency, geared towards self-protection, thus secures her passivity to Diomedes's will.

When Cressida leaves the Trojan world of the court, she does not escape to the forest of Arden, a rehabilitative space facilitating masculine-oriented paradigm shifts. Instead, she moves to a Greek forest of tents, filled "with debauched, demoralized, manipulative inhabitants. To survive, she resorts to their self-serving, duplicitous, expedient actions."[91] As Grace Tiffany argues, "Cressida is, of course, powerfully encouraged by her circumstances to validate male visions and participate in male schemes; the play does not allow her a clear alternative route for physical survival, any more than dramatic convention afforded Shakespeare the freedom to radically alter the Cressida myth."⁹² She has negatively internalized the outcome of her actions, knowing that she has condemned herself, subconsciously insisting that she did possess agency in the face of patriarchal control:

> If I be false, or swerve a hair from truth,
> When time is old and hath forgot itself,
> When water-drops have worn the stones of Troy,
> And blind oblivion swallow'd cities up,
> And mighty states characterless are grated
> To dusty nothing, yet let memory,
> From false to false, among false maids in love,
> Upbraid my falseness! When they've said "As false
> As air, as water, wind, or sandy earth,
> As fox to lamb, or wolf to heifer's calf,
> Pard to the hind, or step-dame to her son",
> Yea, let them say, to stick the heart of falsehood,
> "As false as Cressid."
>
> (3.3.184–96)

In the Greek camp, Cressida's psychological torment creates the psychic space to create another, almost embarrassing persona – the vacillating, servile, perfidious woman of patriarchy, quite unlike the thinking, prudent, engaging woman we meet at the beginning of the play: "I prithee do not hold me to mine oath. / Bid me do anything but that, sweet Greek" (5.2.26–27). John Bayley observes that "Cressida *does* strike us as a real person, in spite of her role as a commonplace in the play's externalized and intellectual scheme", and "when Ulysses calls her a daughter of the game we may feel obscurely that he is wrong, and, if we feel so, it is at this moment that she gives some sort of impression of personality".⁹³ Despite the accuracy of Ulysses's condemnation of Cressida, we do know that Cressida was a different person only moments ago. Her earlier authentic and dimensional Self has vanished, and in its place is substituted a male-authored Cressida. Her one chance at active self-preservation comes at the tragic cost of eternal textual condemnation as the archetypal faithless woman, full of "turpitude" (5.2.112), the final step of her passage into "silent nonbeing".⁹⁴

Mental breakdowns are the end result for both Antoinette and Cressida, and the patriarchal prisons of both women are engulfed in purifying flames and destroyed, forecasting the incendiary future for both nations should their carceral women remain imprisoned within the supposedly protective walls of imperial patriarchy. As Trinh T. Minh-ha observes, "In this chain and continuum, I am but one link. The story is me, neither me nor mine. ... My story, no doubt is me, but it is also, no doubt, older than me."[95]

However, Shakespeare, like Rhys, does recuperate his Cressida in an effort to effect change. While Antoinette's madness leads her home, with a final understanding of who she is, Shakespeare cannot change the "textual psychosis" of Cressida's fate as she is a "creature of intertextuality of Chaucer, Lydgate, Caxton, Henryson, and others endowed with self-consciousness".[96] Cressida, unlike Antoinette, is denied being purified by flames, condemned to watch Troy burn while she is doomed to immortalize female faithlessness. Shakespeare's recuperation involves the correlative dynamic between nation and woman; purging Elizabethan England of its political contagion would offer potential to recoup those marginalized. Shakespeare does not attempt to join the ranks of Trojan and Arthurian encomiasts; his *Troilus and Cressida*, with its contemporary allusions, references the Elizabethan world in the language of disease and rot, a startlingly disparate picture when it is held to the Trojan and Arthurian models of perfection. The last word of *Troilus and Cressida* is given to Pandarus, who completes the *translatio imperii* of noble Troy to base Elizabethan England. This honour is given to a debauched pimp who traded his niece's flesh to his best friend. He stands, throughout the play, as a lecher who connects with the Elizabethan audience, as "brethren and sisters of the hold-door trade" (5.10.52). Their common bond is that they are all "Good traders in the flesh" (5.10.46), and he bequeaths them his diseases. Shakespeare's calculating slaughter of the cultural ambition of the Trojan legend and Arthurian values is summed up in Pandarus, the last figure onstage, who invites the Elizabethan audience to recognize in him the embodiment of their own diseased body politic, created and nurtured by an infected administration.

The concept of nation lies firmly embedded in the state of the Other, the woman. A recovery of the woman allows for the development of a new nation where every Other is able to find a home. National progress in the developing sixteenth-century England is only possible if issues of Otherness, which affect the wombs of the nation, are reconciled to effect a rebirth of minds and bodies formerly shackled by the colonial experience of patriarchal dominance. While Rhys is able to breathe new dimension into a canonical stereotype, Cressida is textually frozen. Shakespeare's recourse is to open an interrogative space for her to negotiate her world and hold it up to scrutiny. He demonstrates that if the woman is not freed, England, like its fictional noble ancestor, will metaphorically implode on itself, leaving its own people dislocated and dispossessed the way they originally were under colonial exploitation, centuries ago. England will cause its own downfall and all the progress made to strengthen the English as a nation since its colonization will have been for naught.

NOTES

1. Charlotte Brontë, *Jane Eyre* (London: Service and Paton, 1897; Project Gutenberg, 2007), ch. 26–27, http://www.gutenberg.org/files/1260/1260-h/1260-h.htm
2. See, for example, Ania Loomba and Martin Orkin, *Post-Colonial Shakespeares* (London: Routledge, 1998); Jyotsna G. Singh and Gitanjali G. Shahani, "Postcolonial Shakespeare Revisited", *Shakespeare* 6, no. 1 (2010): 127–38; and Thomas Cartelli, *Repositioning Shakespeare: National Formations, Postcolonial Appropriations* (London: Routledge, 1999).
3. Benedict Anderson, *Imagined Communities: Reflections on the Origin and Spread of Nationalism* (London: Verso, 1991), 11–12.
4. See Barbara Lalla, *Postcolonialisms: Caribbean Rereading of Medieval English Discourse* (Kingston: University of the West Indies Press, 2008); Kathy Lavezzo, ed., *Imagining a Medieval English Nation* (Minneapolis: University of Minnesota Press, 2004).
5. Derek Walcott, "The Muse of History", in *What the Twilight Says: Essays*, by Derek Walcott (New York: Farrar, Straus and Giroux, 1998), 63.
6. George Huppert, "The Trojan Franks and their Critics", *Studies in the Renaissance* 12 (1965): 227.
7. See Geoffrey of Monmouth, *Historia Regum Britanniae*, trans. Aaron Thompson (Cambridge, ON: In Parentheses Publications, 1999), http://www.yorku.ca/inpar/geoffrey_thompson.pdf.
8. Jeffrey Jerome Cohen, *Medieval Identity Machines* (Minneapolis: University of Minnesota Press, 2003), 219.
9. Robert M. Stein, "Making History English: Cultural Identity and Historical Explanation in William of Malmesbury and Lazamon's *Brut*", in *Text and Territory: Geographical Imagination in the European Middle Ages*, ed. Sylvia Tomasch and Sealy Gilles (Philadelphia: University of Pennsylvania Press, 1998), 114.

10. Found in many Elizabethan encomiastic literary endeavours, most notably Spenser's *The Faerie Queene*.
11. Anderson, *Imagined Communities*, 30.
12. Homi K. Bhabha, "DissemiNation", in *Nation and Narration*, ed. Homi K. Bhabha (New York: Routledge, 1990), 309, 308.
13. Claire McEachern, *The Poetics of English Nationhood, 1590–1612* (Cambridge: Cambridge University Press, 1996), 6.
14. Salman Rushdie, *Imaginary Homelands: Essays and Criticism, 1981–1991* (London: Granta Books, 1991), 11.
15. Heather James, *Shakespeare's Troy: Drama, Politics and the Translation of Empire* (Cambridge: Cambridge University Press, 1997), 21.
16. Eric S. Mallin, "Emulous Factions and the Collapse of Chivalry: *Troilus and Cressida*", *Representations* 29 (1990): 154.
17. Ibid.
18. Quoted in John Neale, "The Elizabethan Political Scene", in *Essays in Elizabethan History* (London: Jonathan Cape, 1958), 79.
19. William Shakespeare, *Troilus and Cressida*, in *The Riverside Shakespeare*, ed. G. Blakemore Evans (Boston: Houghton Mifflin, 1974), 4.2.23. Subsequent references are taken from this edition and appear parenthetically in the text.
20. See John Breuilly, *Nationalism and the State* (Manchester: Manchester University Press, 1993); Ernest Gellner, *Nations and Nationalism* (Oxford: Blackwell, 1983); E.J. Hobsbawm, *Nations and Nationalism since 1780* (Cambridge: Cambridge University Press, 1990); Anderson, *Imagined Communities*.
21. See Gellner, *Nations and Nationalism*; and Hobsbawm, *Nations and Nationalism since 1780*.
22. Keith Stringer, "Social and Political Communities in European History: Some Reflections on Recent Studies", in *Nations, Nationalism and Patriotism in the European Past*, ed. Claus Bjørn, Alexander Grant and Keith J. Stringer (Copenhagen: Academic Press, 1994), 23, 33.
23. See Adrian Hastings, *The Construction of Nationhood: Ethnicity, Religion and Nationalism* (Cambridge: Cambridge University Press, 1996), 4–5.
24. Kathy Lavezzo, introduction to *Imagining a Medieval English Nation*, vii.
25. Hastings, *Construction of Nationhood*, 45.
26. Anthony Smith, "The 'Golden Age' and National Renewal", in *Myths and Nationhood*, ed. Geoffrey Hosking and George Schöpflin (New York: Routledge, 1997), 36.
27. Linda Colley, *Britons: Forging the Nation, 1707–1837* (New Haven: Yale University Press, 1992), 6.

28. Krishan Kumar, *The Making of English National Identity* (Cambridge: Cambridge University Press, 2003), 93.
29. Sir Walter Raleigh, "Ocean to Cynthia", in *Sir Walter Raleigh: Selected Writings*, ed. Gerald Hammond (Harmondsworth: Penguin, 1984), 21st book, 38.
30. Anderson, *Imagined Communities*, 224.
31. Avraham Oz, "Nation and Place in Shakespeare", in Loomba and Orkin, *Post-Colonial Shakespeares*, 111.
32. Richard Helgerson, *Forms of Nationhood: The Elizabethan Writing of England* (Chicago: University of Chicago Press, 1992), 299.
33. Thomas Wilson, *The State of England, Anno Dom. 1600*, ed. F.J. Fisher, Camden Miscellany (London, 1936), 16:34.
34. Thomas Birch, quoting a state paper ("The advantages, which her majesty hath gotten by that, which hath passed at Cadiz ... 1596"): "Her majesty being threatened to be invaded, hath like a mighty and magnanimous prince sent her navy and army to offer her enemy battle at his own door", *Memoirs of the Reign of Queen Elizabeth* (London, 1754; repr., New York: Ams Press, 1970), 2:47.
35. In 1596, an envoy of the Venetian ambassador remarked of his visit to England: "I noticed that in this country they are in great alarm about the enemy; they will not allow anyone to enter who is not quite well known and who has not been thoroughly examined"; *Calendar of State Papers, Venetian, 1592–1603* (London, 1897), 236.
36. Andrew Hadfield, *Shakespeare and Renaissance Politics* (London: Arden Shakespeare, 2004), 1.
37. See John Guy, *Tudor England* (Oxford: Oxford University Press, 1988); C.S.L. Davies, *Peace, Print and Protestantism, 1450–1558* (London: Paladin, 1977); Rosemary O'Day, *The Longman Guide to the Tudor Age* (London: Longman, 1995).
38. See David Loades, *Power in Tudor England* (Basingstoke: Blackwell, 1997); Penry Williams, *The Tudor Regime* (Oxford: Oxford University Press, 1979).
39. See John Guy, "Introduction: The 1590s: The Second Reign of Elizabeth I?", in *The Reign of Elizabeth I: Court and Culture in the Last Decade* (New York: Cambridge University Press, 1995). See also Paul E.J. Hammer, *The Polarisation of Elizabethan Politics: The Political Career of Robert Devereux, 2nd Earl of Essex, 1585–1597* (Cambridge: Cambridge University Press, 1999).
40. See Mark Goldie, "The Unacknowledged Republic: Officeholding in Early Modern England", in *The Politics of the Excluded, c.1500–1850*, ed. Tim Harris (Basingstoke: Blackwell, 2001), 153–94.
41. Lawrence Stone, *The Crisis of the Aristocracy, 1558–1641* (Oxford: Clarendon Press, 1965), 255.

42. For more on Essex's rebellion, see Robert Lacey, *Robert, Earl of Essex: An Elizabethan Icarus* (London: Weidenfeld and Nicolson, 1970); Simon Adams, "The Patronage of the Crown in Elizabethan Politics: The 1590s in Perspective", in Guy, *Reign of Elizabeth I*, 20–45.
43. Mallin, "Emulous Factions and the Collapse of Chivalry", 146.
44. Andrew Hadfield, "Spenser, Drayton and the Question of Britain", *Review of English Studies* 51, no. 204 (November 2000): 583.
45. Władysław Witalisz, *The Trojan Mirror: Middle English Narratives of Troy as Books of Princely Advice* (Frankfurt: Peter Lang, 2011), 35.
46. Norbert Elias examines the relationship between individual behaviour and social power in the Middle Ages, and the correlative impact that change in one dynamic has on the other. Elias examines political authority, monopolization of political power, the division of labour and the chain of mutual dependence in goal fulfilment or achievement, which all led to the establishment of rules to facilitate harmony among social groups with limited personal interaction. Norbert Elias, *The Civilizing Process: Sociogenetic and Psychogenetic Investigations* (Oxford: Basil Blackwell, 1982).
47. George Chapman, preface to *Seaven Bookes of the Iliades*, in *Chapman's Homer*, ed. Allardyce Nicoll (New York: Pantheon, 1956), 1:503.
48. It is worth mentioning that 1563 was a particularly bad year for England with the plague. Also, Essex claimed that illness was the reason behind his frequent withdrawals from court. See "'A Dangerous Image': The Earl of Essex and Elizabethan Chivalry", *Journal of Medieval and Renaissance Studies* 13 (Fall 1983): 313–29.
49. Bruce Smith, "Rape, Rap, Rupture, Rapture: R-rated Futures on the Global Market", *Textual Practice* 9 (1995): 434.
50. Anne McClintock, *Imperial Leather: Race, Gender and Sexuality in the Colonial Contest* (New York: Routledge, 1995), 1–3.
51. Quoted in E. Howard Bloch and Frances Ferguson, eds., *Misogyny, Misandry and Misanthropy* (Berkeley: University of California Press, 1989), 1. See footnote 1 for further elaboration. Some excellent examples of misogyny found in Latin satires are: John of Salisbury's *Policraticus*, Walter Map's *De nugis curialium*, Andreas Capellanus's *The Art of Courtly Love*, as well as in *Les XV joies de mariage* and what is perhaps the most virulent antimatrimonial satire in the vernacular tongue, Jehan Le Fèvre's translation of *Les lamentations de Matheolus*. Misogyny is virtually synonymous with the works grouped under the rubric of *"les genres du réalisme bourgeois"*: the fabliaux (including Middle English and Italian versions); the animal fable (*Roman de Renart*); the comic theatre or farce; and Jean de Meun's portion of the *Roman de la rose*.

52. George Mosse, *Nationalism and Sexuality: Respectability and Abnormal Sexuality in Modern Europe* (New York: Howard Fertig, 1985), 23.
53. Tamar Mayer, "Gender Ironies of Nationalism: Setting the Stage", in *Gender Ironies of Nationalism: Sexing the Nation*, ed. Tamar Mayer (London: Routledge, 2000), 1–2.
54. McClintock, *Imperial Leather*, 23.
55. Evelyn Stevens describes the characteristics of the cult of virility and machismo as "exaggerated aggressiveness and intransigence in male-to-male interpersonal relationships and arrogance and sexual aggression in male-to-female relationships". Evelyn Stevens, "Mexican Machismo: Politics and Value Orientations", *Western Political Quarterly* 18, no. 4 (1965): 848–57. McClintock asserts that "it was white, European men who . . . owned and managed 85 percent of the earth's surface", a powerful male force that has been "unacknowledged or shrugged off as a fait accompli of nature", *Imperial Leather*, 5–6.
56. Jean Rhys, *Wide Sargasso Sea* (Harmondsworth: Penguin, 1997), 62. Subsequent references are taken from this edition and appear parenthetically in the text.
57. Nira Yuval-Davis, *Gender and Nation* (London: Sage Publications, 1997), 39. Much work has been done on the relationship between gender and its role in perceptions of nation. See, for example, Nira Yuval-Davis, "Women, Citizenship and Difference", *Feminist Review* 57 (1997): 4–27; Sarah Radcliffe and Sallie Westwood, *Remaking the Nation: Place, Identity and Politics in Latin America* (London: Routledge, 1996); McClintock, *Imperial Leather*; Tamar Mayer, *Women and the Israeli Occupation* (London: Routledge, 1994); Victoria de Grazia, *How Fascism Ruled Women: Italy, 1922–1945* (Berkeley: University of California Press, 1992).
58. Malcolm Vale, *War and Chivalry* (London: Duckworth, 1981), 167; Stephen Orgel, "Making Greatness Familiar", *Genre* 15 (1982): 41.
59. The Earl of Essex, in a dispute with Elizabeth, turned his back on her with the insult that "her conditions were as crooked as her carcase". Quoted in John Lingard, *A History of England from the First Invasion by the Romans* (1825; repr., Hong Kong: Forgotten Books, 2013), 11:458–59.
60. See Louis Adrian Montrose, " 'Shaping Fantasies': Figurations of Gender and Power in Elizabethan Culture", *Representations* 1 (1983): 79; and Neville Williams, *All the Queen's Men: Elizabeth I and Her Courtiers* (New York: Macmillan, 1972). Examples given are Essex's royal disfavour for marrying without the queen's permission, and Raleigh's imprisonment for secretly marrying Elizabeth Throckmorton.

61. Louis Adrian Montrose, "Gifts and Reasons: The Contexts of Peele's Araygnement of Paris", *English Literary History* 47 (1980): 440.
62. Andre Hurault, sieur de Maisse, *A Journal of All that Was Accomplished by Monsieur de Maisse, Ambassador in England . . . 1597*, trans. and ed., G.B. Harrison and R.A. Jones (England, 1931), 11–12.
63. Stefan Berger, "On the Role of Myths and History in the Construction of National Identity in Modern Europe", *European History Quarterly* 39, no. 3 (2009): 494.
64. Andreas Huyssen, "Monument and Memory in a Postmodern Age", *Yale Journal of Criticism* 6, no. 2 (1993): 249.
65. Berger, "On the Role of Myths", 492.
66. Dennis Walder describes nostalgia not simply as a longing and desire, but also as "a longing for an experience – subjective in the first place, and yet, far from limited to the individual. It is possible to speak of a group or even a whole society as nostalgic". Dennis Walder, *Postcolonial Nostalgias: Writing, Representation and Memory* (London: Routledge, 2011), 2. Eric Hobsbawm, *The Age of Empire: 1875–1914* (London: Abacus, 1989), 3.
67. Wilson Harris, *The Womb of Space* (Westport, CT: Greenwood, 1983), xvii.
68. Salman Rushdie, "The Empire Writes Back with a Vengeance", *Times* (London), 3 July 1982: 8.
69. Edward Said, *Culture and Imperialism* (New York: Alfred A. Knopf, 1994), 66–67.
70. Michael Thorpe, "'The Other Side': *Wide Sargasso Sea* and *Jane Eyre*", in *Critical Perspectives on Jean Rhys*, ed. Pierrette M. Frickey (Washington, DC: Three Continents, 1990), 178.
71. Douglas Cole, "Myth and Anti-Myth: The Case of Troilus and Cressida", *Shakespeare Quarterly* 31 (1980): 77.
72. Preface to *Troilus and Cressida*, in *The Works of John Dryden*, ed. Sir Walter Scott, rev., George Saintsbury (Edinburgh: William Paterson, 1882), vi, 225.
73. Robert Kimbrough, *Shakespeare's Troilus and Cressida and Its Setting* (Cambridge, MA: Harvard University Press, 1964), 73.
74. Rosemary Marangoly George, *The Politics of Home: Postcolonial Relocations and Twentieth-Century Fiction* (Cambridge: Cambridge University Press, 1996), 2.
75. John McLeod, *Beginning Postcolonialism* (Manchester: Manchester University Press, 2000), 217; Homi K. Bhabha, *The Location of Culture* (London: Routledge, 1994), 1.
76. Vijay Mishra and Bob Hodge, "What Is Postcolonialism?", *New Literary History* 36 (2005): 375–402.

77. Richard Kearney, *Strangers, Gods and Monsters* (London: Routledge, 2002), 65.
78. Sanford Sternlicht, *Jean Rhys* (New York: Twayne, 1997), 118.
79. Gayatri Spivak, "Three Women's Texts and a Critique of Imperialism", in *Race, Writing and Difference*, ed. Henry Louis Gates, Jr. (Chicago: University of Chicago Press, 1985), 269.
80. Carolyn Asp, "In Defense of Cressida", *Studies in Philosophy* 74 (1977): 410.
81. Mallin, "Emulous Factions and the Collapse of Chivalry", 161.
82. Ibid., 162.
83. Montrose, "Shaping Fantasies", 68.
84. Coppélia Kahn, *Man's Estate: Masculine Identity in Shakespeare* (Berkeley: University of California Press, 1981), 131.
85. Carol Cook, "Unbodied Figures of Desire", *Theatre Journal* 38 (1986): 254, 257.
86. René Girard, "The Politics of Desire in *Troilus and Cressida*", in *Shakespeare and the Question of Theory*, ed. Patricia Parker and Geoffrey Hartman (New York: Methuen, 1985), 190.
87. G.R. Quaife, *Wanton Wenches and Wayward Wives: Peasants and Illicit Sex in Early Seventeenth-Century England* (New Brunswick, NJ: Rutgers University Press, 1979), 172–82.
88. Mishra and Hodge, "What Is Postcolonialism?", 384.
89. David Cooper, introduction to *Madness and Civilization: A History of Insanity in the Age of Reason* by Michel Foucault (Oxon: Routledge Classics, 2001), viii.
90. Robert Henryson, *The Testament of Cresseid*, Online Medieval and Classical Library Release, no. 6, 1995.
91. Arlene Okerlund, "In Defense of Cressida: Character as Metaphor", *Women's Studies* 7 (1980): 14.
92. Grace Tiffany, "Not Saying No: Female Self-Erasure in *Troilus and Cressida*", *Texas Studies in Literature and Language* 35, no. 1 (1993): 45. See also David Farley-Hills, *Shakespeare and the Rival Playwrights, 1600–1606* (New York: Routledge, Chapman and Hall, 1990), for a discussion of Renaissance performances of the Troilus and Cressida myth.
93. John Bayley, *The Uses of Division: Unity and Disharmony in Literature* (London: Chatto and Windus, 1976), 205.
94. Tiffany, "Not Saying No", 47.
95. Trinh T. Minh-ha, *Woman, Native, Other: Writing, Postcoloniality, and Feminism* (Bloomington: Indiana University Press, 1989), 122–23.
96. Cook, "Unbodied Figures of Desire", 50.

Chapter 4

FAR-OFF PLACES AND THE INVENTION OF ENGLISHNESS
Rereading *Robinson Crusoe* as Romance

RHONDA KAREEN HARRISON

IN THE NARROWEST SENSE, THE IMPORTANCE of the novel to the development of English identity is evidenced in the manner in which early novels located English characters in positions and places outside of England that demanded expressions of Englishness. For this reason, there is an unsurprising marriage between romance and the novel as a mode through which English identity is invented in the eighteenth-century world outside England. In some of the earliest English novels, the Caribbean, both its locale and products, are indispensable factors used in fabricating English nationhood and identity. *Robinson Crusoe*, like many of its contemporaries, presents a hero who clarifies his English identity against non-European threats. Without a doubt, much of the English identity emphasized in *Robinson Crusoe* reflects England's invisible/visible connection with the Caribbean space. These inventions of Englishness in the Caribbean space act crucially to avow English identity in *Robinson Crusoe*, and reflect elements of what constituted a larger part of the project of creating a national and colonizing identity through literature during the eighteenth century. Through this connection, we can observe the relationship between what Ian Baucom describes as English identity "happen[ing] overseas" and the reproduction of that identity in the metropole.[1] On the whole, this paper examines how the synergy created between the Old World and the Caribbean affected the development of English literature and identity through influences on the romance and the novel. In general, the eighteenth-century romance allows for the substitution of cultural and political realities in the creative writings, which, in turn, allows for inventions of Englishness. Looking at reconfigurations and appropriations of utopia and the quest motif, crucial ingredients of the romance genre, this chapter examines the relationship between these traditional romance idioms and the emergence of new English identities in Daniel Defoe's *Robinson Crusoe*. To this end, attention is also given to how the Caribbean affects changes in both the romance and the novel, and becomes central in the project of fabricating eighteenth-century English nationhood and identity. The strongest evidence of this lies in the fact that most of the setting of the *first* English novel is the Caribbean.

ROMANCE AND THE FORMULATIONS OF NATIONAL IDENTITIES

Before beginning the process of rereading *Robinson Crusoe* as a romance, it is necessary to discuss the importance of the insular English romance to the evolution of English identity. Northrop Frye contends that, through the embedding of its values in the romance, the social ideals of any given dominant class are transmitted, and affect the conducting and reinforcing of its cultural hegemonies.[2] Implicit in Frye's suggestion is the idea that romance affects the construction of identity on individual, national and cultural scales. Scholars of Middle English literature insightfully observe that the romance influenced the ways in which English people living in the Middle Ages imagined and understood themselves.[3] Yin Liu suggests that the Middle English romance helped to invent English literary tradition and identity through the establishment of heroes in the wider literary English discourse which, in turn, "invoke[d] the canonical romance tradition".[4] Yin contends that these Middle English romances strongly contributed to the English sense of self.[5]

Susan Crane observes that the Middle English romance had such an impact because it commented on and confronted dominant ideologies that were specific to England's social situation in the Middle Ages.[6] Crane argues that, by commenting on and confronting English ideologies, Middle English writers effectively individualized the romance's relevance to the English context.[7] As the Middle English romance consolidated England's historical past with identity, language and culture through literary form, it allowed

English writers to create representations of Self and Other in the English insular romance – ingredients necessary for the formulation of identity. Significantly, these insular romances fostered the development of a nascent form of English identity and the growth of nationalist feeling in England. These factors were necessary for the feeding of the national psyche. Nathaniel Griffin suggests that, after the advent of the printing press in the fifteenth century, there was an expansion of the English reading public.[8] This expansion in literacy was useful in further solidifying the romance in the national consciousness.[9] Griffin also contends that, through projections of adventure and patriotic allure, the romance gained an even wider appeal.[10]

This appeal grew stronger in the eighteenth century with the emergence of the novel and the inclusion of romance idioms in its text. Ian Duncan insightfully observes that the period between 1750 and 1830 saw the emergence of "national literature" in Britain. The idea of a national literature in the eighteenth century is linked to both the romance and the novel form. The novel form and the eighteenth-century romance help to define English tradition and identity in the Age of Exploration.[11]

The union of the romance and the novel effectively emphasized a national culture via cheaper, more accessible literature in the form of the novel. For Duncan, this relationship occurs because the insular romance has always fostered the idea of national literature through its claim on "imaginative authenticity as a form of national life".[12] In determining the significance of the novel to the development of national identity, Timothy Brennan argues that it is through its power of presentation that the novel engenders the staging of an identity that allows people to see themselves as belonging to a special community that may constitute the nation.[13] Many of these developments, Brennan opines, can be attributed to the fact that the novel allowed a larger portion of the eighteenth-century population access to a form of national print media, and was integral in helping in the standardization of language and the encouragement of literacy.[14] Many of the adventures of these early English novels were located in the New World – more specifically, in the Caribbean. Therefore, the Caribbean became necessary to reinvigorating national consciousness in England.

FORGING ENGLISH IDENTITY IN THE CARIBBEAN

In the Age of Exploration, the Caribbean provided opportunities for experiencing many of the touted aspects of the romance – namely, treasure, adventure and quest. However, the Caribbean also provided a space in which more ideological aspects of the romance – utopia and identity – could be worked out. Hence, the combination of the Caribbean space, with these aspects of the romance genre, and the novel, with its predilection for both fancy and realism, was essential to creating believable fantasies about how the Caribbean space fulfilled English imaginings of self. It is this combination that must be considered as a necessary impetus in the formation of English identity in the eighteenth century. Undoubtedly, much of this is aided by the imperial romance discourse which promotes the primacy of the nation through individual experience, especially as this relates to the economic development of the nation on the whole. In general, we can safely say that the early English novel concerns itself with private life while attempting to eke out a romance about national identity in the face of the imperial project as well as through it. As much of England's early imperial expansions occurred in the Caribbean, the Caribbean becomes central to the process of national myth-making.

Necessarily, the relationship between the romance and the New World, too, calls for examination. The question which emerges is: how do the romance idiom of utopia and the concept of the novel accommodate the New World, and more specifically the British Caribbean? From the onset, the New World space had been aligned with the concept of El Dorado, which, in turn, altered the original concept of utopia. Originary romance ideas of utopia as belonging to a golden world, an Other place of mythic proportions, achieved realistic dimensions in the space of the Americas. Spanish tales of the fabled golden city of El Dorado displaced the mythic golden world in the romance by providing a *tangible* golden world. A literal golden world re-entered the British imagination in the Age of Exploration through the physical sites of Montezuma's Tenochtitlan and the Peruvian Muisca towns. In fact, as the Americas became more prominent in English writings, there was a subtle development in the concept of utopia: it became aligned to economic actualization. Economic actualization began to form a crucial idiosyncrasy of eighteenth-century English identity. More than at any other historical point, the concept of utopia absorbed the romance's penchant for wish-fulfilment, even if that fulfilment occurred without the hero's self-discovery or return to an authentic identity.[15] Easily put, the romances that occur in the Caribbean space do not effect spiritual, cultural or emotional growth in their heroes. Their focus largely rests on the respective hero's desire to achieve economic gains. In short, English attitudes suggest that the English read the Caribbean as materially rich but providing little else. However, from a postcolonial perspective, the obvious influences of the Caribbean on shaping English identity and nationhood cannot be overlooked.

CARIBBEAN CENTRALITY TO ENGLISH IDENTITY: THE WONDERFUL CASE OF ROBINSON CRUSOE

A most obvious place through which to begin a rereading of *Robinson Crusoe* as a romance is the novel's setting. It is best to begin by determining the manner in which the Caribbean island-space can be considered a utopia that engenders a safe space for Crusoe to invent the version of Englishness suitable to the imperial man. Much of the setting of the first English novel is located in places like Africa, Brazil and the Caribbean, considered peripheral to England; and this is one of the first ways through which Defoe enacts the genre of romance in his work. As the romance typically locates itself in a golden age or far-off climes, by situating the main action of the work in "exotic" Africa and the distant West Indies, Defoe secures for his protagonist the safety of a space in which he can dabble in roles that would not have been available to him within England: those of slave trader and colonizer, contemporary eighteenth-century markers of British imperialism.

Thomas Krise contends that Defoe's use of the West Indies in his portrayal of Crusoe's experience projects common British perceptions of the West Indies as "empty, rich and defenceless".[16] In this reworking of the romance, these empty, rich and defenceless lands outside of Britain and Europe became tangible spaces that afforded opportunities for white male explorers to inscribe narratives of power and identity.[17] Therefore, Crusoe's ordering and transformation of his island paradise into his "two plantations in the island" is a means through which he is able to project his identity on the landscape and prepare for opportunities to exercise power in his domain.[18] To this extent, I agree with Peter Hulme's suggestion that "Crusoe's island shares some of the paradisaical elements of certain Utopias, especially the traditions of what might be called 'colonial Utopias', those which stand outside the mainstream of Utopian traditions both by being primarily a sought ideal and only secondarily discursive, and by being constantly anti-authoritarian in impetus".[19]

Although I am more concerned with Crusoe's island experience, the importance of the quest motif is valuable to this discussion. On the whole, the quest is used throughout the novel both to serve as an important marker of the romance and to help assert English imperial identity in various places during the eighteenth century. However, it is also used to emphasize the essentiality of the Caribbean island-colony as a type of utopia in which English identity may be safely hatched, incubated and developed for export back to England.

Leslie Rabine observes that, in its originary form, the quest traces the hero's movement for self-identity.[20] She also observes that the quest takes the form of "an exalted passion for an unattainable heroine".[21] Likewise, Harold Bloom notes that the romance's quest is "a journey toward home, the hero's home" to be exact.[22] However, for Defoe's Crusoe, the quest motif neither traces a movement towards individual self-identity nor demonstrates an exalted passion; neither is the quest a determined movement towards home. Instead, Crusoe's quest is reflective of "the spirit of English colonial and commercial daring" of the eighteenth century, which could only result in material success.[23] Therefore, the romance's quest in *Robinson Crusoe* and the world which it engenders rely on the wish-fulfilment aspect of the romance for its reality. This vital aspect of the romance in *Robinson Crusoe* necessarily includes Crusoe's gaining of material wealth accumulated during the course of his travels.

The spatial movements that Crusoe undertakes deliberately chart journeys to places that provide economic opportunities. We can infer that utopia, for Crusoe, is an economic paradise. Hence, Crusoe's initial foray into Africa as a slaver is, as Roxann Wheeler describes it, a recognition of the value of a "profit-oriented colonial economy dependent on African slaves".[24] However, Crusoe's participation in the act of slaving is also the initial projecting of English ownership into the world outside England and Europe. Ironically, although Crusoe participates in slaving, a defining feature of European identity in Africa, there is no scope for him to inscribe either personal or national identity there. In addition, Africa is framed as threatening. Crusoe's experiences as a slave in a Moroccan house is a threat to his notions of what is entailed in English identity: "this change of my circumstances from a merchant to a miserable slave" (27). It must be noted that it is not his position as a slave that is considered un-English, but his loss of merchandise and merchant-powers. Like Richard Ligon's unnamed sailor, Crusoe values the world outside of Britain through its economic worth.[25] Therefore, it is not surprising that, as soon as Crusoe escapes to freedom, he reacquires goods and shortly sells Xury for "sixty pieces of eight" (52). He resorts to the expressions of Englishness with which he is familiar.

Crusoe's experiences in Africa form the necessary impetus in determining where and how English identity can be inscribed or developed. Africa's inappropriateness is determined by the fact that it is already inscribed with multiple identities – Moors at Sallee, Negroes and Europeans. These multiple identities prevent Englishness from becoming the dominant identity. In short, Africa is far too crowded for the invention of Englishness. Necessarily, Crusoe's African experiences suggest that English identity in the wider eighteenth-century world is being developed for later inscriptions on defenceless lands. Europeans saw the Atlantic World as largely empty despite its Amerindian populace. Defoe's locating of Crusoe's castaway experience in the New World reflects the English communal desire to inscribe their identity upon the non-European world. In analysing *Robinson Crusoe*, Edward Said argues that its advent as the first "modern realistic novel" in English is "certainly not accidental".[26] He suggests that it is an assertion of identity upon a world that is both distant and non-European as much as it is an interpretation of "strange regions of the world".[27] While I largely agree with Said's postulation, the identity that Crusoe asserts on the island is not just the one that he necessarily brings, but one that he invents to meet his needs on the island, and one which is later used as the hallmark of Englishness in the imperial project.

How, then, does Crusoe go about inventing Englishness on his New World island and, by extension, create a utopia? The conditions for inventing and asserting identity are ripe on the island: first and foremost, Crusoe is the only European in sight; second, the island is uninhabited yet fertile with birds and goats. He describes the land primarily in terms of the fauna that he encounters. Interestingly, Crusoe sees almost no island flora. His references to flora are strictly in terms of their usefulness to him: "If I wanted a board, I had no other way but to cut down a tree" (107). As a result, Crusoe's contact with the environment occurs strictly to meet his demands and to make the landscape less Caribbean. This subtle dismissal of the island flora and descriptions of the land as barren open the way for the insemination of Englishness at the level of the soil through the reinvention of the landscape. As such, Ian Watt observes that throughout the novel, "the natural scene on the island appeals not for adoration, but for exploitation".[28] Watt's observation hints at the extent to which the Caribbean space as presented in *Robinson Crusoe* is essential to both the colonial project and the manner in which Englishness and exploitation later become almost synonymous in the Caribbean and other colonial spaces.

At first, Crusoe makes no attempt to reinvent the landscape beyond the needs of his shelter. His inadvertent discovery of the island's fertility is the force that causes him to begin the process of naturalizing the island to some degree of Englishness:

> I saw some few stalks of something green shooting out of the ground, which I fancied might be some plant I had not seen; but I was surprised, and perfectly astonished, when, after a little longer time, I saw about ten or twelve ears come out, which were perfect green barley of the same kind as our *European* – nay, as our *English* barley. . . . and this was the more strange to me, because I saw near it still, all along by the side of the rock, some other straggling stalks, which proved to be stalks of rice. (122–23)

Incidentally, once Crusoe's inadvertent process of naturalizing the landscape to Englishness begins, the tropical island almost immediately starts to reveal its value as an Englishman's paradise. He discovers wild sugar cane in need of cultivation, melon, clusters of grapes, cocoa trees and citrus trees. Defoe's blithe identification of English fruit in the novel's tropical setting is further evidence of the imperial collective tendency to read the non-European world as a blank space that could only come to reality through contact with England. Therefore, it is impossible to ignore the fact that the island flora, which Crusoe now recognizes, constitute items – cocoa and sugar cane – that are in demand in metropolitan England. It is on this discovery that Crusoe articulates "a secret kind of pleasure . . . to think that this was all my own, that I was king and lord of all this country indefensibly, and had a right of possession" (159). Between its receptiveness to English crops and its wealth of desired tropical crops, the island attains a utopic quotient.

Almost immediate to Crusoe's reading of English qualities in the island, his initial dubbing of the island as the "Island of Despair" makes way for his declaration of enamourment (110). This change of attitude when the

Caribbean landscape is familiarized is not unusual for the English colonist. In "America, Found and Lost", Charles Mann observes that, in a bid to reconcile the strangeness of the New World landscape, colonists transformed it into a place that they could understand.[29] So, once Crusoe is able to recognize an environmental aspect with which he is familiar, his attitude changes and he can begin to transform the island into his personal utopia. Hence, the familiarity of the grapevines causes him to build a second home in the wooded section of the island. In addition, impressed by the similarity of the rolling hills, freshness and flourishing greenness of the western section of the island to the English landscape, Crusoe declares it a "planted garden" (159).

Through the act of planting a garden, Crusoe draws similarity both between God and himself and between his island paradise and Eden. Much of this garden comparison is useful in the subtle construction of the colonial utopia and helps in strengthening the romance idiom throughout the novel. Elizabeth DeLoughrey, Renée Gosson and George Handley observe that natural histories comprise a significant part of the colonial process as they are embedded in the historical process of colonialism.[30] Hence, Crusoe's discerning of the island as having "English" characteristics evolves from this perception of the island and contributes to the re-creation of landscape as English and as utopic.

The discovery of the fertility of the soil, coupled with Crusoe's change in attitude towards the island, engenders a new phase in his inventions of Englishness: gardening. Gibson Burrell and Karen Dale argue that social organization lies at the heart of both utopia and gardening.[31] Crusoe's assertion of his ownership of the island is linked to his gardening activities, which are tied to his understanding of the climate of the island: "I sought for a moister piece of ground to make another trial in, and I dug up a piece of ground near my new bower, and sowed the rest of my seed in *February*, a little before the *vernal equinox*; and this having the rainy months of *March* and April to water it, sprung up very pleasantly, and yielded a very good crop" (166). Crusoe's introduction of these European crops to his tropical island constitutes part of what Alfred Crosby describes as "ecological imperialism".[32] Crusoe justifies this ecological imperialism by pointing out a deficit in the island's natural landscape: the absence of cassava roots typically indigenous to the New World. Later, with help from both Friday and the Spaniard, Crusoe is able to expand the size of his European garden. At the peak of his stay on the island, after sowing twenty-two bushels of barley, "we brought in and thrashed out above two hundred and twenty bushels; and the like in proportion of the rice" (396).

Crusoe's pride in his plantations at the end of his island experience comes to represent an aspect of English conquest of the New World environment: steady control and reorganization of the flora in order to give success to English settlement. This strategy suggests a blueprint useful in the process of inventing Englishness in other imperial projects. Much of imperial English identity would later be linked to a reinvention and control of the environment through gardening cultures. Interestingly, Crusoe's success in manipulating the island's environment also translates into economic success on his Brazilian plantation, from which he receives "five chests of excellent sweetmeats, and a hundred pieces of gold uncoined, . . . one thousand two hundred chests of sugar, eight hundred rolls of tobacco, and the rest of the whole account in gold" upon his return to the Old World (454).

Although much of Crusoe's pride lies in his conquest of the island's flora, another aspect of his ecological imperialism lies in his domestication of the wild goats, his release of cats into the woods and, later, in the importation of "five cows, three of them being big with calf, some sheep, and some hogs" (487). These animals also contribute significantly to inventions of Englishness in the New World space. The colonial self-image of Crusoe that emerges is one in which Englishness is also determined by dietary practice. Crusoe accustoms himself to a diet of milk, cheese, butter, raisins and corn bread: all non-tropical dietary items. On the whole, the utopia that Crusoe creates through his gardening and domestic activities shores up his English identity in the tropics primarily through the reinvention of the island's flora and fauna, which, in turn, sustain his Englishness through diet.

The image of the reinvented landscape lends more to the creation of Englishness than the attempt to forge a familiar space in the New World. By creating a utopia through gardening, Crusoe is also able to forge an economic utopia: a most necessary aspect of Englishness in the wider world. Much of the utopic nature of the island, and the ghost plantation, lies in the fact that both places engender economic success either through their respective plantations or through merchandise salvaged from shipwrecks. Economic success from plantations and salvaged treasure come to constitute Englishness in the New World, and are also a large part of the romance element in *Robinson Crusoe*. The fact that the novel ends with the figure of the absentee planter Crusoe reaping the rewards from his various plantations not only serves as proof that metropolitan Englishness is sustained by the controlled fruitfulness of the New World, but also reveals the romance's penchant for wish-fulfilment. By fulfilling this principal dimension of the romance, Defoe not only highlights popular assumptions about English adventurers in the Caribbean but, as Hulme points out, creates Crusoe as the prototype of the British colonist.[33]

WHOSE CARIBBEAN? WHO'S ENGLISH? FRIDAY AND CRUSOE

Crusoe's perceptions of power are skewed by the island experience. When he first arrives on the island, he declares himself the "king and lord" of the island (159). Much of his posturing is evident in the erection of property reflective of his status: at first a plantation, and later a country seat and his castle. Many of the possessive descriptors that he initially uses to emphasize his ownership over the island do not reflect any relationship between his island paradise and the English hierarchical structure. It is not until he regains the society of his fellow Englishmen that he reconciles his position in relation to the English sovereignty. At this point, he declares himself "governor" of the island, thereby recapitulating the unofficial title of king of the island (427). Through this declaration, Crusoe concedes ownership of the island to the English Crown. His concession may be read as his acknowledgement of the role of English explorers in the enlargement of the English empire via securing island properties. Crusoe's declaration also suggests ideas about what constitutes Englishness in the wider world and its relationship to the individual English explorer.

However, Crusoe's ownership extends the expression of property to include the possession of human property in the form of the Kalinago Friday. To a large extent, Friday constitutes an aspect of the landscape that requires anglicizing and a vital aspect of what must also be possessed. If the reinvention of the physical landscape aids in the constitution of Englishness, then the colonizing of the non-English body enacts a performance of colonizing the fertile non-European mind. This is a vital part of inventing Englishness, as it appeals to an identity that "endow[s] properties of place", even if that place is the human body.[34] Traditional views of Friday's placing Crusoe's foot on his head as an act of his submission reflect the perceived manner in which Europeans ranked their relationship with Amerindians in the New World. By placing himself at the level of the soil, Friday aligns himself to part of what must be inseminated with European knowledge.

In *The Rise of the Novel*, Watt postulates that Crusoe's relationship with Friday is egocentric as it is determined exclusively in terms of Crusoe's emotional needs.[35] As Friday generally acquiesces to Crusoe's leading, Crusoe rejoices at the fertile nature of Friday's mind as evident in the results:

> I likewise taught him to say *Master*; and then let him know that was to be my name: I likewise taught him to say Yes and No, and to know the meaning of them. I gave him some milk in an earthen pot, and let him see me drink it before him, and sop my bread in it; and gave him a cake of bread to do the like, which he quickly complied with, and made signs that it was very good for him. (329)

In this excerpt, Crusoe celebrates what he perceives to be Friday's unequivocal submission. Defoe writes a linguistic and cultural passivity into Friday's character that overlaps with the submission of the environment and suggests a concession to Crusoe's superior power. This is implied in the manner in which Friday, from Crusoe's view, readily acquiesces to using the English language, and dressing and eating as an Englishman. Accordingly, Peter Hulme humorously suggests that the "true romance in *Robinson Crusoe* is between Crusoe and Friday. They live in domestic bliss."[36] Their relationship helps to sustain the island-utopia, as it gives Crusoe a sense of dominance over the physical and human aspects of the island.

Crusoe's relationship with Friday is a vital aspect of the romance dimension of *Robinson Crusoe*. First, this relationship is a crucial marker of how English identity is asserted in the Caribbean space. It reflects the English desire for "spiritual fidelity" from the colonized individual in order for the colonial project to succeed.[37] It is in the Caribbean space that Crusoe learns how to colonize the human mind through language, religion and culture, ultimately aimed at reinventing the non-English as English. Defoe also evokes the romance idiom through the assumption that the Kalinago is a cannibal. Cannibals and cannibalism have been long-standing features of the romance idiom and were sometimes used within the context of European romances as metaphors for lust and greed. Within the context of the New World, the image of the cannibal assumes an almost singular meaning: savage. The first stage of Crusoe's reinvention of Friday lies at the level of appetite. Crusoe assumes that Friday, being a Kalinago, must be a cannibal. Hence, he undertakes to wean Friday away from his "hankering stomach after some human flesh" (331). The diet to which he introduces Friday is an English diet that consists of boiled or roasted kid's meat, broth, bread and raisins.

As paradoxical as it seems, this transforming of Friday from his assumed Kalinago cannibal appetite is a first step in trying to reinvent him as English. It constitutes a challenge to the social mores and values that are connected to Friday's attitude to the island environment and are a part of what must be eradicated. In the case of *Robinson Crusoe*, the figure of the cannibal is used as a touchstone against which English civility is measured and proven. By creating the native Caribbean man as a cannibal, Defoe encodes ideas about the inferiority of Caribbean identity, especially in comparison to the English. It is against this notion of the cannibalistic Caribbean man that the "civilized" English man fully emerges. Hence, Crusoe's various acts of inventing Friday as English are active measures to de-cannibalize him and, by extension, de-Caribbeanize him.

Another step that Crusoe takes in the invention process is the clothing of Friday in European-styled garb: "I gave him a pair of linen drawers ... then I made him a jerkin of goat's skin ... and I gave him a cap" (331). The basis of Crusoe's deliberate culturing of Friday in European clothing derives from what Crusoe perceives are European qualities in Friday's physical appearance that make him suitable for such a reinvention: "He had a very good countenance, not a fierce and surly aspect, but seemed to have something very manly in his face; and yet he had all the sweetness and softness of a *European* in his countenance, too, especially when he smiled" (327). In view of Friday's European appearance, complemented by his European outfit, Crusoe anglicizes him through an erasure of material culture previously evident in his Kalinago apparel. Therefore, I agree with Wheeler's observation in "My Savage, My Man: Racial Multiplicity in *Robinson Crusoe*" that Crusoe's defining of Friday's body is consistent with that of a "Europeanized savage".[38] Wheeler's observation of the manner in which Friday and Crusoe, through dress, mirror the reality around them – one a Europeanized savage, the other a "barbaric-looking European" – speaks to the manner in which the Caribbean space complicates identity in the process of colonization.[39]

By the end of the novel, Crusoe and Friday are both olive complected. Friday is perhaps coloured so by Crusoe's imagination; Crusoe, bronzed somewhat by tropical living, is not quite as white as before. Critics have tended to emphasize Crusoe's control over the environment as being reflective of the colonial fantasy and romance element that dominates the novel. However, not much attention has been paid to the manner in which the physical environment of the Caribbean blurs the boundaries of identity between Friday and Crusoe, blending savage and European in a crucible of almost physical sameness, thereby threatening the positive outcome of this New World romance. With the colonial fantasy threatened, the recourse lies in the novel's emphasis on speaking English as crucial in a space where physical identity can be so altered by climate and dress. Hence, the English-speaking voice becomes essential to defining identity and is aligned with authority in the colonial context.

The result is, of course, that the hallmark of inventing Englishness and a subsequent trope of Englishness in the empire lies in the ability to speak English. Bill Ashcroft contends that by installing the imperial language as standard and displacing the native language, the colonizer is able to "plan[t] the language of empire in a new place", thereby effecting cultural control.[40] Therefore, while Crusoe confesses that Friday's presence affords him "some use for my tongue again", it resonates with the innocuous suggestion that the use of the imperial language is restricted to primarily meet his egotistic needs (340). Indeed, Crusoe confesses that Friday "[learned] *English* so well that he could answer me almost any question" (341). However, Crusoe's language relationship with Friday is functional and predicated on the need to control Friday linguistically and culturally. Ultimately, this linguistic control helps to complete Crusoe's utopia, as his subject is not only "spiritually loyal" to his needs, but fulfils his need for an audience.

Crusoe demonstrates no interest in learning Friday's language and remains fairly comfortable with their functional communication. As a result, the initial English words which Friday must learn are "Master", "Friday", "no" and "yes". These words reflect the hierarchy of power that exists on Crusoe's island, as the language relationship is cogently characterized by orders or commands given to Friday. Since interpretations of the manner in which the English language is used in *Robinson Crusoe* are extensively established and accepted as being reflective of power discourses in colonialism, I will not expand further. However, I wish to point out that although the socio-cultural power that Crusoe exercises over Friday are embedded in these orders (first through the act of renaming, and secondly, as a means of comprehending Crusoe's wishes), their linguistic relationship is plagued with problems. In their overall communication, Friday does not have the English words to tell

Crusoe all he wishes to know. Equally important is the fact that Crusoe does not know the Taíno or Kalinago languages and is, at times, unable to fully understand Friday's intent. The compromise lies in the non-verbal expressions and body language that must suffice for the gaps in language: "[Friday] could not tell twenty in *English*, but he numbered them by laying so many stones in a row, and pointing to me to tell them over" (342). Although Crusoe commends Friday's receptiveness and aptitude in learning and understanding English, Friday's use of the English language never evolves beyond that of a contact language.

Although Crusoe's island experience is largely presented as one in which the imperial language dominates for the betterment of the relationship between the colonized and his colonizer, Crusoe suffers anxiety because he is unable to fully understand Friday's language. This is best exemplified when Crusoe observes the "extraordinary sense of pleasure" that Friday exudes at the sight of the mainland; he admits that Friday's reactions, particularly his sparkling eyes and "strange eagerness", put "a great many thoughts into [him]". For this reason, he becomes jealous and withdraws from Friday, returning only to question him about his desire to leave the island paradise and upset their domestic bliss. Crusoe's jealousy makes him "circumspect" and "not so familiar and kind to [Friday]". Although Crusoe attempts to gloss it over, this vexation lasts for weeks. His fears about Friday's desire to leave are partially allayed after considerable probing to prove him as "a religious Christian and ... grateful friend" (357). Friday, however, is more precise in his reading of Crusoe's emotions and body language after the hilltop experience. Friday's question, "Why you angry mad with Friday? what me done?", reveals his suspicions of the motives and attitudes behind the coolness of Crusoe's actions towards him. Although Friday does much to bring about a resolution to the situation, Crusoe is not fully convinced of his sincerity until he sees the tears in Friday's eyes.

Ironically, it is Friday's native language that marks Crusoe as the outsider. As Friday, his father and the Spaniard are able to speak Caribbean native languages, they are able to converse with each other; Crusoe remains outside those conversations as a passive participant who is dependent on translations in order to keep abreast. Crusoe becomes Othered in his own kingdom! This exclusion is something that Crusoe also attempts to gloss over by asserting his role as benevolent king: "My island was now peopled, and I thought myself very rich in subjects.... My man *Friday* was a Protestant, his father was a *Pagan* and a *cannibal*, and the *Spaniard* was a Papist. However, I allowed liberty of conscience throughout my dominions" (385). One must wonder whether Crusoe's assertion of power here is perhaps an attempt to console himself at the moment of his alienation by a language he doesn't understand. Indeed, the feared threat of invasion of his island comes not in terms of armed forces, but in the reality of linguistic exclusion. Crusoe's English does not regain relevance in his island kingdom until he rescues the ship's captain and his mates from the mutineers. With the presence of more English speakers, English once again regains prominence in the island as the imperial language and the native language is once more repressed.

CONCLUSION

On the surface, it would seem that both the landscape and Friday are passive and lack agency during the colonizing process. However, *Robinson Crusoe* is an imperial romance intent on writing English domination onto perceived empty, receptive spaces. After all, it is a type of romance novel about creating a utopia through acts of deliberate cultivation on both the environment and the human body. As Hulme posits, a part of *Robinson Crusoe*'s romance-perennial quality lies in the fact that it "inevitably foregrounds the colonial alibi – the man alone, on a desert island, constructing a simple and moral economy which becomes the basis for a commonwealth presided over by a benevolent sovereign".[41] The radical nature of the novel lies in its invention of a space and an identity suitable for the tasks which imperial conquests require. Through a rereading of *Robinson Crusoe*, the Caribbean critic is well placed to identify an English society beginning to understand the role that their cultural values and the colonial space play in the colonizing process.

Through both literature and exploration, the Caribbean provided much of the necessary synergy and energies needed for creation of imperial and national versions of Englishness in the eighteenth century. Although eclipsed in significance by British imperial expansions into Asia and Africa in the nineteenth century, the Caribbean remained a subtle but pervasive influence on English and British understandings of identity. Hence, I want to close with a final image of the Caribbean's impact on romance from the discovery of the New World through to the twentieth century. Evidence of the manner in which the insular romance is changed by the Caribbean experience is seen in H. Rider Haggard's *King Solomon's Mines*: "'And so,' George Curtis ended, 'we have lived for nearly two years, like a second Robinson Crusoe and his man Friday, hoping against hope that some natives might come here to help us away, but none have come.'"[42] In this statement, there is an intersection of the romance of primitive English imperial identity and the modern English identity in the late 1800s. The perpetuation of this primitive "New World" romance and its engendering of other Robinson Crusoes in other "unknown worlds" attests to the powerful and lasting impact of the Caribbean space on the romance. Haggard's replication of the Robinson Crusoe personae – down to Friday – articulates the impact of the Caribbean space on the genre of the romance, and its impact on English identity and national temper almost two centuries later.

NOTES

1. Ian Baucom, *Out of Place: Englishness, Empire, and the Locations of Identity* (Princeton: Princeton University Press, 1999), 4.
2. Northrop Frye, *Anatomy of Criticism: Four Essays* (Princeton: Princeton University Press, 1957), 186.
3. Yin Liu, "Middle English Romance as Prototype Genre", *The Chaucer Review* 40, no. 1 (2006): 347.
4. Ibid., 344.
5. Ibid.
6. Susan Crane, *Insular Romance: Politics, Faith, and Culture in Anglo-Norman and Middle English Literature* (Berkeley: University of California Press, 1986), 70.
7. Ibid., 7.
8. Nathaniel Griffin, "The Definition of Romance", *PMLA* 38, no. 1 (1923): 54.
9. Ibid., 55.
10. Ibid., 54–55.
11. Ian Duncan, *Modern Romance and Transformations of the Novel: The Gothic, Scott, Dickens* (Cambridge: Cambridge University Press, 1992), 4.
12. Ibid., 5.
13. Timothy Brennan, "The National Longing for Form", in *Nation and Narration*, ed. Homi K. Bhabha (London: Routledge, 2004), 49.
14. Ibid.

15. Leslie Rabine, *Reading the Romantic Heroine: Text, History, Ideology* (Ann Arbor: University of Michigan Press, 1985), 2.
16. Thomas W. Krise, introduction to *Caribbeana: An Anthology of English Literature of the West Indies, 1657–1777* (Chicago: University of Chicago Press, 1999), 4.
17. Anne McClintock, *Imperial Leather: Race, Gender and Sexuality in the Colonial Contest* (New York: Routledge, 1995), 30.
18. Daniel Defoe, *Robinson Crusoe* (1719), http://www.planetpdf.com/planetpdf/pdfs/free_ebooks/Robinson_Crusoe_BT.pdf, 241. Subsequent references are taken from this edition and appear parenthetically in the text.
19. Peter Hulme, *Colonial Encounters: Europe and the Native Caribbean, 1492–1796* (London: Methuen, 1986), 187.
20. Rabine, *Reading the Romantic Heroine*, 2.
21. Ibid., 2–3.
22. Harold Bloom, *The Ringers in the Tower: Studies in Romantic Tradition* (Chicago: University of Chicago Press, 1971), 3.
23. Bruce McLeod, *The Geography of Empire in English Literature, 1580–1745* (Cambridge: Cambridge University Press, 1999), 178.
24. Roxann Wheeler, "The Complexion of Desire: Racial Ideology and Mid-Eighteenth-Century British Novels", *Eighteenth-Century Studies* 32, no. 3 (1999): 325.
25. Richard Ligon, *A True and Exact History of the Island of Barbados* (1657), in Krise, *Caribbeana*, 30.
26. Edward Said, *Culture and Imperialism* (London: Chatto and Windus, 1993), xii.
27. Ibid., xii–xiii.
28. Ian Watt, *The Rise of the Novel* (Berkeley: University of California Press, 1957), 70.
29. Charles C. Mann, "America, Found and Lost", *National Geographic* (May 2007): 44.
30. Elizabeth M. DeLoughrey, Renée K. Gosson and George B. Handley, introduction to *Caribbean Literature and the Environment: Between Nature and Culture* (Charlottesville: University of Virginia Press, 2005), 6.
31. Gibson Burrell and Karen Dale, "Utopiary: Utopias, Gardens and Organization", in *Utopia and Organization*, ed. Martin Parker (Oxford: Blackwell/Sociological Review, 2002), 121.
32. Quoted in Mann, "America, Found and Lost", 44.
33. Hulme, *Colonial Encounters*, 216.
34. Baucom, *Out of Place*, 4.
35. Watt, *Rise of the Novel*, 69.
36. Hulme, *Colonial Encounters*, 212.

37. Ibid., 212.
38. Roxann Wheeler, "My Savage, My Man: Racial Multiplicity in *Robinson Crusoe*", *English Literary History* 62, no. 4 (1995): 846.
39. Ibid.
40. Bill Ashcroft, *Caliban's Voice: The Transformation of English in Post-Colonial Literatures* (London: Routledge, 2009), 1.
41. Hulme, *Colonial Encounters*, 222.
42. H. Rider Haggard, *King Solomon's Mines* (1885), ch. 20, http://www.pagebypagebooks.com/H_Rider_Haggard/King_Solomons_Mines/Found_p2.html.

Chapter 5

FROUDE, KINGSLEY AND TROLLOPE
Wandering Eyes in a Trinidadian Landscape

JAK PEAKE

WHILE THE LEGACY OF IMPERIAL, VICTORIAN British literature in the postcolonial Caribbean is considerable, travel writing stands out as one of the most significant British literary genres dealing with the region in the nineteenth century. It is perhaps no accident that travel writing became the *modus operandi* for Victorian writers at a point when Britain's empire was at its height. As Tobias Döring has argued, the genre "has special relevance for the rhetoric of empire with its discursive prominence of 'discovery' and 'exploration', constructing a global space to be traversed, surveyed, mapped, administered and so transformed into a knowable geography as the basis for imperial rule".[1] Yet just as imperial travel writing could be said to produce a "knowable geography" of colonized lands, it likewise exposes a number of anxieties beneath the surface of the text, unveiling that which lies – to paraphrase Fredric Jameson – within the political unconscious of the text.[2]

While a corpus of criticism has accrued over the last forty years in which colonial mythologies have been well documented, it is worth noting that many of the foundational postcolonial works emerged around the 1960s–1970s era of West Indian decolonization. Just as Fanon emphasized the link between language and a colonial culture in *The Wretched of the Earth* (1961), so postcolonial and Marxist critics like Said and Jameson, in the succeeding decades, would further implicate "literature" as anything but "innocent" in the political sphere.[3] In the wake of these foundational figures, a plethora of postcolonial, Caribbeanist and Americanist criticism has emerged, much of it geared either towards consideration of the "postcolonial" moment or deconstruction of the colonial moment.

As Caribbean, and specifically anglophone, literary talent came to British and consequently international prominence from the 1950s onwards, with the likes of George Lamming, V.S. Naipaul and Samuel Selvon, the corpus of early Caribbeanist criticism tended towards a progressive evaluation of these new, decolonizing and, subsequently, postcolonial voices. In turning to the postcolonial, this first wave of literary criticism, though keenly aware of the colonial legacy of the region, rarely sought to investigate colonial texts themselves. This task was more often than not left to the creative writer, historian or anthropologist. However, from the 1980s onwards, starting perhaps with Peter Hulme's *Colonial Encounters* (1986), a steady trickle of literary scholars began to tackle the vault of colonial literature dealing with the Caribbean. In *Imperial Eyes* (1992), which deals in part with tropical America, Mary Louise Pratt extended Said's thesis regarding literature's complicity with imperial ideology. According to Pratt, imperial travel literature often engaged in "anti-conquest" narratives which amounted to "strategies of representation whereby European bourgeois subjects seek to secure their innocence in the same moment as they assert European hegemony".[4]

In many respects, this chapter seeks to continue in this vein of postcolonial critique. The aim is to draw together the travel writing of James Froude, Charles Kingsley and Anthony Trollope and the historical contexts – not to mention the additional subtexts – in which their writing emerged to reveal the ulterior views underpinning apparently transparent ways of *seeing* or *knowing* Trinidad and its landscape. The term *landscape*, as W.T.J. Mitchell asserts, is itself a medium which is never, as it were, neutral, but always subjective, being "embedded in a tradition of cultural signification and communication, a body of symbolic forms capable of being invoked and reshaped to express different meanings and values".[5] While landscape may often be deemed primarily the subject of the visual arts, it is equally important in literature, as Mitchell reminds us: "all media are mixed media".[6]

Accordingly, the discussion here seeks to trace the role of Trinidadian landscape – or rather, the writers' authorial moulding of it – alongside the influence of visual aesthetics on the British travellers' writing. Particular attention will be given to the picturesque, a genre which became hugely popular in late-eighteenth-century Britain and which played a significant role in shaping the ideological perspectives, if not the material geography, of the colonial Caribbean. With respect to the British Caribbean, Krista A. Thompson observes that the picturesque was "intrinsically connected to the politics of space, the colonial state's governance and the control of land and society".[7] Thompson also contends that "the picturesque undoubtedly shaped physical transformations of parts of the islands' landscapes".[8] While it is difficult to assess with any certainty how the travelogues of Froude, Kingsley and Trollope led directly to the alteration of Trinidadian land, it is not too great a claim to say that they were ideologically supportive of a colonial regime which in turn shaped Trinidad's geography.

In *Consuming the Caribbean*, Mimi Sheller argues that imperial travel writing often operated within "a politics of the picturesque", whereby "the framing of scenery became an exercise of colonial domination over Caribbean people, informed by literary precedents".[9] In her view, books such as Kingsley's *At Last* contributed to subsequent tourists' and travellers' perceptions of the Caribbean. Furthermore, travel writing dealing with particular places often influences subsequent travel literature on the area in question. Travelling to Trinidad some seventeen years after Kingsley, Froude is a good case in point, as the sixth chapter of his book *The English in the West Indies* opens with an homage to his friend Kingsley's exploits in Trinidad: "I might spare myself a description of Trinidad, for the natural features of the place, its forests and gardens, its exquisite flora, the loveliness of its birds and insects, have been described already, with a grace of touch and a fullness of knowledge which I could not rival if I tried, by my dear friend Charles Kingsley."[10] Froude's indebtedness to Kingsley's prior travel writing on Trinidad also suggests an endless, intertextual corpus that exists between all travel writers with respect to the places about which they write. For, as Froude points out, Kingsley "had followed the logs and journals of the Elizabethan adventurers till he had made their genius part of himself" (*EWI*, 52). Acquiring knowledge from previous travellers was, no doubt, part of the course for the professional Victorian travel writer. In the case of Froude, Kingsley and Trollope, their readings appear largely circumscribed to writing that reinforces European cultural and racial chauvinism and that ultimately supports British imperialism.

All three British travel writers' views of tropical America conform to the common European paradigm in which the region is rendered Edenic, lush and vital on the one hand, and overwhelming, corrupt and hellish on the other.[11] This notion of a superabundant natural world which could be both salubrious and noxious even carries traces of older European fantasies concerning the Orient.[12] Yet what is clearly distinct about these travelogues, as opposed to the European travel narratives of previous centuries, is the impact of scientific and empirical literature. As John Gillis asserts, from the Enlightenment onwards, scientific travel established the "authority of the eye" with "the focus . . . now on facts".[13] Although, as Gillis notes, "travel fiction remained immensely popular" in this period, he argues that "science divorced itself from literature in terms of both style and content".[14] While literature seems to be equated implicitly here with fiction, Gillis does not quite explore the bridge between non-fictional, observational travel writing and scientific discourse. In the eighteenth and nineteenth centuries, a plethora of travel accounts emerged in which the thrust of science can be detected through an indebtedness to empiricist methodology and the "authority of the eye". Yet where the object of scientific writing from the Enlightenment onwards was to strive towards truth, uncovering the working principles of the universe through observation, scientific accounts were themselves given to particular unobserved biases, musings and opinions.

Alexander von Humboldt was perhaps the most illustrious of scientific explorers from Europe to investigate the American tropics thoroughly, inspiring hosts of educated travellers like Kingsley, who mentions him repeatedly in his account of Trinidad. While Humboldt undoubtedly raised the level of scientific knowledge concerning the region, he was still predisposed to European myths regarding the retardation of "civilization" in hot places.[15] The non-fiction travelogues under discussion in this chapter are very much influenced by a scientific movement which valued the "eye", and yet was also inextricably linked to other nineteenth-century intellectual discourses and, ultimately, a European tradition of framing tropical America. This chapter, therefore, seeks to reveal that the adoption of an apparently neutral "eye/I" in the three Victorian accounts of Trinidad was anything but – following Said's and Jameson's leads – apolitical.

Another facet informing the approach taken here is the view which held that the Caribbean was very much connected to the American continent. Alexander von Humboldt arguably set the precedent for the geographical conception of Trinidad's attachment to the South American mainland. Though he never visited Trinidad, sailing within sight of Tobago and Chacachacare, the westernmost island in the Bocas del Dragón, Humboldt not only wrote of Trinidad from a mainland perspective, but also as a recent remnant of the mainland cast adrift:

> The current produced by the Orinoco between the South American Continent and the asphaltic island of Trinidad is so powerful, that ships . . . can scarcely make way against it. This desolate and fearful spot is called the Bay of Sadness (*Golfo Triste*), and its entrance the Dragon's Mouth (*Boca del Drago*). Here isolated cliffs rise tower-like in the midst of the rushing stream. They seem to mark the old rocky barrier . . . which, before it was broken through by the current, connected the island of Trinidad with the coast of Paria.[16]

Humboldt's reflections also find striking parallels with the ideas of modern Caribbean theorists and critics, foremost among them Édouard Glissant and Antonio Benítez-Rojo. In Glissant's words, the Caribbean is "the part that breaks free of the continent and yet is linked to the whole", while for Benítez-Rojo it is "an island bridge connecting in 'another way' North and South America".[17] Both Caribbean theorists associate the Caribbean with the continent, and particularly with the tropical and sub-tropical parts of the continent – or at least those areas in which the impact of the plantation has been significant, such as the US South.[18] From a wider Atlantic perspective, Gillis contends that there has often been too great a tendency to essentialize the difference between islands and continents, belying the fact that they are cultural constructs of "one interconnected world".[19]

The approach taken here builds on these strands of Caribbean and Atlantic theory, locating discourse on Trinidad within a tropical American framework, placing the island in dialogue with the other islands and the tropical American mainland. The prevalence of this vision of a wider Caribbean in the nineteenth century, which connected what in twentieth-century terminology might be dubbed the "insular" Caribbean islands to the tropical American mainland, is evidenced by the travel routes and discussion of all three travellers. Where Trollope journeyed to Trinidad as part of a Caribbean tour which included trips to the Central and South American mainland (Costa Rica, Colombia and Panama), both Froude and Kingsley refer repeatedly to European antecedents – Drake, Henry Morgan and Humboldt – who made their mark on the Caribbean coast of the continent as well as the islands.

As with these earlier figures, Froude, Kingsley and Trollope clearly perceive the Caribbean as linked to all the lands – both islands and mainland – around the Caribbean Basin. Indeed, an island such as Trinidad which represented a stepping stone to South America, perched so close to Venezuela and the headwaters of the Orinoco, no doubt served as a reminder of what British possessions had been lost in the wider continent, namely the United

States. It is this awareness of Britain's waning power in the Americas which colours all three accounts with nostalgia. Rather than operating solely as a retrospective remembrance of Britain's prior glory, nostalgia here seems to be double-edged, inviting a response to, if not a defence of, what remains of the Empire. Each writer touches upon a history in which Britain's foothold in the continent was stronger in contrast to its precarious present-day circumstances. This nostalgia is politically motivated, as the ramifications of Britain losing yet another colony in the Americas, itself a symbol of the Empire's waning grasp on the region, is no doubt intended to act as a call to a British readership. It may be that each writer saw himself as a vanguard of Empire, travelling to the far reaches for the benefit of the nation – and, by extension, the Empire. It is perhaps unsurprising that hope for the future can also be gleaned in their writing of Trinidad, as its potential for development, under British tutelage, plays into a lingering fantasy of imperial expansion and British influence in the region. Its close proximity to the South American mainland made the island an excellent *entrepôt* for trade with the new South American republics, highlighting how small islands might still play an important role in vast empires like Britain's.

SETTING THE "SEEN"

In 1859, 1869 and 1886, respectively, Trollope, Kingsley and Froude traversed the Atlantic to set foot on Trinidadian soil. The three English men were middle-aged and their literary reputations well established at their points of departure. While Froude's and Trollope's voyages consisted of Caribbean tours, Kingsley spent the majority of his trip in Trinidad. Arriving in Trinidad in the wake of the abolition of slavery, Froude, Kingsley and Trollope all succumbed to the racist essentialism of the era. The "Sybarite" Negro is "lazy" and the British Caribbean, to stay in British hands, requires further labour from the Orient. Accordingly, the indentured Indian or Chinese émigré – the new plantation labourer – is generally ranked above the African in the tally of racial taxonomy.[20] For the connection between the soil, sugar and the new sugar cultivators is inextricably linked to the elevation of Indians or Chinese in nineteenth-century racial taxonomies of the British Caribbean.

As with many eighteenth- and nineteenth-century accounts of the Caribbean, Froude's, Kingsley's and Trollope's travelogues are loaded with nostalgia.

Froude's *The English in the West Indies* opens with the following sentence: "The Colonial Exhibition has come and gone." It continues, "The British race dispersed over the world have celebrated the Jubilee of the Queen with an enthusiasm evidently intended to bear a special and peculiar meaning" (1). The year Froude undertook his Caribbean voyage, the Colonial and Indian Exhibition had been fêted and followed a year later with Queen Victoria's Golden Jubilee. While the colonial exhibition trumpeted Britain's colonial exploits, the Jubilee signalled not only Britain's imperial possessions, but also its new relationship with its partially self-governing colonies of Canada, Australia, New Zealand and the South African Cape. Their semi-autonomous position suggested a possible fracture, and also hinted at the potential for self-rule for Britain's possessions in the Americas. For Froude, where self-rule among those of "the same blood, the same language, the same habits, the same traditions" would not leave the British Empire "shattered into dishonourable fragments", the Caribbean was entirely contrasting, as "the mass of the population were [once] slaves.... To throw countries so variously circumstanced under an identical system would be a wild experiment" (*EWI*, 3, 5).

The future of the colonies, in Froude's narrative, is hanging in the balance and Britain's dealings in the Caribbean may set a marker for the whole empire. Acknowledging that federation may offer the best chance to the colonies, he perceives the Haitian Revolution, Spanish American republicanism and annexation to the United States as distinct threats to the British Caribbean. For Froude, the question of Britain's lingering presence in the Caribbean is one which extends beyond current market evaluations (9–10). If, as Froude reasons, "great nations always treasure the heroic traditions of their fathers", then to let these colonies go – colonies which cost "hundreds of thousands of English lives" – is to falter before the honourable duties to *patria* and patriarchy. Froude contrasts the banality of his era's politics with a golden age in which British daring was proven in the Caribbean Sea. "There Drake and Hawkins", writes Froude, "intercepted the golden stream which flowed from Panama into the exchequer at Madrid"; similarly, "Adventurers, buccaneers, corsairs, privateers" are all lionized as "extraordinary" men, serving their nation "whether disowned or acknowledged" against the imperial forces of the Spanish and French (9). In Froude's words, "The Bow of Ulysses is unstrung." The Classical allusion, which serves as both a secondary title for his travel book and a running trope throughout his account, suggests that the old supremacy of Britain is dissipated. All that is needed is "the true lord and master" to restring the bow to banish from the kingdom the "pretenders" courting "Penelope Britannia" (14). The allusion asserts the nineteenth-century historian's ideological mission statement: that the Caribbean requires new *British* heroes for a further wave of reconquest.

Froude's harking back to a golden age of imperial exploits bears many parallels with Kingsley's and Trollope's tropical American travelogues. Trollope voices the plaintive longings of Trinidad's planter class to return to the past, "when planters were planters, and slaves were slaves, [and the island] produced cutton [sic] up to its very hill-tops. Now", Trollope writes, "it yields nothing but the grass for a few cattle" (*WISM*, 177). While it is true that cotton had enjoyed a short spell of high yields between 1783 and 1789, beginning with the arrival of settlers from the French Caribbean and ending with the spread of parasites across the island, Trinidad's agricultural development had never been extensive in the eighteenth or nineteenth centuries. Rather, Trollope sees the island as representative of a paradigm of decay and retrogression in the American tropics generally.

Like Froude, Kingsley glories in the past military feats of the British in the Caribbean, recounting the naval successes of admirals Sir Samuel Hood and Baron George Rodney. In summarizing Britain's exploits in the Caribbean Sea, Kingsley highlights "what these islands have cost us in blood".[21] In his historicism of tropical America, the old conquistadors are represented as figures from a brutish past distinct from the latter generations of European settlers. Just as the "present Spanish landowners of Trinidad . . . do not derive from those old Ruffians", so the nineteenth-century gentleman and explorer bear no ties to the "dumb generation and . . . unlettered" conquistadors (*AL*, 27, 190). Kingsley summarizes the difference between these two phases of colonialism in the American tropics accordingly: "They did not, as we do now, analyse and describe their own impressions: but they felt them nevertheless . . . because they could not utter them; and so went, half intoxicate . . . with the beauty and wonder . . . till the excitement overpowered alike their reason and their conscience" (27).

Enlightenment ideals of analysis, observation, empiricism, reason, temperance, order and utterance are considered the markers which distinguish the men such as Kingsley from their predecessors. Unlike Kingsley's contemporaries, these earlier Europeans are represented as degenerate figures "gone native", having lost their wits through overstimulation in tropical America. Yet in spite of his partial historicism, Kingsley envisions himself as following a path from Europe to the Americas in the wake of "three great names": Christopher Columbus, Walter Raleigh and Alexander Von Humboldt (*AL*, 65).[22] In aligning himself with these three figures, Kingsley positions himself as a successor to a mythological European lineage of exploration in the Americas whose *telos* is increasingly scientific.

Throughout *At Last*, Kingsley envisages the American tropics as a laboratorial site of experimentation, in which human, animal and plant life can be observed and measured. The colonial mission of appropriating nature continues as a leitmotif, especially in the case of plants and animals, as Kingsley often notes specimens worthy of the English "hothouse" or "zoological garden".[23] Overwhelmed in the bowels of the forest by the sublime and "strange" sights of plants "growing out of the bare yellow loam", Kingsley explicitly identifies Trinidad as "one of Nature's hottest and dampest laboratories" (*AL*, 166). The idea of the island and forest specifically as an outdoor laboratory recurs in a later episode in which Kingsley attempts to describe the mountains and valleys of Trinidad's Northern Range. Finding "clumsy words" inadequate to the task, he instructs the reader as follows: "The reader must fancy for himself the loveliest brook which he ever saw in Devonshire or Yorkshire, Ireland or Scotland. . . . Then let him transport his stream to the great Palm-house at Kew, stretch out the house up hill and down dale" (264). As with the prior episode in the forest, the image of the laboratory is employed at the moment when enunciation fails and the tropical landscape is rendered incommensurable. The allusions to British landscapes and Kew Gardens suggest that these "colonial grafts" are employed to shore up Kingsley's vision when it is most threatened with dissolution or a "topos of ineffability".[24]

Kingsley's promiscuous discourse – as he transplants images from one landscape to another – provides impetus for a utilitarian vision which appropriates the natural world in the name of science, even as it is evinced as all-important to man.[25] This promiscuity is illustrative of the combined techniques employed to justify the manipulation and transplantation of nature in the American tropics. Kingsley's promiscuity even affects the language he employs to describe the nature he finds in Trinidad. While the purpose of the authentic travel book was, in some sense, to represent the unfamiliar in familiar terms to the target audience, it likewise sought to validate the exoticism of the foreign place through reliable knowledge of peculiar inhabitants, cultures and languages. Kingsley's use of words like "bower", "The High Woods", "English lawn" and "garden" set against the tropical environment suggests a continual exchange of terms with shifting meaning dependent on geographical location. As Froude remarks of various trees in the Port of Spain Botanical Gardens, "They had Old World names with characters wholly different" (*EWI*, 61).

In the age of science, the tropical "paradise" of the Americas appeared capable of restoring lost paradisiacal comforts to the temperate world through a range of products: medicines, decorative flora, foods, spices, fruits and woods. Kingsley considers this – mankind's (and metonymically Europe's) utilitarian benefit – to be the chief rationale and motivation for man's active uprooting and re-rooting of nature. With reference to the famous landscape architect William Andrews Nesfield, Kingsley remarks that he is able to "make landscapes . . . more beautiful than they are already by Nature". Continuing, he writes, "if foreign forms, wisely chosen for their shapes and colours, be added, the beauty may be indefinitely increased" (*AL*, 252). Though Kingsley is discussing botany, it is not difficult to see the analogy with the transplantation of people to the tropics. As the Americas and indeed islands so often represented *tabulae rasae* in European discourse, Caribbean islands, especially, were perceived as de facto laboratories for a number of professional European investigators: anthropologists, medical men, travellers, writers, poets and artists.

In Froude's travelogue, the delimitation of the term "experiment" takes on a more hysterical or cautionary note as he regularly returns to the potentially cataclysmic results of the laboratory. For Froude, self-governance in the British Caribbean is a "wild experiment"; to "try [such] an experiment . . . which if it fails is fatal" ultimately risks a second "Hayti, where they eat the babies, and no white man can own a yard of land" (*EWI*, 5, 50, 80). As is evident, nineteenth-century scientific discourse inflected travel narratives of the era, imbuing the terms *laboratory* and *experiment* with a protean meaning that manoeuvred from the vegetative to the societal. Nature and science were at the forefront of a revivification of a wider aesthetic appreciation of the world which relied on both observation and notions of the sublime. The eye of the traveller, artist and scientist and his or her respective "sense" impressions could be deemed part of an inseparable field of nineteenth-century discourse on nature in the American tropics.

INNOCENT EYE/I IN THE TROPICAL PICTURESQUE

In his autobiography, Trollope describes his Caribbean travel book as "the best way of producing to the eye of the reader, and to his ear, that which the eye of the writer has seen and his ear heard".[26] What he aims to universalize for the reader is primarily the visual and secondarily the aural. Sailing through the smallest of the Bocas, the Boca de Mona (Monkey's Mouth), Trollope declares the entrance "by far the prettiest" and effuses that "No scenery can be more picturesque than that afforded by the entrance to Port of Spain" (*WISM*, 176). At root, the picturesque relies on the power of vision to substantiate a sight worthy of beholding. This emphasis of *worthiness* makes the picturesque conversely not merely a matter of sight alone, but a genre equally reliant on judgement and taste – holding a mirror up to art and seeking a reflection of artistry in nature. The location of the spectator of the scene, his or her fixed position or movement through places, remains tantamount; likewise, reference to past scenes, sights and landscapes corroborate the spectator's authority as a visual guide. What qualifies as picturesque requires special faculties of aesthetic appreciation on the part of the viewer: he or she must be "conversant with ... art".[27] The picturesque therefore signals a shift from a "way of looking" into a "way of *knowing*".[28]

Trollope, as a novelist, essayist, journalist and travel writer firmly yoked in the canon of great English literary figures, positions himself both in the Trinidadian scene and ideologically within the realms of those who are privileged to see. He is the connoisseur, the "knowing eye/I" who judges a whole range of sense impressions received by the eye through the mediating "I": that which is *tasteful*, sensible, delightful, sublime, fantastic, well-ordered, pleasurable and so on.[29] Ostensibly his vision purveys the myth that the "eye" is impartial and transparent, ordering the tropical world coherently.[30] This element of ostensible transparency is also notable in Froude's and Kingsley's travelogues. At the start of his voyage, Froude, aged sixty-eight, claims that "old people can see some objects more clearly than young people.... They have no interest of their own to mislead their perception" (*EWI*, 15). Clarity, perspicacity and neutrality are proclaimed repeatedly by Froude, Kingsley and Trollope as the hallmark of their truthful observation. More often, the seemingly objective eye is deployed to displace the egoistic, subjective "I". After a day in the mountains of Trinidad's Northern Range, Kingsley writes, "the eye grows tired ... with the monotonous surges of green woodland"

(AL, 262).³¹ In introducing Port of Spain to the reader, Kingsley forgoes the typical subjective first-person "I" who sees, in favour of the second-person pronoun "you". This second-person narrative address circumscribes rather dictatorially the scene which the reader would witness if *in situ*. Possibility of choice appears denied; the experience is universalized as that of the sensible traveller to the tropics; yet conversely it is a universalizing discourse which excludes many others – namely those born in, alongside long-term residents of, tropical America. In an attempt to remove the subjectivity of his views, Kingsley deploys the second-person pronoun to direct the supposed inevitable shock of Port of Spain's cosmopolitan spread of people: "When you have ceased looking – even staring – at the black women and their ways, you become aware of the strange variety of races which people the city. Here passes an old Coolie Hindoo, with nothing on but his lungee round his loins, and a scarf over his head; a white bearded, delicate-featured old gentleman, with probably some caste-mark of red paint on his forehead" (AL, 89). Dictatorially, Kingsley virtually mobilizes his readers – speaking for and directing their actions, impressions and sensations. However, the action of the Other in this scene, the "Coolie Hindoo", is marked by an unusual transition from definitive description to a hypothetical kind. From his definitive appearance (his "lunge", "scarf" and white beard) at the outset, he is transformed into a far more impressionistic and protean figure, a man who is "probably" marked with a tilak on his forehead. This transition into the impressionistic illustrates a link to painting and the picturesque. The picturesque is largely defined by two principles: firstly, by "a desire to impose an order on landscape"; "secondly, by a willingness to manipulate a view so that it fits the order being imposed upon it".³² Kingsley's impressionism is indicative of such graphic manipulation, as he adds the finishing touches – a daub of red paint to the man's forehead – just as he suggests that a "bright-eyed young lady" is "probably" this man's daughter-in-law (AL, 89). Such manipulation belies the notion that such forms of seeing are innocent. No indication of the wider issues or voices of the subjects is attendant: poverty, hunger, violence, frustration and upset are kept out of the picture.³³

Though far from static, another drive of the picturesque was its generally gravitational pull towards scenes of nature.³⁴ For Kingsley in Port of Spain, as with Trollope in Cienfuegos and Humboldt in tropical America more generally, the urban is either uninteresting or inferior to Europe; the "Government buildings [are] brick-built, pretentious, without beauty of form" (AL, 87).³⁵ If the civilized world is Europe and its cities are the most advanced, then urban tropical America, by contrast, remains neophyte and lacking. Yet while the Port of Spain buildings are represented as "ugly", the saving grace of the city is its apparently fluid communication with nature. As Kingsley conjectures, even the buildings "after a few years" will begin "to look beautiful, because [they will be] embowered among noble flowering timber trees" (*AL*, 87).

The picturesque, far from being passive or innocent, actively operates in colonial narratives to propel the spectator towards the natural view which is never *here*, but always over *there*. In this sense, the genre could be considered another strategy of the innocent eye/I, justifying further exploration into the interior, the still contested *terra incognita*, under the guise of aesthetic wonder. That the colonial mission in Trinidad – whereas Trollope noted much of the island had "never been properly surveyed" – required further manpower to explore its interiors remains an unspoken subtext of the imperial traveller's romance with particular natural views (*WISM*, 184). The picturesque is merely represented as an innocent "way of seeing", primarily referential to art and beauty, propelling the eye/I deeper into the picture, which remains ever-elusive, always out of reach. Scanning the vista from Port of Spain, Froude picks out some waterworks in the hills of the Northern Range. It is this "first sight of the interior of the island" which impels him to enter, and penetrate, the "seen" scene "through jungles of flowering shrubs which were running wild" (*EWI*, 67). As he journeys along the mountain path, he encounters ex-slave freeholders' cabins and is struck by the surrounding tropical cornucopia: "luscious granadilla climbs among the branches; plantains throw their cool shade over the doors; oranges and limes and citrons perfume the air" (68). His progression into the heart of the view hints at a greater overload of sensory impression. He is all too aware of the latent danger lurking in this paradise: "There are snakes . . . as there were snakes in Eden."[36] Finally, Froude reaches the waterworks, which are "even more beautiful than we had been taught to expect. A dam has been driven across a perfectly limpid mountain stream" (69). What accounts for beauty under Froude's assessing eye is the waterworks' function and symbolism as a man-made device harnessing the power of nature for man's utility. Froude's description blends the industrial and non-industrial or "natural" landscapes into a harmonious aesthetic. Simon Ryan argues that "in the picturesque the utilitarian pressures of agriculture and aesthetic demands are reconciled".[37] Equally likely is that the picturesque may face utilitarian pressures from all sides, the industrial included, as in Froude's evocation of the waterworks in which aestheticism and utility are inseparable.

In attracting the wandering eye/I to the heart of the view, the picturesque may also function paradoxically, enticing the traveller into places of potential physical or psychic threat, danger and dissolution. As the eye often draws its subjects to places spied many miles away, the reality of penetrating an opaque backdrop cannot be guaranteed by the visible. On entering hills, forests and traces skirting between landmarks, the traveller, though initially motivated by the visual, must discover all that was previously invisible. The picturesque, therefore, may well entice spectators into its antithesis, a non-picturesque world of the abject, a *locus terribilis*. Journeys into interior places in the American tropics are often played out within explorers' psyches as sites of potential dissolution. On hearing of the "Blue Basin", Froude's eye leads him through a trail, occasionally tailored for the "British tourist", until he reaches the illustrious waterfall (*WISM*, 71–72). In the tranquillity of the basin, Froude sketches the waterfall. Although, for him, the spot remains an Edenic, picturesque site for picnicking, swimming and sketching the waters' descent, the waterfall carries with it a profound, psychic "landscape for contemplating final things".[38] While the "perpendicular" fall poses no direct threat, Froude offers an unusual insight a few paragraphs later: a man poised to dive in the basin sees beneath him "a large dead python". Death, and the noxious reminders of terminal endings, lingers on the periphery of this otherwise idyllic scene.

In *At Last*, the rainforest – a well-established site of anxiety for the European slave-holding elite – serves a similar role for Kingsley, who is clearly drawn to investigate its interiors for some experience of the sublime in nature, much like the Romantic writers in the earlier part of the century. Yet on "entering the high woods", Kingsley's sense of self appears profoundly disturbed, as he writes of being overcome by "helplessness, confusion, awe, all but terror". He is "afraid at first to venture in fifty yards. Without a compass or the landmark of some opening to or from which he can look, a man must be lost . . . such a sameness is there in the infinite variety. . . . You can only wander on as far as you dare . . . carrying away a confused recollection of innumerable perpendicular lines" (157–58). The wild abundance of the forest vegetation, its incommensurability, impassability, prickliness and armoury, threaten Kingsley with physical and psychic destruction. An age-old trope of man and nature at war is rehearsed. A "labyrinth of wire-rigging" forces

Kingsley's party to hew their way through the bush with cutlasses, a "strong sedge-like Sclerias, with cutting edges to their leaves" risks abrasions, while the "Croc-chien", a plant with a "long, green, curved whip, armed with pairs of barbs" threatens to tear off human flesh (158, 168). The forest is reinvented as a terrifying anthropophagus devouring human beings in its midst. In both instances, Froude and Kingsley catalogue the potential dangers of Eden: that with beauty comes danger. Like all travellers' tales, their narratives emphasize the daring of their deeds and their survival in the face of peril. In this respect, their narratives highlight the risks of physical, as opposed to armchair, travel. The motivation here could be said to be twofold: to elevate their own actions, while presumably inspiring other courageous travellers to venture forth from the mother country to the colony.

The picturesque is one strategic device employed to reconcile European aesthetics with an alien tropical world, rendering the unfamiliar familiar. In the same instance that a sight is declared worthy of admiration, so it is often assessed – either consciously and subconsciously – for its potential utility, whether for society's leisure, economic profit, scientific expeditions, agriculture, industry, tastes, whims or aesthetics. Trollope's picturesque vision of Port of Spain's bay reveals no "pure" aestheticism, but rather one that links the land to its use by man and, perhaps more vitally, its *potential* use. As he nears Trinidad, he is struck by its abundant vegetation and fertility as trees sprout "forth from the sides of the rocks as though no soil were necessary for them". Flora here is teeming with possibilities and seemingly needs little subsistence to grow. "Soft-green smiling nooks" appear the "very spot for picnics", while "a little further" on, they reach a whaling station where the cetaceous prey "render up their oily tributes" (*WISM*, 177). In every instance, the landscape is rendered amenable, useful and consumable.[39]

If the eighteenth-century explosion of landscape gardening raised fresh controversies over "the ratio of art to nature", as tastes for the formal symmetry of the classical garden declined, so art as means of controlling nature remained a dominant post-Enlightenment ideology.[40] As Kingsley insists, "That Art can help Nature there can be no doubt."[41] The notion of a perfect natural world untouched by man, Kingsley argues, is for sentimentalists who "wish to controvert science" (*AL*, 252). Nature stands in contradistinction to "Art" and "science" – symbols of man's intervention in nature – as a potentially savage, anti-social entity threatening humankind. In the tropics particularly, "social plants are rare" and nature is always "grander . . . more tyrannous and destroying" (95, 161). For this reason, it must be contained, as to yield to nature is to risk the degeneration or annihilation of civilization.

In the forests of the Northern Range, Kingsley stumbles across a camp "not yet arrived at so high a state of civilization". Submerged in a "tangle of logs, stumps, branches, dead ropes and nets of liane", the grounds of the house pose a difficult entrance. Yet, a "second glance" reveals some Indian corn which will be ready for cropping and, he surmises, will "richly repay the clearing" (283). Agriculture and civilization are closely entwined in Kingsley's vision, as the owner's clearing of the land shows his partial advance towards "civilization".[42] Man's hand in nature is necessary for his development, progress and survival in Kingsley's aesthetic, making a "mere clearing . . . a more beautiful place than the forest" (252). As a consequence of Kingsley's utilitarian view, a lodging-house in Tortuga is a "little paradise . . . far more beautiful than the forest out of which it had been hewn" (253). Conversely, the bush, a place inhabited by the "lawless squatter", a prevalent figure in nineteenth-century Trinidad due to the large tracts of unsettled land, represents a "contact zone" of anxiety.[43] Underlying Kingsley's vision is a utilitarian outlook, partly traceable to the "greatest happiness principle" championed by Mill and Bentham, but arguably more closely aligned with Hume's utilitarian aesthetics.

In his philosophical treatise, Hume proposes that the "beauty" of objects "is chiefly derived from their utility, and from their fitness for that purpose".[44] By way of exemplar, he states that "nothing renders a field more agreeable than its fertility. . . . I know not but a plain, overgrown with furze and broom . . . as beautiful as a hill covered with vines or olive trees."[45] This Humean aesthetic is detectable in Froude's, Kingsley's and Trollope's travel writing on Trinidad and tropical America.[46] Kingsley's vision of botany is also coloured by the usefulness of plants, as he distinguishes the myrtle for its "size, beauty and use" (AL, 274). In a similar vein, he justifies deforestation of the rainforest on the basis of utility, proposing that only "the useless timbers" should be cleared. Yet his industrialism is tempered by a proportionate ecological utility, as he cautions that "if that jungle be once cleared off, the slow and careful work of ages has been undone" (311). The aestheticization of utility bears a long legacy in colonial Caribbean, with the plantation itself representing the paragon of such an idyllic vision – marrying the vision of the rural, abundant landscape with the productive management of the farmstead or garden.

In his autobiography, Trollope judges his Caribbean travelogue as "short ... amusing, *useful*, and true" (*Autobiography*, 109; emphasis mine). As with Kingsley, utility shapes his notion of beauty. As a corollary, he lionizes British Guiana, the then greatest sugar-producing British colony in the Caribbean, as "the Elysium of the tropics ... the transatlantic Eden" (*WISM*, 137). Pondering the flatness of its landscape, he ruminates, "what is the use of mountains? You can grow no sugar on them" (138). In short, the most beautiful Caribbean colony was the most productive. Beauty for beauty's sake, or the Kantian equivalent of non-useful aesthetic appreciation, is clearly out of the question in Trollope's account. A further Humean outlook on utility is evident in Trollope's perception of the market, value and money, all of which are equated with use. In contrast to Adam Smith and Karl Marx, Hume conflated utility and market value: "Fertility and value have a plain reference to use; and that to riches, joy, and plenty."[47]

This aggregation of value and utility separates, at least on the surface, Trollope from Kingsley, as the former champions the competitive marketplace as *useful*, while the latter, as a clergyman and advocate of Christian socialism, is sceptical of the moral benefits of laissez-faire capitalism. "The love of money", Trollope expounds, "is a good and useful love" (*WISM*, 154). Yet despite his criticism of "the mere brute tendencies of supply and demand", Kingsley nevertheless succumbs to the racist rhetoric of the plantocracy, positing the lazy "Negro" as pernicious. According to Kingsley, the "coaling system" demoralizes black labourers because they can "earn enough in one day to keep them in idleness, even in luxury" (*AL*, 21).[48]

The year that Trollope journeyed to Trinidad, Charles Darwin's *The Origin of Species* was published, altering forever man's place within the natural world. While Darwin's evolutionary hypothesis made polygenist theories untenable, scientific rationale for racism shifted to the possibility of degeneration.[49] At the start of his voyage, Froude remarks of a black boy on board his ship, "he had little more sense than a monkey". Describing his movements behind a grating, Froude writes that he is "curiously suggestive of the original from whom we are told now that all of us came" (*EWI*, 22). That Darwinian theory poses a crisis to Froude and Kingsley particularly is evident through their limited application, miscomprehension and alternative readings of competing evolutionary ideas.[50] Deeming the Sapajou monkey "a man and brother, plus a tail", Kingsley demonstrates a reading of evolution not entirely dissimilar to Jean-Baptiste Lamarck's theory of inheritance of acquired characteristics, as he suggests the primate may "gradually cure himself and his children of those evil passions . . . and rise to the supremest heights of justice, benevolence, and purity" (*AL*, 111). While Lamarck subscribed to evolutionary progressivism and the notion that practised behaviour was inheritable, Kingsley places the natural world in an eschatological framework. Competing evolutionary theories collapse and concentrate anxieties over civilization. Both Froude and Kingsley consider the disparity between Britain's – generally England's – populace and their predecessors troubling. Both men abhor the idea, even as they consider it, that the British or English race has degenerated.[51] What each Victorian writer exposes is a great anxiety over the position of the white race in the natural world, particularly the tropics. In voyaging to the region, Froude, Kingsley and Trollope eschew myths of white degeneration, elevating their standing as superior specimens of human evolution in contrast to the tropical inhabitants they encounter.

The issue of whether the white race – and particularly the white male – was suited for the tropics, however, weighs heavily in the Victorian travelogue. Trollope, somewhat pessimistic about the "English" race's prospects, perceives them as civilizing birds of passage: "When sufficient of our blood shall have been infused . . . [with] those children of the sun . . . we may be ready, without stain to our patriotism, to take off our hats and bid farewell to the West Indies" (*WISM*, 68). As with Froude, who considered Britain's greatness to be bound up with those who sow the seed ("men who cleared and tilled the fields . . . and spread our race over the planet"), Trollope considers white male virility and autonomy as intrinsically linked to land cultivation (*EWI*, 31; *WISM*, 85).

Froude, Kingsley and Trollope seek to recast and redeploy the image of the tropical paradise to counter the possible nightmarish landscape which might ensue. From Kingsley's dismissals of the tropical degeneration of white men, to the repeated efforts by all three writers to re-inscribe "paradise" onto the tropics by means of the picturesque, the new mission presents itself as the repopulation of the British Caribbean by white men and women – especially those hailing from the mother country.[52] As Kingsley asks rhetorically, "Why should not many a young couple, who have education, refinement, resources in themselves, but are . . . unable to keep a brougham and go to London balls, retreat to some such [a Trinidadian] paradise as this[?]" His response is equally revealing: "A cultivated man and wife . . . might be useful also in their place; for each such couple would be a little centre of civilization for the Negro, the Coolie" (*AL*, 130). The mission is made explicit, glimpsed momentarily. Ulysses's bow, which Froude contends must be strung for Britain's return to glory, must first be eulogized by writers, so that new heroes may come forward to take up the challenge. As Naipaul writes, the overriding concerns of Froude, Kingsley and Trollope appeared to be to "keep the estate productive", shoring up British possessions against risk.[53] Art, the picturesque-scanning eye of the travel writer and, ultimately, the product of the voyage, the travel book itself, were all to be kept in the service of empire.

The question as to why paradisiacal representations of Trinidad emerge alongside moments of potential danger in these travel accounts requires us to decode, as Jameson phrased it, the "political unconscious" inherent in the apparent textual contradictions.[54] All three writers discuss the contingency in which Trinidad will persist as a paradise to emphasize the equal or even greater loss to Britain – and, as they deem it, the world – if the colony is not properly managed. To read between the lines, between the written on the one hand, and the *impensé* ("unthought") and *non-dit* ("unspoken") on the other, reveals a discourse of latent political intentions. British influence in Trinidad and tropical America appears equally under threat in light of a new rising hegemonic power in the region: the United States. Froude observes that "opinion in Cuba" holds "that America [the US] is the residuary legatee of all the islands, Spanish and English equally" (*EWI*, 293). Similarly, Trollope recalls a map he sees, entitled "The United States as they now are, and in prospective", which contains the cartography of "Mexico, Central America, Cuba, St. Domingo, and even poor Jamaica" (*WISM*, 191–92). The lament for Jamaica exposes the subtext rather nakedly. As the only British possession illustrated on the US map, its loss is rendered elegiac in sentimental tones. Service and relocation to the British Caribbean by British subjects is, therefore, a further bulwark against encroachment into British territory by the United States. The nostalgic potted histories recounted by Froude and Kingsley particularly, which tell of British blood spilt in the Caribbean Sea, are there to remind Britons of the cost of such Caribbean possessions to their Empire. While the probability of British Caribbean possessions being yielded up to others, either through means of self-government or Spanish, French or US administration, is considered almost inevitable by Froude and Trollope, a "sufficient" mingling of British blood with island residents is perceived by the latter as a palliative against complete cultural atrophy. In such a case, he surmises that "some white Governor with a white aide-de-camp and a white private secretary – some three or four unfortunate white men" will lend "dignity" to "the throne of Queen Victoria's great-grandchild's grandchild". While avidly racist, Trollope's viewpoint reveals an insidious mission which is temporarily unmasked and unambiguous: "It is not enough for us to beget nations, civilize countries and instruct in truth and knowledge. . . . All this will not suffice unless also we can maintain a king over them!" (*WISM*, 68). In this lucid declaration, Trollope's political outlook is brought into the light. Britain's hegemony must be maintained, even when it appears to have waned. The subtext appears out in the open, revealed in a way which is left undisclosed in both Froude's and Kingsley's accounts. While it is impossible to know whether Froude or Kingsley would have concurred with Trollope, it is very likely that his text – the first published of the three – formed the reading material of his successors. As a literary precedent for their generation of travellers, it set the stage for Froude and Kingsley, who were both to follow in his footsteps. Both sought, in their own ways, solutions to a common imperial mission of ensuring that the British Caribbean not only remained in civilized hands, but would remain so in future.

The romance of all three writers appears to arise from a belief that each may be the last of a particular line of imperial travellers from the mother country to visit the island while it remained in British hands. They were not the only Victorians to write about Trinidadian travels, as figures like Baroness Brassey, Mrs A.C. Carmichael and William G. Sewell all published notable accounts of their visits or brief residency in Trinidad. However, Froude, Kingsley and Trollope collectively covered the post-emancipatory era when questions of self-governance were starting to come to the fore.[55] In some respects, they can be seen as representative of the last of a particular Victorian set of travellers, even if they were not the last British travellers to write about the island before its independence. The most notable British literary traveller to visit pre-independence Trinidad was probably Patrick Leigh Fermor, a figure who extended a British tradition of travel writing in which a mixture of sharp wit, keen observation and erudite acumen were all ingredients of the narrative. Yet where Leigh Fermor differs from his Victorian antecedents is with respect to his treatment of Caribbean nature and culture.[56] As opposed to his Victorian antecedents, his interest in Caribbean culture is much more pronounced and not divorced from his enjoyment of Caribbean nature, as he takes time to describe the Saga Boy culture of Port of Spain after the Second World War. Froude, Kingsley and Trollope pay far less attention to Trinidad's urbanity, seeking rather the sublime sights of rural or natural Trinidadian landscapes. The bulk of their accounts are dedicated to abundant plantations or landscapes as yet unexploited by man. While V.S. Naipaul's infamous comments concerning an apparent lack of creativity in the Caribbean ("nothing was created in the West Indies") have on occasions been attributed to a reading of the colonial era, Froude, Kingsley and Trollope all appeared deeply concerned with the creative production of the island.[57] From new tropical medicines to unknown foodstuffs, Trinidad represented a treasure trove of new creative potential, all of which required fresh expertise and, most importantly, eyewitnesses to assess the untapped value lying just below the surface. The attention due to the human beings who were expected to labour for these goods would be left to later generations of writers.

NOTES

1. Tobias Döring, *Caribbean-English Passages: Intertextuality in a Postcolonial Tradition* (London: Routledge, 2002), 40.
2. Fredric Jameson, *The Political Unconscious* (London: Routledge, 2002).
3. Frantz Fanon, *The Wretched of the Earth*, trans. Constance Farrington (London: Penguin, 2001); Edward W. Said, *Orientalism* (New York: Penguin, 2003), 27; Jameson, *Political Unconscious*, 5.
4. Mary Louise Pratt, *Imperial Eyes: Travel Writing and Transculturation* (London: Routledge, 1992), 9.
5. W.J.T. Mitchell, "Imperial Landscape", in *Landscape and Power*, 2nd ed. (Chicago: University of Chicago Press, 1994), 14.
6. W.J.T. Mitchell, *Picture Theory: Essays on Verbal and Visual Representation* (Chicago: University of Chicago Press, 1994), 5.
7. Krista A. Thompson, *An Eye for the Tropics: Tourism, Photography, and Framing the Caribbean Picturesque* (Durham: Duke University Press, 2006), 22.
8. Ibid., 21–22.
9. Mimi Sheller, *Consuming the Caribbean: From Arawaks to Zombies* (London: Routledge, 2003), 61.
10. James Anthony Froude, *The English in the West Indies, or, The Bow of Ulysses* (Marston Gate: Adamant Media, 2005), 51–52. Subsequent references are taken from this edition and appear parenthetically in the text as *EWI*.
11. For more on this, see Basil A. Reid, *Myths and Realities of Caribbean History* (Tuscaloosa: University of Alabama Press, 2009), 98.

12. David Lowenthal, *West Indian Societies* (New York: Oxford University Press, 1972), 14.
13. John R. Gillis, *Islands of the Mind: How the Human Imagination Created the Atlantic World* (New York: Palgrave Macmillan, 2010), 106.
14. Ibid., 107.
15. Nancy Leys Stepan, *Picturing Tropical Nature* (Ithaca: Cornell University Press, 2001), 42.
16. Alexander von Humboldt, *Views of Nature, or, Contemplations on the Sublime Phenomena of Creation*, trans. Elise C. Otté and Henry G. Bohn (London: H.G. Bohn, 1850), 155.
17. Édouard Glissant, *Caribbean Discourse: Selected Essays*, trans. Michael Dash (Charlottesville: University Press of Virginia, 1981), 117; Antonio Benítez-Rojo, *The Repeating Island: The Caribbean and the Postmodern Perspective*, trans. James Maraniss, ed. Stanley Fish and Fredric Jameson (Durham, NC: Duke University Press, 1992), 4.
18. Édouard Glissant's interest in Faulkner is a good example of the perceived relationship between the Caribbean and the US South. See, for example, Édouard Glissant, *Faulkner, Mississippi* (Chicago: University of Chicago Press, 2000).
19. Gillis, *Islands of the Mind*, 2.
20. The romanticized position of Asian labourers in the post-slavery landscape partly owes to Orientalist narratives, which pitted such peoples as belonging to an ancient civilization over the typically de-historicized "Negro". While such racial and hierarchical constructs were generally reified as the summation of a whole body and ethnographic discourses, the additional motivator for elevating these new labourers often lies sublimated in the subterranean subtext of the Trinidadian narrative. Anthony Trollope, *The West Indies and the Spanish Main* (Marston Gate: Adamant Media, 2006), 64, 66. Subsequent references are taken from this edition and appear parenthetically in the text as *WISM*.
21. Charles Kingsley, *At Last: A Christmas in the West Indies*, *The Works of Charles Kingsley* (London: Macmillan, 1880), 14:46. Subsequent references are taken from this edition and appear parenthetically in the text as *AL*.
22. D. Graham Burnett demonstrates how Raleigh was recast in the nineteenth century as an embryonic scientist and mercantile explorer. While Humboldt claimed to have demythologized El Dorado, locating it in Lake Amucu, Robert Schomburgk, the renowned explorer and surveyor of British Guiana, wrote "of the general correctness of Raleigh's descriptions". D. Graham Burnett, *Masters of All They Surveyed: Exploration, Geography, and a British El Dorado* (Chicago: University of Chicago Press, 2001), 27. See Alexander von Humboldt, "Preface",

trans. Walter E. Roth, in *Robert Hermann Schomburgk's Travels in Guiana and on the Orinoco During the Years 1835–1839*, ed. Otto Alfred Schomburgk (Georgetown: Argosy Company, 1931), viii. See also Robert H. Schomburgk, introduction to *The Discovery of the Large, Rich, and Beautiful Empire of Guiana, with a Relation of the Great and Golden City of Manoa (Which the Spaniards Call El Dorado) . . . By Sir W. Ralegh, Knight* (London: Hakluyt Society, 1848), ix.

23. On Monos, a Trinidadian island lying in the northern Bocas, Kingsley notices a "low tree" and "racemes of little white flowers" smelling of honeysuckle and reflects that "it ought to be, if it be not yet, introduced to England". As regards the rare Guacharo bird which, as Kingsley notes, "the great master" Humboldt "discovered . . . or rather described . . . to civilized Europe", he regrets the bad weather that prevents his being able to "get one safe to the Zoological Gardens . . . [or] one or two corpses for the Cambridge Museum" (*AL*, 136, 40).

24. Döring describes the process by which tropical nature disrupts European concepts and, consequentially, enunciation, as a "topos of ineffability" (*Caribbean-English Passages*, 156, 31). See Jill H. Casid, *Sowing Empire: Landscape and Colonization* (Minneapolis: University of Minnesota Press, 2005), 19.

25. Casid defines the term *promiscuous* in eighteenth-century colonial discourse as not merely sexual or reproductive, but equally related to "intermixture" (Casid, *Sowing Empire*, 20).

26. Anthony Trollope, *An Autobiography* (Berkeley: University of California Press, 1947), 109. Subsequent references are taken from this edition and appear parenthetically in the text.

27. Richard Payne Knight, *An Analytical Enquiry into the Principles of Taste* (London: T. Payne and J. White, 1808), 152.

28. John Barrell, *The Idea of Landscape and the Sense of Place, 1730–1840: An Approach to the Poetry of John Clare* (Cambridge: Cambridge University Press, 1972), 50, 59.

29. I am indebted to Nancy Stepan for this phraseology. Stepan, *Picturing Tropical Nature*, 36.

30. Pratt discusses the power of the imperial "eye" to both essentialize and cloak the viewer in narratives of "anti-conquest" – a mode of discourse whereby Europeans represent their innocence, while avowing their superiority equally.

31. After a week in the West Indies, Trollope proffers a similar ostensible truism that "the eye soon becomes accustomed to the black skin and the thick lip" (*WISM*, 44).

32. Barrell, *Idea of Landscape*, 58.

33. In a discussion of the urban picturesque, Benedict Giamo maintains that the

genre is characterized by its inability "to confront the descriptive analogues of poverty, such as hunger, desensitization, hopelessness, dependency, and withdrawal". Benedict Giamo, *On the Bowery: Confronting Homelessness in American Society* (Iowa City: University of Iowa Press, 1989), 62.

34. See Allen Carlson, *Nature and Landscape: An Introduction to Environmental Aesthetics* (New York: Columbia University Press, 2009), 27.

35. In the opening chapter of *At Last*, "Outward Bound", Kingsley declines a visit to the town on Water Island, claiming that he "came to see Nature, not towns" (17). For more on Humboldt's perspective on the New World, see Stepan, *Picturing Tropical Nature*, 40–41.

36. Though Raleigh likened tropical America to paradise, he rejected it as the site of paradise, along with theoretical positioning of paradise as the "whole earth" or a spot "south of the equinoctial line". Following biblical testimonies, he believed that paradise resided in Mesopotamia. See Charles W.J. Withers, "Geography, Enlightenment and the Paradise Question", in *Geography and Enlightenment*, ed. David N. Livingstone and Charles W.J. Withers (Chicago: University of Chicago Press, 1999), 71.

37. Simon Ryan, *The Cartographic Eye: How Explorers Saw Australia* (Cambridge: Cambridge University Press, 1996), 76.

38. Burnett, *Masters of All*, 192.

39. There are echoes of Jonson's poem "To Penshurst" and its Arcadian world of plenty, where in the estate's ponds, "Bright eels . . . leap on land / Before the fisher, or into his hand". Trollope considers that "the whaling huts are very picturesque", yet adds that they "do not say much for the commercial enterprise of the proprietors". In Trollope's portrayal, a seeming contradiction or opposition presents itself between the aesthetic and utilitarian; yet, again, if the remit of the picturesque is expanded to potential utility there is no contradiction. See Margaret W. Ferguson, Mary Jo Salter and Jon Stallworthy, *The Norton Anthology of Poetry* (New York: W.W. Norton, 1996), 297.

40. Ronald Paulson, *Emblem and Expression: Meaning in English Art of the Eighteenth Century* (Cambridge, MA: Harvard University Press, 1975), 20.

41. A similar view of the relationship between art and nature is expressed by Addison in a 1712 edition of *The Spectator*: "we find the Works of Nature still more pleasant, the more they resemble those of Art". See Joseph Addison, *The Spectator*, ed. Donald Frederic Bond (Oxford: Oxford University Press, 1965), 3:550 (no. 414, 25 June 1712).

42. Robert Young contends that the Romantic tradition saw "culture", synonymous in early English usage with soil cultivation and "agri-culture", as "the term that

came in between the nature/civilization opposition". Robert Young, *Colonial Desire: Hybridity in Theory, Culture and Race* (London: Routledge, 1995), 31, 42.
43. Pratt, *Imperial Eyes*, 6.
44. David Hume, *A Treatise of Human Nature: Being an Attempt to Introduce the Experimental Method of Reasoning into Moral Subjects* (London: T. and J. Allman, 1817), 44.
45. Ibid.
46. Even a notable critic of the plantocracy, William Sewell, is not immune to this utilitarian aesthetic, as he "surveys the splendid picture of cultivation" of the Naparima district. See William G. Sewell, *The Ordeal of Free Labor in the British West Indies* (New York: Harper and Bros., 1862), 120.
47. Hume, *A Treatise of Human Nature*, 44–45. Hume's position conveniently smooths over Smith's example of diamonds and water, whereby the former possesses great value but is of little use, in antithesis to water, which has little value but is of great use. Karl Marx defines the distinction between utility and market value accordingly: "when commodities are exchanged, their exchange-value manifests itself as something totally independent of their use-value". See Karl Marx and Friedrich Engels, *The Marx-Engels Reader*, ed. Robert C. Tucker (New York: Norton, 1978), 305.
48. The "coaling system" of which Kingsley wrote refers to the industrial organization of coal stations, whereby labourers, generally men and women of African heritage, were paid to haul coal in baskets for refuelling ships. For more on this, see Anyaa Anim-Addo, " 'A Wretched and Slave-like Mode of Labor': Slavery, Emancipation, and the Royal Mail Steam Packet Company's Coaling Stations", *Historical Geography* 39 (2011): 65–84.
49. Young, *Colonial Desire*, 13, 16.
50. With reference to Kingsley, Amar Wahab cites S.K. Sharma's discussion of the "Victorian compromise", which sought to reconcile Christian ideology and scientific discourse. See Amar Wahab, " 'Wild, Yet Prospect': Inventing Tropical Nature in Victorian Trinidad", in *"What Is the Earthly Paradise?": Ecocritical Responses to the Caribbean*, ed. Chris Campbell and Erin Somerville (Newcastle: Cambridge Scholars Publishers, 2007), 56.
51. Kingsley writes, "There were heroes in England in those days. Are we, their descendants, degenerate from them? I, for one, believe not." Froude's response is even more adamant: "I do not believe in the degeneracy of our race." See Froude, *English in the West Indies*, 14; Kingsley, *At Last*, 6.
52. "And yet men say that the Englishman loses his energy in a tropic climate"; see Kingsley, *At Last*, 224.

53. V.S. Naipaul, *The Loss of El Dorado: A Colonial History* (London: Picador, 2001), 352.
54. See Jameson, *Political Unconscious*.
55. Perceiving civilization as "retrograding" in the Republic of New Granada, where universal suffrage was granted to all, Trollope is especially sceptical of its results. It is more than likely that he has Britain's Caribbean possessions in mind here. See Trollope, *WISM*, 197.
56. Recent ecocritical studies of the Caribbean, such as the critical collection edited by Elizabeth DeLoughrey et al., draw attention to the fact that "the dialectic between Caribbean nature and culture has not been brought into productive relation" – a particular legacy of the colonial era. Elizabeth M. DeLoughrey, Renée K. Gosson and George B. Handley, eds., *Caribbean Literature and the Environment: Between Nature and Culture* (Charlottesville: University of Virginia Press, 2005), 1–2.
57. V.S. Naipaul, *The Middle Passage: Impressions of Five Societies – British, French and Dutch – in the West Indies and South America* (Harmondsworth: Penguin, 1993), 29.

Chapter 6

A STUDY OF THE IMPERIAL GAZE

Jenkins's *Lutchmee and Dilloo:*
A Study of West Indian Life

J. VIJAY MAHARAJ

CARIBBEAN STUDIES SCHOLAR STUART HALL, NOT unlike other postcolonial theorists such as Edward Said, argues that the "imperializing eye" of *"Présence Européenne"* gazed upon the colonized Other "as different and other within the categories of the West". Hall's concern is that this bequeathed a monstrous legacy of self-alienation to the present, in that it taught us to "see and experience ourselves as 'Other' ".[1] A growing volume of critical engagement with European representations of the Caribbean indicates widespread recognition of the enormity of the problem as well as a desire to confront it directly. Moreover, despite the impossibility of neatly connecting the past to the present in straight lines, the critical enterprise nonetheless attempts to forge a double movement, in Hall's words, of "recogniz[ing] its [colonialism's] irreversible influence, while resisting its imperializing eye".[2] This undertaking is performed simultaneously from diverse angles, including postcolonial rewriting of history based on critiques of colonial historical representations; "writing back" to, as well as criticism of, the colonial literary canon; analyses of the colonial picturesque; and republication of uncanonized, often forgotten, works about the Caribbean.

The Centre for Caribbean Studies at the University of Warwick has, in fact, launched one of these republication drives, one of many Caribbean Classics series. It comprises literature about the Caribbean, "of more than historical interest", published prior to the familiar literary boom of the

1950s and 1960s that forms the core of a contemporary Caribbean canon.³ Through this impetus, un/wittingly, the Warwick project participates in a widespread enterprise of expanding the Caribbean and, by extension, the postcolonial canon; but it also, in some instances, by default, expands the British canon by including work done by British visitors to, or residents of, the Caribbean. However, each text is edited and introduced by a well-known Caribbean scholar. And one of the more important tasks of the introductory paratext is to go beyond helping the reader to hypothesize how the work was asking to be read by the European reader at the time of its initial publication, to activating competing sense-making frames appropriate to the libidinal investments of Caribbean or other readers interested in such sociopolitical meanings and psychological overcoming as outlined by Hall. The Warwick scheme, like other canon-making efforts, thus responds to shifting academic as well as social, cultural, political and historical currents and contributes to the ongoing shaping of these currents.

One text first published in 1877 and republished in the Classics Series in 2003, John Edwards Jenkins's *Lutchmee and Dilloo: A Study of West Indian Life*, is a prime example of the Caribbean-specific expansion of the British canon. This novel came out of Jenkins's involvement with the work of the abolitionists, and with it he produced one of a very few fictional representations of a people, often referred to as "coolies", who, from 1838 to 1917, were brought from India to labour on Caribbean plantations after the abolition of slavery. David Dabydeen wrote the introduction, in which he wryly observes that, not unlike the fate of another significant figure in indentureship discourses, "Charles Freer Andrews, revered in India and forgotten in England", Jenkins's novel "was soon forgotten and Jenkins himself written out of the history of Victorian literature".⁴ Attesting to the importance of the republication for Caribbean self-understanding, however, Dabydeen continues: "As a descendant of one of Jenkins's indentured coolies it is now my privilege to make [certain] fact[s] known, to recover his voice and to bring him once more into print, into the life of English letters."⁵

The republication of *Lutchmee and Dilloo* is certainly critical for making many previously unknown facts known, especially "given that the historical record before the mid-twentieth century is sadly lacking when it comes to Indo-Caribbean [the term often used today to refer to the descendants of the coolies] peoples' own views of much of anything in their New World environments".⁶ But, more importantly for the purpose of this chapter, it offers a sound basis for understanding some of the ways in which the "imperializing eye" shaped the indentureship experience, and continues to "make us see and experience ourselves as 'Other' ". This chapter aims to take advantage of the base it provides in order to open out analyses of representations of the indentured and experiences of indentureship so as to speculate on their possible repercussions in the present, and to ask some hopefully pertinent questions about what can or should be done about these effects, especially but not only from within academia.

A convenient starting point for the theoretical framework and subsequent discussion is provided by Amar Wahab's timely essay on the "coolie–West Indian" picturesque, "Mapping West Indian Orientalism: Race, Gender and Representations of Indentured Coolies in the Nineteenth-Century British West Indies".[7] Gilmore remarks that in *Lutchmee and Dilloo*, "Jenkins is good on descriptions of scenery, and his pictures of life and work on the sugar plantations are drawn from personal observation".[8] In addition, Dabydeen argues that in *Lutchmee and Dilloo*, "the Guianese coolie in particular and the Indian diaspora in general are for the first time in English fiction portrayed with a degree, however limited, of psychological realism and aesthetic artistry".[9] However, *Lutchmee and Dilloo* is not included in the archive Wahab constructs for study, and this essay thus redresses that shortcoming in his work. Additionally, however, by foregrounding the types of questions with which Wahab ends his work, the essay goes well beyond showing how "orientalist thought [was organized] as a disciplinary mechanism for positioning the indentured coolie".[10] In fact, the chapter will show how reading Jenkins's representation of indentureship within the paradigm of Orientalism allows one to observe the obvious suppressions, omissions and deletions that Orientalism involves. Most importantly, it asks questions about the possible repercussions of Orientalist epistemology on ontological designations in existence today.

READING *LUTCHMEE AND DILLOO*

In "Mapping West Indian Orientalism", Wahab states that he examined "literary and visual representations of colonial travel writers to demarcate the significance of Orientalist discourse in the reinvention of colonial hegemony in the post-emancipation West Indies".[11] With this gesture, Wahab situates his study within a considerable body of research that performs this kind of analysis of European representations of the Middle and Far East. In fact, works such as Sara Suleri's *The Rhetoric of English India*, in which she draws on previous studies like Mildred Archer's *Early Views of India* to examine the feminine picturesque, come to mind immediately.[12] The now classic theoretical formulation of Orientalism is, of course, Edward Said's book *Orientalism*, in which Said argues that "Orientalism is a style of thought based upon an ontological and epistemological distinction made between 'the Orient' and (most of the time) 'the Occident' . . . [which takes] the basic distinction between East and West as the starting point for elaborate theories, epics, novels, social descriptions, and political accounts concerning the Orient, its people, customs, 'mind', destiny, and so on".[13]

One of the more significant impacts of Said's concept of Orientalism is the way in which it grounds studies by scholars like Ashis Nandy, who looks at how "colonialism tried to supplant the Indian consciousness to erect an Indian self-image which, in its opposition to the West, would remain in essence a Western construction". Therefore, for Nandy, as for Hall, the ongoing ramifications of Orientalism are important. Nandy further notes, for example, that "if the colonial experience made the mainstream Western consciousness definitionally non-Oriental and redefined the West's self-image as the antithesis or negation of the East, it sought to do the reverse with the self-image of the Orient and with the culture of India".[14] It is not surprising that Said's critique of the Orientalist "style of thought" would be used in this way as a model to elucidate the impact of imperialism in India. Wahab's application of the Orientalism concept to the Caribbean is, however, less expected.

Wahab begins with Mimi Sheller's question in *Consuming the Caribbean*: "How did it [Orientalism] shift from this geographical referent [the East] to take on a wider significance as a generic 'regime of difference' in the Caribbean, understood as another 'Indies'?"[15] He answers via Lisa Lowe's succinct justifications of its use to position his own research.[16] He notes, for example, that "Lowe further observes: 'the British representations of India and Indians establish as British the position of narrative agency or subjectivity; the Indian people, landscapes, and images occupy the position of *objects brought into focus* by the British subject's point of view' ".[17] But this familiar, albeit much criticized, dichotomous subject-object basis allows him to conduct his investigations to show that

> as *East* Indians [another term often used to refer to indentured Indians and their descendants] crossed the boundary of a constructed Old World into the New World, British orientalist discourse was challenged to re-establish racialized boundaries and a sense of distance between the Old World and the New, reifying persistent orientalist tropes, while inverting others to meet the specific demands of re-establishing order in the British West Indies . . . a repeating matrix of discursive measures of distancing and approximating to British ideals that might be termed "West Indian Orientalism".[18]

The practices that Wahab dubs "West Indian Orientalism" are certainly evident in *Lutchmee and Dilloo*. In fact, in a text that is subtitled *A Study of West Indian Life*, the emphatic use of Orientalist constructions of India necessarily raises warning flags in view of Hall's warning about "irreversible influence". The "British subject's point of view" is evident in the very form the novel adopts, as Jenkins uses the Victorian melodrama as a fictional schema to tell a tale about the "coolies" within the noble savage paradigm.[19] The format would have had resonance for an audience familiar with stories about encounters with the "native" informed by a variety of legends such as those of Inkle and Yarico, and Pocahontas.[20] In keeping with the schematic framework, the plot is filled with intrigue and violence, at the centre of which are "noble" coolies, Dilloo and Lutchmee, and an irredeemably evil villainous one, Hunoomaun, who pursues them relentlessly from India to the Caribbean.

However, for the Caribbean reader, the more important aspect of the novel is that, in many respects, Jenkins's characterization, among other elements of the text, substantiates Wahab's assertion that "representations of 'orientals' as backward, irrational, and possessing immutable or *natural* qualities that were antagonistic to Western self-conceptions were formulated and recirculated through a growing British visual and literary tradition moored in a wider project of justifying imperial rule".[21] Furthermore, Jenkins's representations of events in India also conform to Wahab's enumeration of three sub-theories in Said's theory of Orientalism: "Said's profound argument about Orientalism as a discourse highlights Western constructions of 'oriental society' as free of social differentiation (i.e. a theory of despotic/arbitrary power), the absence of a tradition of civil rights and a theory of social change (theory of social stagnation), and a theory of sexuality, sensuality, and irrationality."[22]

These Western "theories" of Indian social formation and stagnation, exotic sexuality and irrationality are but a few of the many aspects of Orientalist thought arrayed in Jenkins's narrative. If one were to consider that they may have bequeathed the contemporary burden of an always already identifiable Indian sensibility to ethnic self-perception as well as the perceptions of people of Indian origin by other groups in Caribbean, then it is important to itemize these legacies and to understand them well. Only then can they be addressed as part of the overall project of decolonization – of taking action with regard to colonialism's seemingly "irreversible influence" – by social action and policy or cultural transformation, or other means when necessary. Investigating *Lutchmee and Dilloo* through the lens provided by Said's concept of Orientalism is, therefore, an urgent task today for Caribbean criticism.

"WEST INDIAN ORIENTALISM" IN *LUTCHMEE AND DILLOO:* INDIA IN THE CARIBBEAN?

Jenkins sets the beginning of his tale in the Indian village of Bihar, one of the areas from which many indentured labourers came to the Caribbean. Interestingly, this region had a history of revolts against the British, a fact which should have implications for Caribbean scholarship on indentureship.[23] However, possible links between the revolutionary background and indentees' decision to migrate have been underexamined, except for some work done by Caribbean historians such as Brinsley Samaroo. In the essay "The Caribbean Consequences of the Indian Revolt of 1857", for example, Samaroo notes that after the 1857 "Indian Revolt", Bihar was one of the areas from which the "outflow of immigrants" was greatest following the British "scorched earth policy . . . in those areas where the Revolt had been hottest".[24] Additionally, Patrick Brantlinger asserts that the Revolt had a decisive impact in terms of the "ontological and epistemological distinction" to which Said refers, on the imperial project in the imagination of writers throughout the latter half of the nineteenth and the early twentieth centuries.[25]

One is struck, therefore, by the realization that in *Lutchmee and Dilloo*, traces of the Indian Revolt and Bihari history of revolts permeate the story, but actual events and their possible aftermath in the village setting are submerged. Instead, Jenkins is careful to present Bihar as an unchanging pre-industrial agrarian location.[26] In fact, the Bihar Jenkins represents is not a real place at all; it is a conceptual space. Here, the concept of the coolie as being of ancient subordinate peasant stock contradicts the very modern streaks of revolution that adhere to the text. Jenkins's representation is embedded in the same cognitive framework that gives Charles Kingsley the right to speak of the coolies as "strange, uncivilized, violent, heathen, miserly, and possessing oriental instincts and Indian habits that have been fixed in special groves for tens of centuries".[27] These observations are not meant to imply that scholarship should involve replacing a stereotyped image of peasant passivity by one of revolutionary activity. It merely points to the two-dimensionality of the view of Indians brought to the Caribbean, and the possibility of its imposition on the perception their descendants as simply "industrious, docile, cheerful, contented and obedient" or, alternatively, "strange, uncivilized, violent, heathen, miserly".[28] It also gestures to the urgency of being wary of the epistemic embeddedness of received knowledge.

Jenkins's representation of the Bihari village is also important to this study in other ways. In *Lutchmee and Dilloo*, the Bihari village is representative of India's innumerable villages and is presented almost as a stage set. It is a self-contained site of about four thousand people living in a peace established by British policing. Village life is relatively undisturbed despite the physical proximity of the village to one of the central administrative arms established through the system of direct state governance instituted in the eighteenth century, which replaced the seventeenth-century methods of the agents of the East India Company. The villagers are separate and apart from the British. Reconstructions of the history of the early European presence in South Asia, such as those by Maya Jasanoff, Durba Ghosh and William Dalrymple, for example, suggest that this construction belies the extensive interaction that existed prior to the 1857 uprising and continued even after.[29] Ghosh argues, in fact, that "interracial sexual relationships were a crucial and constituent part of early colonial state formation and governance in British India, laying the foundations for the colonial social order".[30] The narrative perspective is thus a sign of textual investment in the construction of boundaries between people based on notions of race and nation. These boundaries were manifested in a new system of governance that stressed a zone of non-convergence between ruler and ruled, and emphasized the differences between separate and distinct ethnicities, races and nations.

On the contrary, however, the village can be seen, within the ambit of Jenkins's own representation as well as in terms of historical reconstructions, as what Mary Louise Pratt has famously called a "contact zone". The concept of the contact zone as put forward by Pratt refers to those spaces where "peoples geographically and historically separated come into contact with each other and establish ongoing relations, usually involving conditions of coercion, radical inequality, and intractable conflict".[31] Pratt's concern is that the "interactive, improvisational dimensions" of colonial encounters which transformed both colonizer and colonized have been ignored by earlier scholarship.[32] The erasure of interaction in Jenkins's representation provides some context for scholarly avoidance as it speaks to the hegemony of notions of racial purity set in opposition to ideas of hybridity, or in Pratt's terms, "transculturation". It is also embedded in current exercises in India as well as in the Caribbean. Writers like Salman Rushdie can be seen as facing up to it – for example, in his comments on his aim in *Midnight's Children*: "My view is that the Indian tradition has always been, and still is, a mixed tradition. The idea that there is such a thing as a pure Indian tradition is a kind of fallacy, the nature of Indian tradition has always been multiplicity and plurality and mingling.... So the book comes out of that, that sense of a mixed tradition."[33]

The idea of racial purity and immunity to the transculturation intrinsic to interaction, by the same token, underwrites perceptions of Indians in the Caribbean – as evident in Edward Paton's contention that "the coolies are emigrants, it is true, but they appear to have brought their country with them; they orientalize ... that part of the New World into which they have come – they are not *new worldified* by crossing the seas".[34] As Wahab points out, in statements like these, Paton can be seen as "rehearsing an orientalist script". On the image with which Paton supports his remark, Wahab contends further that it "conveys the message that coolies in the New World could only exist as oriental subjects, reifying conventional notions about the impermeability and non-malleable nature of their identity *even* in the crucible of the nascent Atlantic world".[35] They are represented as "culturally-saturated others within, *but not of* the New World, and ... alien to Creole society". This positioning, of course, "served to symbolically foreclose any claims to cultural authenticity by coolies in the West Indian landscape, save for their position as laborers".[36] One could argue it not only "served" but continues to serve foreclosure of Indo-Caribbean belonging in the region via the impact of Orientalist thought on Caribbean studies. The recognition of this effect is slowly infiltrating some studies. One example of this is Raymond T. Smith's contention in *The Matrifocal Family* that a postcolonial academic genealogy underpins Caribbean perceptions of eternal essentializing ethnic differences among groups.[37] But much more of this type of questioning of the postcolonial continuation of colonial modes of seeing and doing is required.

As with Paton's representation, in *Lutchmee and Dilloo* the boundaries Jenkins discursively maintains between groups is similarly evident in the Caribbean as much as in India. In fact, the repudiation of hybridity is even more pronounced, particularly in the representation of the overseer rank of management on the Caribbean plantation. Most overseers are portrayed as products of either racial or cultural mixing or both, and *Lutchmee and Dilloo* registers deleterious effects on their moral values. The narrator declares that, for the most part, the overseers are "of that low type of Briton and half-breed common in tropical latitudes: their morality was only restrained by the capacity of their desires, or by considerations of opportunity and safety" (85). They are thus misfits who are, moreover, in a relation of direct power over the indentured labourers. In *Colonial Desire: Hybridity in Theory, Culture and Race*, Robert Young argues that hybridity became the object of a broad discourse when those in power began to question the impact of ubiquitous practices of mixing on the status quo. Pratt suggests that, consequently, "much of European literary history" is obsessed with the subject of hybridity, a point on which Young concurs. In fact, Young traces the indisputably hybrid states of culture and identity produced throughout imperial history and observes that it is "striking how many novelists . . . write almost obsessively about the uncertain crossing and invasion of identities".[38] Jenkins can certainly be located within the circle of common obsession, and his self-positioning as guardian of the status quo is visible in the care taken to distinguish the mixed groups from the pure by the degeneracy of the former. The resonance of Jenkins's depiction with Edward Long's in *History of Jamaica* suggests the ubiquity of practices of mixing and the problems it presented for the maintenance of colonial social stratification in the Caribbean.[39]

Their orientalist refusal of mixing is today arguably a part of the naturalization of mutually exclusive boundaries among groups in the Caribbean, but Orientalism is seldom perceived as a source of the problem. In fact, assumptions that the refusal is an intrinsic Indo-Caribbean trait are rife. As Wahab notes, for example: "According to Governor Light of British Guiana, East Indian men married and cohabited with black women in the early phase of indenture, and in correspondence to Secretary of State for the Colonies, Lord Glenelg, stated that 'the magnificent Features of the Men . . . promise well for the Mixture of the Negress with the Indian.'" He observes, however, that "contrary to this report, Verene Shepherd claims that, 'The male dominated nature of Indian immigration (by itself) does not even seem to have forced

Indian men to find sexual partners among Creole women.'"[40] Such is the current truth value of the assumption! Indeed, the "even" tells of the value of mixing in Caribbean society and summons the perception that under the most trying of conditions people of Indian origin were and are unlikely to mix. In addition, as a corollary, as Aisha Khan contends, "one of colonialism's most significant triumphs . . . was the legacy of race as an organizing principle" in Caribbean societies.[41]

Perhaps out of awareness of the enormity of the current problems these issues entail, in a rare instance at the end of his essay, Wahab pushes his discussions in the same direction as this essay to argue that "tracking this historically-specific discursive formation into contemporary decolonizing projects such as nation-building forces us to consider whether Paton's nineteenth-century claim that *coolies orientalize but are not new worldified by contact* has, in fact, undergone further inflections and challenges or whether it has conveniently endured to complicate the terms of authenticity for East Indians in the Caribbean".[42] But even the probability of such "irreversible influence" seems to advance many other critical questions, such as: To what extent has scholarship on the indentured and their descendants been informed by Orientalist thought on race and hybridity? Can a level be identified or should the concern be what steps are necessary to address the damage already done? Is the contemporary value of mixing in Caribbean society a reaction or resistance to Orientalist valuing of purity? If it has, as a consequence, become a hegemonic discourse, how does it affect persons at individual and institutional levels? What kind of pressure is exerted to ensure conformity, and how do individuals respond? In other words, what are the psychological, social, political and other side effects?

To move on, however, perhaps because of the Orientalist notion of enclosed groups, in *Lutchmee and Dilloo* interpersonal interactions are largely confined within groups, and this functions to emphasize the idea of Indian social stagnation and hierarchy. For example, the narrative presents the power structure in the village as traditional, one on which the British presence has had no impact. Power rests in the hands of *zamindars*. This category of Indians is inscribed through the lens of European feudalism as landlords who ruthlessly tax the villagers, "tenants [of] small plots of ground" owned by the *zamindars*. This is a skewed perspective of the *zamindari* system. According to Irfan Habib, the form to which Jenkins refers was a British-instituted system.[43] During Mughal rule, the Emperor Akbar attempted to rationalize the process of tax collection from land revenue in 1571. However, it was not until the East India Company had uncontested control of Bengal, Bihar and Orissa from 1756, and attention was focused on revenue collection, that the *zamindari* system referred to was effected. Concerned only with the revenue collector or *zamindar*, the system erased the actual tillers and customary possessors of the land out of existence.[44] In this aspect of the narrative in particular, Jenkins can thus be seen as imposing the Orientalist's "monumental form of encyclopedic or lexicographical vision" on the setting.[45] His representation of life in the village is, moreover, reminiscent of Mary Poovey's assertion that what is noteworthy in the archives she studies is that "for ... most prominent English commentators on India, empirical evidence was either unnecessary or dispensable".[46]

In *Lutchmee and Dilloo*, the tillers comprise nuclear families, established by "conventional arrangements between parents", who live in huts of "mud and wattle", till their plots of rented land and are kept in thrall to the *zamindaris*' whims because they depend on them for their existence. A supposed Indian sensibility transmitted in this way is notoriously common in Caribbean discourse today, including in fictional representations such as, for example, the Naipauls' work and Earl Lovelace's well-known *The Dragon Can't Dance* and *Salt*.[47] To what extent, one wonders, are the notions of conventional family arrangements and social hierarchy based in reality, versus on Orientalist-derived perception? Jenkins's depictions, however, serve the ideological purpose of establishing the continuity of the Indian village on the Caribbean plantation and are, therefore, a part of the narrative economy. So despite the people's confinement within a rigid social hierarchy, their manifestations of nobility are indisputable. Pastoral village wholesomeness is maintained by healthy recreational activities: regular sporting events include wrestling and "lattey" fighting, and evening gatherings for sharing news and communality are everyday occurrences. These take place in the middle of the village, in common ground which, apart from recreation, also serves as the space where matters of village importance are enacted and mediated (35–36). In this setting, the peasants are represented as living together in relative harmony, involved in their domestic affairs and as unconcerned about happenings in the wider world as they are about those not in their own class.

This is transferred to the Caribbean via ascription of a similar kind of group consciousness on the plantation, notwithstanding that it is one that responds to hostile plantation management as opposed to the distant but beneficent imperial governance in India. In the Caribbean, Dilloo, for example, identifies himself as the plantation identifies him to insist that "all Coolies should agree to help each other, and not quarrel among themselves" (98). He warns Lutchmee that she "must not quarrel with anyone [because] we are now obliged to live among them for five years, and your peace and our safety depend on our being on good terms with these people" (94). The change in group consciousness allows Jenkins to argue for plantation conditions that would more closely approximate the assumed social arrangement of the Indian village, with a more paternalistic and caring upper class than the *zamindars*.

Not surprisingly, in both contexts, Jenkins downplays the possibility of conflict between class and group, and confines it to intra-group conflict. In the village setting, the villagers' idyllic life is shattered by two of their "own people", Dost Mahommed and Hunoomaun, who it would seem invigorate their innate corruptions. They are thus respectable, law-abiding subjects of empire, except when they give in to corruptions endemic to their culture. In addition, signifying another issue which calls for Caribbean-specific forms of analysis, for Jenkins, as for most Orientalists, Hindu and India are coterminous and the Muslim is an inside-outsider. Some work has been done on the creation of this divide in David Gilmartin and Bruce Lawrence's collection of essays, *Beyond Turk and Hindu*, which shows that the formation of boundaries now seen as inherent in the terms *Hindu* and *Muslim* was an act performed during British rule.[48] Such boundaries were not present in the pre-colonial setting, in which groups were identified and self-identified mainly in terms of linguistic affiliation. Khan, in for example *Callaloo Nation*, and V.S. Naipaul, in for example *A Way in the World*, are among the few who have pointed to the Caribbean development of previously non-existent boundaries between Muslims and Hindus.[49]

In *Lutchmee and Dilloo*, the divide is craftily promulgated through the portrayal of Dost Mahommed as the *arkatiya*, or recruiter of indentured labour. However, perhaps betraying the inability of discourse to contain the subject, the two iniquitous figures, Mahommed and Hunoomaun, can be seen as revealing a capacity for flexibility and transmutation in the subject positions that people occupy. The ideology of one system calls the individual to occupy a certain subject position; the ideology of a new system does not call for a new subject position but transmutes the old. The ideological underpinning of pre-colonial village governance had given rise to such positions as *chokedar* and *pagi*; the new turned them into outlaw and recruiter. But although Dost Mahommed, the ex-*pagi* and now recruiter, is in a new class of servants of the Raj and an instrument of the new system of rule, considerable effort is expended on describing his agency, his wilful, irrational choice of the role of persuader to ends he has not thought through. As with Hunoomaun, the material causes of Mahommed's subjectivity are elided. The reader encounters him when he disturbs the normal pace of village life by installing himself on the common ground in a position of authority as representative of "the Protector of Emigrants at Calcutta [who acts] in the name of Her Majesty the Queen ... by authority of the Government of India" (39). He convinces his listeners of the benefits of immigration through a finely tuned discourse of likeness and difference. He talks of "boundless riches, and unalloyed happiness" in a place where "the sun is warm like the sun of Bengal and the waters plentiful and pure like the streams and tanks of India" (41). He uses the inequities of the *zamindari* system to promise the villagers that they can become *zamindars*.

The Victorian myth of the empire as family, with the benevolent queen as mother, by means of which subject peoples were kept in their assigned places, is demonstrated in operation in Mahommed's behaviour. According to Adrienne Munich, this myth established and perpetuated hierarchical systems and limiting categories by perpetrating the idea of Victoria/England as mother/land and source of order and powerful knowledge and the subject as subordinate child, in need of protection and redemption. It worked invisibly to undermine resistance to hegemony, as Antonio Gramsci conceptualizes this operation of power.[50] It is such subordinated positions that Mahommed and the villagers occupy, but the figures of hegemonic control in their lives are conspicuous by their absence. Mahommed is shown as using his powers of persuasion wilfully to convince the villagers of the quasi-divine status of the queen, of their British subjecthood and of the Crown's protection of their well-being and provision for their food, housing and medical needs. He may well have been using common *arkatiya* rhetoric, since in post-Revolt India the idea of the queen/mother was well established. In 1858, for example, even as Queen Victoria asserted her power, and brought the subcontinent fully under the authority of the Crown, she proclaimed: "We desire to show our mercy, by pardoning those who have been thus misled."[51] The narrative recognizes the role of the queen/mother in convincing the villagers to become indentured but ascribes agency to Mahommed's fraudulence, not to imperial rule. From

Jenkins's Orientalist perspective, therefore, the Indians are directly responsible for their involvement in the indentureship scheme.

Jenkins's abolitionist-inspired intervention to allay the negative effects of the indentureship scheme through the composition of texts like *Lutchmee and Dilloo*, therefore, becomes an act of paternalistic care of the naïve Other. His writing and other work on and in the Caribbean were imbricated in the work of the abolitionists who had continued to take an interest in New World plantations after slavery was abolished. In fact, the abolitionist George William Des Voeux was one of the more prominent voices raised against indentureship, which he called "the new system of slavery".[52] In 1869, Des Voeux predicted eruptions of labour unrest in British Guiana if the reforms he suggested were not made to the indentureship scheme, and the Royal Commission of Enquiry into the Treatment of Indian Immigrants was appointed in 1870.[53] Jenkins represented the Aborigines Protection Society and the Anti-Slavery Society at the enquiry. His Orientalist perspective in *Lutchmee and Dilloo* thus engenders questions about Orientalism and abolitionist discourse and activity.

Some studies have begun to look into the possible overlap between such seemingly opposed discourses, although the focus, to date, is largely on African subjectivity and abolitionist discourse. Lynn Festa's work is a good case in point. She has examined "the way eighteenth-century abolitionists used tropes and figures borrowed from sentimental literature to delineate the parameters of the human". She notes that these tropes were used to "excite the 'humanity' of metropolitan readers toward the suffering of enslaved people in distant climes".[54] Certainly Jenkins's claim that *Lutchmee and Dilloo* was written to "arouse popular sympathies" by "throw[ing] the problems of coolie labour in our colonies into a concrete and picturesque form" places it squarely within this paradigm (28–29). Festa asserts, however, that the pattern involves a "double movement of empathy and usurpation" and "sentimentality generates a situation in which the subjects who sympathize and the objects who elicit sympathy confront one another across an affective and cultural divide in which one set of people feels *for* – has feelings about and instead of – another".[55] She claims, moreover, that this "produces hierarchy and difference as much as it creates reciprocity and likeness".[56]

Christopher Leslie Brown similarly argues that the abolitionists followed a "self-concerned, self-regarding, even self-validating impulse" and many "took up the issue of slavery less because they cared about Africans than because they regretted its impact on society, on the empire, on public morals, or on the collective sense of self . . . [they] wanted, above all, to be free of slavery, and thus free from danger or free from corruption or free from guilt".[57] Deirdre Coleman, in particular, develops this observation further, arguing that racism can be seen in many anti-slavery tracts. She notes, in addition, that white women's claims for emancipation at the same time were made at the expense of Africans: "The belief in a common humanity, the sentimental identification of the African as brother: these recuperative features of abolitionism always co-exist with a panicky and contradictory need to preserve essential boundaries and distinctions."[58] The misalignment of the affective dimension and the actions undertaken by the abolitionists are the common concerns here. The Orientalism of Jenkins's novel is cause for similar concern and points to a gap in scholarship on the relation of the abolition movement to the indentureship arrangement.

With regard to the issue of the law, which receives a considerable level of attention in *Lutchmee and Dilloo*, Jenkins also adopts an Orientalist position. For example, the crumbling of village systems of self-policing under British rule is shown in the displacement of Hunoomaun from his traditional role as *chokedar*, or village watchman, by "Government police".[59] The new policing system consists of the white magistrate and his "sub-officials": the *darogah* at the top, the *jemmadars* below and beneath them the *burcandazes* (36). These positions were parts of the earlier system of Mughal policing adopted and reconstructed by the British. The *chokedar*, however, is displaced from the system and is now an outlaw. From a nineteenth-century perspective of social hierarchies, the narrator contends that the *chokedars* were "of a low order . . . their most active occupation consisted in winking at the operations of the rural dacoits (or robbers), and in lending themselves to the corrupt designs of one villager or village family upon another" (35). The *chokedar* is portrayed as a subject category characterized by corruption and innate criminal tendencies.[60] Though the replacement of the *chokedar* by "Government police" may well have been a reason for his involvement in questionable activities and for the "cunning" he exercises, Hunoomaun is portrayed as naturally evil. He patrols the village at night as his traditional duty required, but for the purpose of cowing the villagers by terror and depravity.

Hunoomaun may thus be located in the discourse of the thug embedded in British self-congratulations on their introduction of the rule of law to the subcontinent inscribed in nineteenth-century conceptions of the British Raj in India.[61] Criminal control, first consolidated in the development of the Cornwallis Code in 1793, was an aspect of British efforts to discipline India. The discourse of the thug was part of the new control. According to Sandria B. Freitag, Mughal rule left responsibility for criminal control in local hands, but the British viewed crime as defiance of the state and used the Mughal system they inherited, exercising it in a new, more controlled fashion.[62] In Jenkins's depiction of events in India, it is clear that he writes out of the prevalent perspective that rule of law had been introduced into a decadent, lawless India by the British.[63] One may read the surfeit in the representation of Hunoomaun within the tenebrous presence of the Revolt as well as in Orientalist constructions of the criminal thug. To read in this way is not to suggest that types like Hunoomaun did not exist, but to indicate another way in which not only setting but also character portrayals in *Lutchmee and Dilloo* are influenced by a legacy of discursive constructions of India and fears about "native" resistance. This reading does not render Hunoomaun resistive or anti-imperial, but merely points out the impact of the discourse of the thug and the belief in British introduction of the rule of law.

Hunoomaun is depicted not as dispossessed but as naturally cowardly and criminal in his actions. For example, he would not have attacked Lutchmee "but for a dose of arrack with which he had fortified his courage". Yet, "he knew well how to revenge himself" (37). He exacts revenge in small-minded ways by petty theft from Dilloo and destruction of his crops. It is this kind of cowardice that is responsible for migration to the Caribbean, which he must undertake to escape British anti-criminal vigilance which has turned in his direction. It is also, ironically, responsible for Lutchmee's decision to migrate to join her husband so that she will be protected. To read Jenkins's representation of indentureship within the paradigm of Orientalism is, therefore, to observe the glaring elision of historical causality that underpins Orientalist epistemology and corresponding baseless ontological ascriptions.

ANOTHER ORIENTALISM IN *LUTCHMEE AND DILLOO*

Lutchmee and Dilloo, Jenkins's noble coolies, on the other hand, are depicted within the terms of another strand of Orientalist scholarship, often called "Romantic Orientalism", through which the idea of an Indian golden age was established.[64] This Orientalism speaks of the "mystical East", site of spiritual power as opposed to the materialism of the "Occident". Richard Fox speaks of it as an "affirmative Orientalism".[65] James Clifford refers to it as a "sympathetic non-reductive Orientalist tradition".[66] However, in Vinay Lal's trenchant terms, one may see it as "bold attempts by individual colonial officials to transform themselves into the guardians of traditional repositories of authority and venerated customs, the British endeavor to out-Hindu the Hindu".[67] In a Romantic Orientalist vein, Lutchmee and Dilloo are presented as different from others like the villain Hunoomaun or the treacherous Mahommed.[68] Dilloo, for example, is "of unusually fine development . . . a fine, strong, ready young fellow, with a taste for athletics and adventure" and exemplary traits of "thrift and industry", unlike Hunoomaun, who is "as avaricious, sensual and dishonest as any Indian in the province" (35–36). However, at the same time that Dilloo's romanticized individuality is established, the exposition shows that even though he may be different, he shares in a common decadence. He is no less violent, rash, impulsive and emotionally unstable than Hunoomaun. The plot develops through these predispositions the characters are shown to possess from the moment of inception of their journeys in India. Dilloo's impetuosity, for example, results in Lutchmee being left alone in a British magistrate's mansion in India while he submits to making their future in a distant place of which he knows little (44). Their depiction involves the homogenization of individual differences into a common irrationality.

Furthermore, through the confrontations between Dilloo and Hunoomaun, both characters are constructed as potentially murderous. The conflict begins when Dilloo, who is "a formidable obstacle", uses his "lattey" (stick) to render Hunoomaun senseless after he attacks Lutchmee and then threatens him: "I'll finish you with a knife, and not let you off with a beating." Hunoomaun's equally vengeful nature is established by Lutchmee's fear: "But . . . what will he do to you? He will kill you", and supported by the assertion that "the ruffian followed them vowing a frightful vengeance" (34). In the encounter, while there is no direct reference to the Revolt, nuances of the exposition suggest its presence. Those in Dilloo's depiction, in particular, ironically mark him with the signs of the revolutionary. He wields his "lattey" with skill and dexterity and is willing, in other ways, to act to change his circumstances. This establishes the context for future events in the Caribbean when Dilloo carries out the threat against Hunoomaun and becomes embroiled in activities aimed at changing conditions on the plantations. However, Dilloo's conflict with Hunoomaun is the point of Jenkins's emphasis.

This focus ensures that although Jenkins is ostensibly writing on behalf of the coolies ensnared within the webs of the system of indentureship, as Lowe might have it, he is ultimately incapable of according them agency. This is particularly pertinent in the Caribbean setting in *Lutchmee and Dilloo*, in which Dilloo is depicted as being in constant conflict with the law and the estate management in the battle between annihilation and resistance. For the purposes of narrative closure, however, Dilloo is ultimately undone by his conflict with Hunoomaun. Dilloo dies and his demise frames, forecloses and renders null the idea of a successful collective uprising against the plantation and the possibility of its transformation. His death is not tragic; it is meaningless. Nothing in the plantation world will change because of it. Festa's observations about the abolitionists' sentimentality are thus apropos:

> Sentimentality cannot envision rights as something that must be declared or enacted by the parties in question, inasmuch as the very structure of sentimental description produces subjects whose suffering victimhood renders them incapable of making a performative declaration. Inasmuch as one cannot declare rights for another, that is, the ventriloquizing structure of the sentimental traps the slave in a structure of grief that cannot be converted to grievance, of complaint that never leads to vindication.[69]

Furthermore, according to the narrator, Dilloo and Hunoomaun's conflict demonstrates that "forgiveness is not a Hindu virtue" (43). This establishes the narrator's moral superiority to the characters but, at the same time, it can be seen as corroborating the viewpoint that Indians "possess a culture that was alien to and incongruent with the Eurocentric secular and religious norms of West Indian Creole society".[70] Citing Verene Shepherd's work on the subject, Wahab further notes that "even the local Baptist Union in Jamaica criticized the Hindu religion as pagan and given to moral depravity as a central argument against the indentureship system". This depravity was made "the very rationalization for later Christian conversion initiatives".[71] There are many who argue that Said pays too little heed to some of the positive aspects of "Orientalist conceptions".[72] Some distinguish between the eighteenth-century study of India under Hastings and Jones and the later Anglicism of Macaulay and argue that the Hastings-Jones Orientalism is not the kind to which Said refers.[73] As this interpretation of *Lutchmee and*

Dilloo shows, regardless of the form it takes as a discourse of domination, it is incapable of acting or thinking outside "categories of the West".

As in Dilloo's portrayal, Jenkins draws on a pre-colonial genealogy, in this case of Indian femininity as developed by "Romantic Orientalism" in Lutchmee's depiction. As Dabydeen observes, she is the idyll of Indian womanhood, exhibiting complete devotion to home and husband, conjured not only in the *Ramayana* but in the *Manu Smriti*.[74] But she is also "of refined indolence", the epitome of femininity expounded in the *Kama Sutra*, the *Ananga Ranga*, and *The Perfumed Garden*, brought to European attention by Richard Burton between 1883 and 1886.[75] Jenkins thus draws on a de-historicized idyll informed in no small measure by Judeo-Christian conceptions of femininity inscribed, for example, in Milton's well-known Eve in *Paradise Lost*. The narrator in *Lutchmee and Dilloo* others Lutchmee in the same way Adam others Eve, with the epithet "perfect" and the declaration "What there thou seest, fair creature, is thyself."[76] Lutchmee is rendered in prelapsarian tones of nakedness and disingenuous sexual freedom. She is "a young Indian girl, whose loose white robe and jacket... scarcely hid one line of the delicate mould of her form, displayed, as it was, by the *abandon* of her posture, in all its grace, litheness and perfection". The narrative begins with her risqué song, a "free paraphrase of the *Gitagovinda*" which reiterates her sexuality and "abandon" (31–32). The *Gitagovinda* is a religious text which, in presenting sexuality and spirituality together, sacralizes and concurrently naturalizes sexuality as intrinsic parts of Indianness.[77] Her exotic difference is, thus, indisputable.

In addition, while Lutchmee's knowledge of the *Gitagovinda* may be, as Dabydeen notes, an aspect of Victorian interest in the culture of the subcontinent, it is a critical aspect of narrative economy. It establishes the currency of Hindu "theology" in the general population and proceeds to demonstrate that even though the indentured possess the culture out of which the *Gitagovinda* comes, which endows them with a fine, albeit different, sensibility, they are still lacking in their credulousness and in their incapacity for rationality. This lack is developed in the depiction of the circumstances that lead to indentureship and their subsequent behaviour on the plantations. As with Dilloo's impetuosity, it is Lutchmee's Indian femininity that creates the problems that result in indentureship and ensuing problems on the plantations and ensnares her, her husband and Hunoomaun in a doomed triangle of blood, lust and sex, no doubt on account of "the fiercer passions of their Eastern blood".[78] Therefore, one can contend that Lutchmee's knowledge serves to connect her to an "ancient and noble" Indian civilization and to demonstrate that even ordinary people are aware of the religious texts which provide the philosophical bases of their lives. At the same time, it establishes her cultural difference from the Victorian reader and rationalizes the "civilizing mission".

Ironically, following historian Ron Ramdin, Wahab notes that "East Indian indentured laborers experienced a series of abuses, hostilities and brutal 'punishments' on the part of planters and Creole society on the whole". In addition, they "occupied the lowest rung in the labor hierarchy, excluded from the working class of Creole society, possibly representing more so its underclass (as most indentured laborers worked for wages below the free wage)".[79] However, Orientalist (especially of the Romantic variety) "aesthetic celebration of East Indian indentureship served as an offensive against the conscious Afro-proletariat".[80] To read Jenkins through the discourse of Orientalism is thus to better understand the nuances of what is meant by "divide and rule", the colonial political practice seen as the cause of so many contemporary political and social problems in the Caribbean.

CONCLUSION AND CAVEAT

At the time of Jenkins's writing, the British had been changing daily life on the subcontinent for over two centuries – longer than Indians have been in the Caribbean. Railroads, telegraph and postal services had been established and village life had been substantially changed. The educated elite had also responded to the British presence with schools, newspapers and debating societies and organizations, such as the Brahmo Samaj founded by Ram Mohan Roy. But in Jenkins's representation, the Bihari village remains a static pastoral site. The structure of village life with *zamindars* above and tenants below, the natural Hindu criminal tendencies elaborated in Hunoomaun's behaviour, and the villagers' distance from the system of governance make way for the wiles of the recruiter. The depiction of characters and events in *Lutchmee and Dilloo* is thus consistent with Said's charge that Orientalist studies are characterized by "the defeat of narrative by vision" and corroborates Pratt's contention that the idea of "a non-interventionist European presence" in places the West infiltrated is fraudulent.[81]

The narrative draws on Orientalist discourses of India's golden age constructed in the eighteenth century by groups like the Asiatic Society of Bengal.[82] At the same time, discourses of decadence, which removed the idea of a golden age in order to read the history of Hindu India as an unmitigated story of degeneration requiring the presence of the moral and civilizing order of British rule, are also inscribed in the text. This establishes the grounds on which the removal to the plantation could be viewed as being of benefit to those dislocated by the imperial shuffling of the Indian population to service its needs. Moreover, the myth of a golden age and present dereliction make visible, to use Homi Bhabha's words, the "cultural 'mummification' " consequent to "the colonizer's avowed ambition to civilize or modernize the native".[83] In *Lutchmee and Dilloo*, people who are "at once an 'other' and yet entirely knowable and visible" ostensibly sign an indenture contract based on private problems and needs, such as those caused by Hunoomaun and the *zamindari* system, and the guarantee of benign government care of its subjects is provided by recruiters like Mahommed.[84] Some are running from British anti-criminal vigilance that resulted from British institution of the rule of law. The breakdown in traditional structures which the British presence on the subcontinent would have wrought is repressed, and the subsequent hybridity and capacity for hybridity are made invisible. Jenkins's depiction of India in his study of West Indian life thus provides a sense of the magnitude of the scholarship that would be required to offset the "irreversible influence" of Orientalist constructions of people who would, in time, become Caribbean subjects.

It is for this reason that this chapter is grounded in the subject/object dichotomy that critics claim is intrinsic to the application of Said's theory of Orientalism, despite full awareness of objections raised to its use. One is certainly aware that the whole field of Subaltern Studies developed out of attempts to recover the subaltern as the subject of Orientalist history, as evident, for example, in Ranajit Guha's essays "On Some Aspects of the Historiography of Colonial India" and "The Prose of Counter-Insurgency".[85] Moreover, Said himself, in the foreword to the collection in which these essays appear, works out his "contrapuntal" style of reading as a means of mining the imperial archive not just for the perspective of British colonial administrators but also for that of the people they were trying to rule.[86] Reading "contrapuntally" becomes, of course, a subject of discourse in *Culture and Imperialism*, and here Said reminds us that the act of criticism is important "not only to define the situation, but also to discern the possibilities for active intervention, whether we then perform them ourselves or acknowledge them in others who have either gone before or are already at work".[87] Bhabha is also concerned about shortcomings in the concept of Orientalism. In essays such as "Of Mimicry and Man" in *The Location of Culture*, he therefore begins from the contention that discourses are always ambivalent and that contra Said's notion of a monolithic Orientalist discourse, there is no absolute binary between two opposed forces in colonizer/colonized relationships; rather, there is a proliferation of multiplicities. The notion of multiplicitous proliferation is certainly relevant to *Lutchmee and Dilloo*, but this would imply another kind of reading for different purposes.[88]

In the Caribbean, similar objections to Orientalism, a similar desire to uncover the voice of the subaltern and to find a place for "active intervention", can be seen, for example, in criticisms of Sheller's *Consuming the Caribbean*. In Harvey Neptune's review of Sheller's book, "Moving History in the Aftermath", he pointedly asks if "the politics of postcolonial histories holds little regard for the experience of Caribbean people?"[89] One may say that Neptune's review recognizes the value of Sheller's work in demonstrating how the colonized were perceived "as different and other within the categories of the West", but he is concerned about how it falls short of interpreting how this "makes us see and experience ourselves as 'Other' " or helping us to "recognize its irreversible influence, while resisting its imperializing eye". Perhaps similarly constrained, "Mapping West Indian Orientalism" does attempt to identify some marks of influence in the present, yet it surprisingly does not analyse Jenkins's work. One would certainly have anticipated the inclusion of Jenkins's work in Wahab's study because, in contrast to places like India, which has an expansive visual archive, the Caribbean picturesque is severely limited – perhaps, as Geoff Quilley argues, because the slave plantation did not easily conform to the sublime, the poetic or the aesthetic.[90] In an undertaking such as Wahab's, Jenkins's efforts, which encompass a variety of genres including documentaries, travel narratives, woodcuts and fiction, would have been very useful. However, as Dabydeen rightly argues, Jenkins is "no clichéd Imperialist", and this may well account for the absence of *Lutchmee and Dilloo* in Wahab's selection of objects of study.[91] When the lines become blurry and categorical denunciations through Orientalist methodologies are not possible, representations that blur would tend to be marginalized or ignored.

However, there may be other explanations, such as the one that underwrites the reason this chapter follows Wahab in his selection of Orientalism as the most useful theoretical framework. In Wahab's own words, it allows for "complicating an understanding of colonial power and the processes that shaped early East Indian identity in the West Indies".[92] This chapter, on the other hand, specifically complicates prior use of George Lamming's early conceptual metaphor taken from Shakespeare's *The Tempest* to posit the dialectic of Caribbean society as the conflict between Prospero the colonizer and Caliban the native.[93] This is an imperative undertaking in the twenty-first century Caribbean, fraught with the trials of intergroup relations. As the questions raised in this essay demonstrate, Orientalism promotes Said's injunction that criticism should "not only . . . define the situation, but also . . . discern the possibilities for active intervention" without any need for modification.[94] Moreover, as Nandy points out, it also opens the way for addressing the fact that the "White Sahib . . . [is not] the conspiratorial dedicated oppressor that he is made out to be, but a self-destructive co-victim with a reified life style and a parochial culture, caught in the hinges of history he swears by". Also, if we are to agree with Nandy that "all theories of salvation, secular or nonsecular, which fail to understand this degradation of the colonizer are theories which indirectly admit the superiority of the oppressors and collaborate with them", then there is no need for further justification.[95]

NOTES

1. Stuart Hall, "Cultural Identity and Diaspora", in *Colonial Discourse and Post-Colonial Theory: A Reader*, ed. Patrick Williams and Laura Chrisman (Hemel Hempstead: Harvester Wheatsheaf, 1994), 394.
2. Ibid., 400.
3. John Gilmore, series editor's preface, *Lutchmee and Dilloo: A Study of West Indian Life*, by John Edwards Jenkins (1877; repr., London: Macmillan, 2003), vi. Subsequent references to the novel are taken from this edition and appear parenthetically in the text.
4. Ashis Nandy, *The Intimate Enemy: Loss and Recovery of Self under Colonialism* (Delhi: Oxford University Press, 1983), 46; David Dabydeen, introduction to *Lutchmee and Dilloo*, 21.

5. Dabydeen, introduction, 21.
6. Aisha Khan, "Sacred Subversions? Syncretic Creoles, the Indo-Caribbean, and 'Culture's In-between' ", *Radical History Review* 89 (Spring 2004): 171.
7. Amar Wahab, "Mapping West Indian Orientalism: Race, Gender and Representations of Indentured Coolies in the Nineteenth-Century British West Indies", *Journal of Asian American Studies* 10, no. 3 (2007): 283–311.
8. Gilmore, series editor's preface, ix.
9. Dabydeen, introduction, 16.
10. Wahab, "Mapping West Indian Orientalism", 287.
11. Ibid., 284.
12. Sara Suleri, *The Rhetoric of English India* (Chicago: University of Chicago Press, 1992); Mildred Archer, *Early Views of India: The Picturesque Journeys of Thomas and William Daniell, 1786–1794* (London: Thames and Hudson, 1980), 75–110.
13. Edward Said, *Orientalism: Western Representations of the Orient* (London: Verso, 1978), 2.
14. Nandy, *Intimate Enemy*, 72.
15. Mimi Sheller, *Consuming the Caribbean: From Arawaks to Zombies* (London: Routledge, 2003). Quoted in Wahab, "Mapping West Indian Orientalism", 283.
16. Lisa Lowe, *Critical Terrains: French and British Orientalisms* (Ithaca: Cornell University Press, 1991).
17. Wahab, "Mapping West Indian Orientalism", 284.
18. Ibid.
19. For a discussion of the impact of this discourse in the thought and writing of the Classical period and of early modern Europe as well as Rousseau's use of the concept, see Stelio Cro, *The Noble Savage: Allegory of Freedom* (Waterloo, ON: Wilfrid Laurier University Press, 1990). For discussion of its transference to the colonies, see also Hayden White, *Tropics of Discourse: Essays in Cultural Criticism* (Baltimore: Johns Hopkins University Press, 1978); Peter Hulme, *Colonial Encounters: Europe and the Native Caribbean, 1492–1797* (London: Methuen, 1986); Hulme, *Remnants of Conquest: The Island Caribs and Their Visitors, 1877–1998* (Oxford: Oxford University Press, 2000); Peter Hulme and Neil L. Whitehead, eds., *Wild Majesty: Encounters with Caribs from Columbus to the Present Day: An Anthology* (Oxford: Oxford University Press, 1992).
20. The tale of Inkle and Yarico was made known to the public from at least 1657 through Richard Ligon's *A True and Exact History of the Island of Barbadoes*. See *English Trader, Indian Maid: Representing Gender, Race, and Slavery in the New World: An Inkle and Yarico Reader*, ed. Frank Felsenstein (Baltimore: Johns Hopkins University Press, 1999), 55–81. For an account of the dissemination

of the Pocahontas tale, see Robert S. Tilton, *Pocahontas: The Evolution of an American Narrative* (New York: Cambridge University Press, 1994).
21. Wahab, "Mapping West Indian Orientalism", 284.
22. Ibid., 283.
23. The area was most well known for its peasant and tribal rebellions. In 1770 there was the Sannyasi Rebellion and in 1820–21 there was the Ho uprising, which initiated a series of uprisings throughout the nineteenth century. See Stanley Wolpert, *A New History of India*, 6th ed. (New York: Oxford University Press, 2000), ch. 13–16; and John Keay, *India: A History* (New York: Grove, 2001), ch. 16. This past infects the present even today. See, for example, Shishir K. Jha, "Prospects of Radical Change in Bihar: Recuperating the Diseased Heart of India", http://www.proxsa.org/politics/shishir.html.
24. Brinsley Samaroo, "The Caribbean Consequences of the Indian Revolt of 1857" (paper presented at the conference Asian Migrations to the Americas, University of the West Indies, St Augustine, Trinidad and Tobago, 2000), 1. This paper identifies the other areas as Bengal and Oudh. In addition, Samaroo uses the term "Indian Revolt" and this usage is followed here. Karl Marx's reference to the event as the "First War of Indian Independence" is often preferred.
25. According to Patrick Brantlinger, apart from the numerous eyewitness accounts, journal articles, histories, poems and plays, no less than fifty novels were written about the Mutiny in the second half of the nineteenth century, and at least thirty in the first half of the twentieth. *Rule of Darkness: British Literature and Imperialism, 1830–1914* (Ithaca: Cornell University Press, 1990).
26. Alternative views to the one presented in *Lutchmee and Dilloo* are available in M.N. Srinivas, ed., *India's Villages* (Calcutta: West Bengal Government, 1955) and Srinivas, *The Remembered Village* (Berkeley: University of California Press, 1980); André Béteille, "The Indian Village: Past and Present", in *Peasants in History: Essays in Honour of Daniel Thorner*, ed. E.J. Hobsbawm et al. (Calcutta: Oxford University Press, 1980); the stories written by the Indian writer Premchand (1880–1936); and the Naipaul brothers' attempts to interrogate village life in India.
27. Quoted in Wahab, "Mapping West Indian Orientalism", 297.
28. Ibid., 295.
29. Maya Jasanoff, *Edge of Empire: Lives, Culture, and Conquest in the East, 1750–1850* (New York: Knopf, 2005); Durba Ghosh, *Sex and the Family in Colonial India: The Making of Empire* (New York: Cambridge University Press, 2008); William Dalrymple, *White Mughals: Love and Betrayal in Eighteenth-Century India* (London: HarperCollins, 2003).

30. Ghosh, *Sex and the Family*, 2.
31. Mary Louise Pratt, *Imperial Eyes: Travel Writing and Transculturation* (London: Routledge, 1992), 6.
32. Ibid.
33. Quoted in David Goonetilleke, *Salman Rushdie* (London: Macmillan, 1998), 45.
34. Quoted in Wahab, "Mapping West Indian Orientalism", 296.
35. Ibid.
36. Ibid., 296–97.
37. Raymond T. Smith, *The Matrifocal Family: Power, Pluralism, and Politics* (London: Routledge, 1996).
38. Robert Young, *Colonial Desire: Hybridity in Theory, Culture and Race* (London: Routledge, 1995), 2.
39. Edward Long, *History of Jamaica, or, General Survey of the Antient and Modern State of that Island, with Reflections on its Situation, Settlements, Inhabitants, Climate, Products, Commerce, Laws and Government* (1774; repr., Kingston: Ian Randle, 2003).
40. Wahab, "Mapping West Indian Orientalism", 310, fn. 88; Verene Shepherd, "Control, Resistance, Accommodation and Race Relations: Aspects of Indentureship Experience of East Indian Immigrants in Jamaica, 1845–1921", in *Across the Dark Waters: Ethnicity and Indian Identity in the Caribbean*, ed. David Dabydeen and Brinsley Samaroo (London: Macmillan, 1983).
41. Aisha Khan, *Callaloo Nation: Metaphors of Race and Religious Identity among South Asians in Trinidad* (Kingston: University of the West Indies Press, 2004), 9.
42. Wahab, "Mapping West Indian Orientalism", 306.
43. Irfan Habib, *The Agrarian System of Mughal India, 1556–1707* (New York: Asia Publishing House, 1963).
44. The Permanent Settlement Act of 1793 effected the *zamindari* system to which Jenkins refers. See, for example, Habib, *Agrarian System of Mughal India*; Robert Eric Frykenberg, ed., *Land Control and Social Structure in Indian History* (Madison: University of Wisconsin Press, 1969); and Richard Gabriel Fox, *Kin, Clan, Raja and Rule: State–Hinterland Relations in Preindustrial India* (Berkeley: University of California Press, 1971). In the traditional *zamindari* system in Bengal, Bihar and Orissa, the *zamindar* was a chief with custodianship over the entire village, but the productive powers of the land were by customary law and religious sanction the property of the villagers. The act made the *zamindars* actual landlords who had to pay the government assessed revenue from rents collected from the peasants. If the peasant could not pay, the *zamindar* now had the power to evict him.

45. Said, *Orientalism*, 240.
46. Mary Poovey, "The Limits of the Universal Knowledge Project: British India and the East Indiamen", *Critical Inquiry* 31, no. 1 (Autumn 2004): 186.
47. Earl Lovelace, *The Dragon Can't Dance* (Essex: Longman, 1984); Lovelace, *Salt* (London: Faber and Faber, 1996).
48. David Gilmartin and Bruce Lawrence, eds., *Beyond Turk and Hindu* (Gainesville: University Press of Florida, 2000).
49. V.S. Naipaul, *A Way in the World: A Sequence* (New York: Knopf, 1994).
50. Antonio Gramsci, *Selections from the Prison Notebooks*, ed. and trans. Quintin Hoare and Geoffrey Nowell Smith (New York: International, 1971).
51. Veena Talwar Oldenburg, *The Making of Colonial Lucknow, 1856–1877* (Delhi: Oxford University Press, 1989), xix–xx.
52. Dabydeen mentions that "the British Secretary of State, Lord John Russell, called [the indenture scheme] in 1840 'a new system of slavery' ", introduction, 1. But Hugh Tinker and Joseph Beaumont both use this term also to refer to the system of indentureship, and it has been widely adopted since. See Hugh Tinker, *A New System of Slavery: The Export of Indian Labour Overseas, 1830–1920* (London: Hansib, 1993), and Joseph Beaumont, *The New Slavery: An Account of the Indian and Chinese Immigrants in British Guiana* (London: Ridgway, 1871). The resonance of Jenkins's texts with the reformist legacy is apparent when they are compared to George William Des Voeux's *Experiences of a Demerara Magistrate, 1863–1869*, ed. Vincent Roth (Georgetown: Daily Chronicle, 1948), and John Scoble, *Hill Coolies: A brief exposure of the deplorable condition of the Hill Coolies in British Guiana and Mauritius, and of the nefarious means by which they were induced to resort to these colonies* (London: Harvey and Darton, 1840), http://www.indiana.edu/~librcsd/etext/scoble/about.htm.
53. For more on this, see Dabydeen, introduction. For further information on Des Voeux and his activities and concerns, see Walton Look Lai, *Indentured Labour, Caribbean Sugar: Chinese and Indian Migrants to the British West Indies, 1838–1918* (Baltimore: Johns Hopkins University Press, 1993), 134–40 and 174; Walter Rodney, *A History of the Guyanese Working People, 1881–1905* (Baltimore: Johns Hopkins University Press, 1981), 179; Alan H. Adamson, *Sugar without Slaves: The Political Economy of British Guiana, 1838–1904* (New Haven: Yale University Press, 1972), 127, 131 and 264; and Keith O. Laurence, *A Question of Labour: Indentured Immigration into Trinidad and British Guiana, 1875–1917* (Kingston: Ian Randle, 1994), 15–18, 132–34, 508.
54. Lynn Festa, "Humanity without Feathers", *Humanity* 1, no. 1 (2010): 9.
55. Ibid.

56. Ibid., 17.
57. Christopher Leslie Brown, *Moral Capital: Foundations of British Abolitionism* (Chapel Hill: University of North Carolina Press, 2006), 26.
58. Deirdre Coleman, "Conspicuous Consumption: White Abolitionism and English Women's Protest Writing in the 1790s", *English Literary History* 61, no. 2 (1994): 358–59.
59. For an interesting analysis of the changes in policing systems, reflected in this change from *chokedar* to *dacoit*, which were established through the establishment of the Cornwallis Code in 1793 and tightened after the 1857 "Mutiny", see Basudeb Chattopadhyay, *Crime and Control in Early Colonial Bengal, 1770–1860* (Calcutta: K.P. Bagchi, 2000).
60. The representation of the *chokedar* in Jenkins's novel may be inflected by the constant harassment of the British in Bihar by the Santhal tribals, which Samaroo discusses in "The Caribbean Consequences" (5).
61. The discourse of the thug constructed by the British is a complex and extensive one. See, for example, Parama Roy, "Discovering India, Imagining Thuggee", *Yale Journal of Criticism* 9, no. 1 (1996): 121–45.
62. See Sandria B. Freitag, "Collective Crime and Authority in North India", in *Crime and Criminality in British India*, ed. Anand Yang (Tucson: University of Arizona Press, 1985), 158–61; and Om Prakash, ed., *Lord Cornwallis: Administrative Reforms and British Policy* (Delhi: Anmol Publications, 2002).
63. According to Young, this was an intrinsic aspect of the development of the idea of Englishness. He notes, for example, that Kingsley traces the introduction of law as the special gift of the English to Western civilization – and compares it to the Goth contribution to a dying and effeminate Roman empire. *The Idea of English Ethnicity* (Oxford: Blackwell, 2008), 169–70.
64. The progressive changes in these types of discourses from the seventeenth century to the twentieth century are the concern of Jyotsna Singh's *Colonial Narratives/Cultural Dialogues: "Discoveries" of India in the Language of Colonialism* (London: Routledge, 1996), and the reading of the play of discourses in Jenkins's narrative is influenced by her arguments.
65. Richard Gabriel Fox, "East of Said", in *Edward Said: A Critical Reader*, ed. Michael Sprinker (Oxford: Oxford University Press, 1992), 146.
66. James Clifford, *The Predicament of Culture* (Cambridge: Cambridge University Press, 1988), 261.
67. Vinay Lal, "The Rhetorical and Substantive Basis of the 'Rule of Law' under Colonialism: The Suppression of Terrorism in Bengal in the Early Twentieth Century", http://www.vinaylal.com/RP/9.pdf, 48.

68. Aisha Khan claims that this type of dichotomous representation substantiates Mintz's claim that British interpretations of India were based on "paired polarities". See Khan, *Callaloo Nation*, 34–36.
69. Festa, "Humanity", 16.
70. Wahab, "Mapping West Indian Orientalism", 287.
71. Ibid.
72. Richard King, "Orientalism and the Modern Myth of 'Hinduism' ", *Numen* 46, no. 2 (1999): 150.
73. David Kopf, "Hermeneutics versus History", in *Orientalism: A Reader*, ed. Alexander Lyon Macfie (New York: New York University Press, 2000), 194.
74. Dabydeen, introduction, 16–17.
75. See, for example, Charles Fowkes's *The Illustrated Kama Sutra, Ananga Ranga, Perfumed Garden: The Classic Eastern Love Texts* (London: Octopus, 1987).
76. See Lee Morrissey, "Eve's Otherness and the New Ethical Criticism", *New Literary History* 32, no. 2 (2001): 327–45.
77. The illicit aspects, from a Western perspective, of the love between Radha and Krishna were often the facet of the story that fascinated Europeans. See Barbara Stoler Miller, ed. and trans., *The Gitagovinda of Jayadeva: Love Song of the Dark Lord* (New York: Columbia University Press, 1977).
78. Froude quoted in Wahab, "Mapping West Indian Orientalism", 298.
79. Wahab, "Mapping West Indian Orientalism", 306.
80. Ibid., 293.
81. Said, *Orientalism*, 239; Pratt, *Imperial Eyes*, 78.
82. For more on the Asiatic Society, see Gauri Viswanathan, *Masks of Conquest: Literary Studies and British Rule in India* (New York: Columbia University Press, 1988).
83. Homi Bhabha, "Remembering Fanon: Self, Psyche and the Colonial Condition", in *Colonial Discourse and Post-Colonial Theory*, 116.
84. Homi Bhabha, *The Location of Culture* (London: Routledge, 1994), 70.
85. Ranajit Guha, "On Some Aspects of the Historiography of Colonial India", in *Selected Subaltern Studies*, ed. Ranajit Guha and Gayatri Chakravorty Spivak (New York: Oxford University Press, 1988), 37–44; "The Prose of Counter-Insurgency", in *Selected Subaltern Studies*, 44–86.
86. Said, foreword to Guha and Spivak, *Selected Subaltern Studies*, v–x.
87. Said, *Culture and Imperialism* (New York: Vintage, 1993), 140.
88. See J. Vijay Maharaj, "In a Tongue that is Forked; Not False", ch. 1 in "A Caribbean Katha: Re-visioning the 'IndoCaribbean' 'Crisis of Being and Belonging' through the Literary Imagination" (PhD diss., University of the West Indies, St Augustine, 2008), in which such a reading is undertaken.

89. Harvey Neptune, "Moving History in the Aftermath", *Small Axe* 8, no. 2 (2004): 219.
90. Geoff Quilley, "Pastoral Plantations: The Slave Trade and the Representation of British Colonial Landscape in the Late Eighteenth Century", in *An Economy of Colour: Visual Culture and the Atlantic World, 1660–1830*, ed. Geoff Quilley and Kay Dian Kriz (Manchester: Manchester University Press, 2003), 106–28.
91. Dabydeen, introduction, 8.
92. Wahab, "Mapping West Indian Orientalism", 303.
93. George Lamming, *The Pleasures of Exile* (1960; repr., London: Allison and Busby, 1984).
94. Said, *Culture and Imperialism*, 140.
95. Nandy, *Intimate Enemy*, xv.

Chapter 7

STRANGE CREATURES AND FANTASTIC WORLDS

The Other in Selected Nineteenth-Century Children's Texts

GISELLE RAMPAUL

SINCE ITS DISCOVERY AND COLONIZATION, THE Caribbean has always been a subject of the British literary imagination. Although this is clear in canonical books written for adults that have been the usual subjects of critical scrutiny, representations of the Caribbean in children's literature are not often the focus of attention – owing to what Peter Hunt and Karen Sands refer to as "colonial blindness . . . in the criticism of children's literature" – although "children's books, always fundamentally involved in reflecting and transmitting culture, were the witting or unwitting agents of the empire-builders".[1] In this chapter, I would like to focus on a few canonical texts emerging in the nineteenth century, considered the "Golden Age" of children's literature. Although these texts do not all specifically make references to the Caribbean, reading them with British imperialism and the colonization of the Caribbean in mind helps to contextualize the ways in which ideas of difference and discovery were treated in children's books. These books were important because they had a cultural and imperial agenda and perpetuated ideas and ideals about British civilization in the face of newly discovered places and people. According to Mary Louise Pratt, "books written by Europeans about non-European parts of the world created the imperial order for Europeans 'at home' and gave them their place in it".[2] Children's books, especially, helped to consolidate the superiority of the British and the primitivism of the colonized in the minds of the next generation. This chapter will thus examine the ways in which Other landscapes and peoples were constructed in selected children's texts.

In *Soon Come Home to This Island: West Indians in British Children's Literature*, Karen Sands-O'Connor has done a remarkable job of detailing and documenting the several appearances of West Indian characters and the Caribbean setting in children's books from the eighteenth to the twentieth centuries.[3] However, only a few of the texts Sands-O'Connor examines might be considered British "canonical" texts, although they would have been in circulation at the time and were, perhaps, also popular. This chapter takes as its point of departure the canonical and extremely influential *Robinson Crusoe*, which eventually became a children's classic and which laid the foundation for how subsequent canonical children's books treated with different landscapes and peoples. Significantly, the main events for which *Robinson Crusoe* has become famous involve his shipwreck in the Caribbean, his confrontation with the Caribbean landscape, and his encounter with and colonization of an Amerindian character. This literary engagement with and representation of the Caribbean was, therefore, significant to subsequent constructions of the Other in the imperial context.

ROBINSON CRUSOE AND THE FANTASY OF THE CARIBBEAN

Several children's texts emerging in the nineteenth century showed an awareness of the wider world, and exploited the imperial situation to present to their readers tales of adventure that included encounters with new and different people and lands. These texts were following in an already established "exoticist discourse" that developed after the rediscovery of the Americas by Columbus and the subsequent imperial thrusts into the region, and that "allowed an *avant-garde* of writers and intellectuals to escape to strange places and romanticize the liberating otherness of new colonial possessions".[4] Patrick Brantlinger argues that *The Tempest* "might be taken as the starting point for a full account of British imperialism in literature".[5] Jacqueline Lazú agrees, as the play features an island setting peopled by Otherworldly creatures such as the airy spirit Ariel; the witch Sycorax; and a half-human, half-beast, Caliban.[6] Martin Green, however, suggests that the rise of the British Empire should be dated to the *end* of the seventeenth century (or beginning of the eighteenth century) with the union of England with Scotland in 1707 and, more significantly for our purposes, with the publication of *Robinson Crusoe* in 1719, when the adventure tale began to be written. Indeed, the full title of the novel, as published in 1719, was *The Life and Strange Surprizing Adventures of Robinson Crusoe*. Green sees Defoe (who was one of the government agents involved in the negotiation of the union), rather than Shakespeare, then, as a preferred "candidate for the prototype of literary imperialism".[7]

M. Daphne Kutzer dates the rise of imperialism to later – the second half of the nineteenth century – and sees it as concomitant with the development of children's literature: "The rise of imperialism is roughly contemporaneous with the golden age of children's literature (approximately 1860–1930), and the two grew up together."[8] She thus sees Rudyard Kipling as "the logical beginning point for a study of empire and imperialism in children's books".[9] However, her argument might be influenced by her choice of study, which focuses on the presence of imperialism in children's books that feature India and Africa, and not the Caribbean. Nevertheless, she argues that "the omnipresence of empire in what are known as 'classic' works for children . . . suggests how deeply the culture of empire was embedded in Britain, and how important adults thought empire was to the rising generation of children".[10] This point is also important to the argument of this chapter.

I shall take the publication of *Robinson Crusoe* as my starting point for an examination of how the Caribbean informed perceptions of exoticism and difference in nineteenth-century children's texts for a few reasons. *Robinson Crusoe* has long been regarded as the first English novel; its publication date of 1719 is considered the "birthdate" of the novel. Moreover, although emerging as a book written for adults, *Robinson Crusoe* found its way eventually to children's libraries and became a children's classic.[11] Green further points out that although it was a popular book in the eighteenth century and inspired several other such stories, in what came to be called the "Robinsonade", it was not until it was given significant attention by Jean-Jacques Rousseau in *Emile, or On Education* in 1762 that it was taken seriously.[12] Rousseau argued that *Robinson Crusoe* was "the first and only book one should read", and "he transferred Defoe's book from the category of 'Pastime Reading for the Non-literary' to the category 'Textbooks of the Times' ".[13] This was an important development because *Emile*, a treatise on education, contributed to the philosophical conceptualization of childhood in the eighteenth century, and it had a profound effect on the establishment of children's literature as a genre.[14] That it endorsed Defoe's novel so emphatically might have been the reason for *Robinson Crusoe*'s enduring influence on boys' adventure stories in the nineteenth century, when children's literature became an established genre. Indeed, as Jeffrey Richards tells us, *Robinson Crusoe* was at the top of the list of individual favourite titles in a survey published in 1888 of 790 boys in different kinds of schools.[15] By the end of the nineteenth century, its influence was, therefore, still clear. According to Richard Phillips, "The production of *Robinsonades* peaked in the Victorian period, with an average of more than two per year. In addition, 110 translations appeared in print before 1900, alongside at least 115 revisions."[16] In fact, Green argues that the novel might be "the most widely read book in the whole world".[17] Of course, *Robinson Crusoe* is also an obvious beginning point to examine how constructions of the Caribbean influenced subsequent children's books because it is known for the Caribbean island setting in which most of the action takes place, and for the colonization of the Amerindian Friday. But it is also "the first novel that sets itself in the New World", according to Barish Ali, and "one of the great cultural repositories of the imagery of empire", according to Rashna B. Singh.[18] Still, as Peter Hulme points out, the novel has not traditionally been seen as "a Caribbean book", although Hulme himself (like this chapter) tries "to return [it] to the Caribbean".[19] Finally, *Robinson Crusoe* is a good place to start because, as Green points out above, it marks the rise of the British Empire.

Another novel that was a contemporary of *Robinson Crusoe* and that made the crossover from a book for adults to a children's classic is Jonathan Swift's *Gulliver's Travels* (1726), a parody of the very genre of travel writing to which Defoe's novel belonged. Both novels, as adventure tales, had an interesting relationship with realism and fantasy, and it is instructive to examine not only the effect *Robinson Crusoe* had on *Gulliver's Travels* as material for parody, but also the ways in which the latter illuminates the fantasy elements of the former. Children's literature as a separate genre of writing catering specifically to a child audience or reader only developed in the nineteenth century, and this development was simultaneous with the fantasy genre coming into being. But these eighteenth-century novels were already experimenting with the creation of fantastic worlds, and it is the aim of this chapter especially to examine the ways in which Defoe created a fantasy of the Caribbean that had such an enduring influence on later fantasy novels.

Defoe and Swift both presented their novels as authentic compositions written by a real Crusoe and a real Gulliver respectively, who supposedly existed and supposedly had really experienced these adventures. Defoe's story was actually based on the shipwreck of the Scottish sailor Alexander Selkirk on the South Pacific island of Juan Hernandez, and was influenced by the many nautical stories being circulated at the time, the most famous collection of which was Hakluyt's *Voyages*. Swift was also influenced by the stories brought back to Britain about unfamiliar environments peopled by strange creatures beyond the seas. As Pratt points out, "Travel books . . . gave European reading publics a sense of ownership, entitlement and familiarity with respect to the distant parts of the world that were being explored, invaded, invested in, and colonized. . . . They created a sense of curiosity, excitement, adventure, and even moral fervor about European expansionism."[20] Elizabethan writers especially (such as Sir Walter Raleigh) had written enthusiastic propaganda about the new lands in an attempt to secure investments by city merchants.[21] Many of the stories coming back to England were, therefore, based on gross exaggeration and sometimes were even completely apocryphal. Swift thus created his own fictional lands in his satiric travelogue *Gulliver's Travels*, originally titled *Travels into Several Remote Nations of the World*. While I am not suggesting that eighteenth-century readers believed that Swift's novel was actually based on fact, as far-fetched as Swift's settings and characters are, stories about Houyhnhnmland and the Yahoos might have been as plausible as other stories circulating about hostile and sometimes impenetrable rainforests full of scantily clad, dark-skinned, man-eating savages.

Both novels, therefore, contributed to the development of the fantastic yet realistic world of the adventure tale, and the desert island of Defoe's novel and the miniature and other imaginary worlds in Swift's have influenced numerous subsequent adult and children's books.[22] Now, clearly, Defoe's setting of the Caribbean was more "real" than Swift's fictional lands. Swift's novel was, after all, a satire, and therefore employed gross exaggeration to parodic effect. However, although Defoe is careful to give us details about the position of Crusoe's island to suggest its actual existence in the Caribbean (Crusoe describes the island as lying in the mouth or the gulf of the Oroonoko and the "land which [he] perceived to the W. and N.W. was the great island of Trinidad, on the north point of the mouth of the river"), and although *Robinson Crusoe* has been hailed as the forerunner of modern realistic fiction, the island itself was a figment of the imagination.[23] Likewise, Swift provides maps and refers to actual places like India and Japan to situate his fictional countries in the real world. The novels, therefore, construct their foreign lands in terms of realism and fantasy in similar ways, and Swift's fictional lands, instead of emphasizing the "realness" of Defoe's Caribbean island, draw attention to the fact that Defoe was constructing a fantasy of the empire.

Furthermore, both novels depict British protagonists sailing to far-off lands and encountering "strange" and "exotic" peoples and landscapes, then describing them in minute detail so that the reader, through the first-person narrative perspective, could see what the protagonists saw, experiencing these worlds through the dominant perceptual and conceptual perspectives of the British sailors. These detailed descriptions contributed to the realistic settings and characters, but the distance from the ordinary and familiar setting of Britain helped to construct these places as Other-worldly, as places that the British reading public could only access through imaginative complicity with the narrators of these texts. These settings were, therefore, more fantastic than the familiar solidity of everyday Britain. In this way, the novels established ideas of a stable home (Britain) and of foreign lands beyond the seas that were constructed as at once realistic and fantastic. As Kutzer explains, "In adventure fiction, we appear still to be in the real world, but one that provides much more excitement and exoticism than can be found in dreary and domesticated England. The treatment of foreign lands as both realistic and fantastic is common in fiction of empire."[24]

Hulme has also described *Robinson Crusoe* as a "colonial romance" and "colonial fantasy" for several reasons, not least its utopianism.[25] The landscape that is so easily cultivated by Crusoe's British hands, the Amerindian Friday who is so willing to be moulded and civilized, and the good fortune of being shipwrecked on an island where the natives are not familiar with firearms as late as the seventeenth century are all part of the colonial fantasy. Peter Redfield also refers to the novel as "cultural myth", and Ann Marie Fallon describes it as "a kind of myth of the modern condition".[26] Hulme explains that the novel is "mythic in the sense that [its portrayal of the Caribbean has] demonstrably less to do with the historic world of the mid-seventeenth-century Caribbean than [it does] with the primary stuff of colonialist ideology".[27] V.S. Naipaul similarly discusses the novel in terms of an "enduring human fantasy" (206) and the colonizer's "dream of total power".[28]

Kutzer further argues that "the story of empire is often presented as a kind of fairy tale, in which the valiant but unrecognized hero travels to strange realms, overcomes obstacles and villains, all in order to reach the pot of gold ... at the end".[29] This, as Maria Nikolajeva points out, also defines the basic plot of the fantasy novel (which grew out of the fairy tale): "the hero leaves home, meets helpers and opponents, goes through trials, performs a task, and returns home having gained some form of wealth".[30] Crusoe does indeed gain wealth from his estates in Brazil at the end of the novel, and it was in the spirit of adventure, which Hulme argues is synonymous with the quest for treasure, that both Crusoe and Gulliver set out from Britain to explore the world.[31] And this was certainly the story of several other characters that would appear in nineteenth-century boys' adventure tales. The influence of *Robinson Crusoe* on the establishment of a literary fantasy of the Caribbean, therefore, cannot be overlooked.

"STRANGE ISLANDS AND ADVENTURES": THE BOYS' ADVENTURE TALE[32]

Charles Kingsley's *Westward Ho!* (1855) and Robert Louis Stevenson's *Treasure Island* (1883), for example, followed suit with their presentations of the Caribbean as an exotic and Other world, full of riches to be found. Both novels fit into the same genre of boys' adventure story as *Robinson Crusoe* and *Gulliver's Travels*, and featured a similar androcentric world of exploration, discovery and imperialism. They harked back to a romantic past (that of the seventeenth and eighteenth centuries) peopled by seafaring adventurers and pirates who were looking for El Dorado.[33]

There are several specific references to the Caribbean in *Treasure Island*. The schooner setting sail for the Caribbean island on which the treasure is buried is called the *Hispaniola*, and the treasure is the booty acquired by the bloodthirsty buccaneer Captain Flint, whose career was established mainly in the West Indies and some of the American colonies: describing Flint as the "bloodthirstiest buccaneer that ever lived", Squire Trelawney says to Dr Livesey, "I've seen his top sails with these eyes, off Trinidad, and the cowardly son of a rum-puncheon that I sailed with put back – put back, sir, into Port of Spain" (38). Stevenson's swashbuckling pirates might have been influenced by real-life historical heroes of empire, the sixteenth- and seventeenth-century seamen, pirates and privateers like Sir Walter Raleigh, Sir John Hawkins and Sir Francis Drake (and many more) who combed the seas and raided foreign ships, and who were also searching for treasure in the form of El Dorado in the Caribbean region. In fact, other real-life pirates such as William Kidd, Blackbeard, Edward England, Howell Davis and Bartholomew Roberts, some of whom operated in the West Indies, are also referred to in the novel. Similarly, the main character in *Westward Ho!*, Amyas Leigh, follows Sir Francis Drake to sea, and part of the novel follows his adventures searching for gold in the Caribbean as well.

Stories about the great wealth to be found in the New World had circulated around Europe since Columbus's entrance into the Caribbean, but the myth of El Dorado associated with Guyana and the Orinoco was most associated with Sir Walter Raleigh, whom D. Graham Burnett refers to as Guyana's "colonial father".[34] Burnett further argues: "the figure of Sir Walter Ralegh and the nebulous figure of El Dorado – the gilt king of a legendary empire – both loomed large in British conceptions of the [Caribbean] region".[35] The link between piracy, treasure and the Caribbean, therefore, became an established characteristic of boys' adventure stories. The prospect of going to sea is exciting for Jim Hawkins, the young protagonist of *Treasure Island*, because of the mystery and adventure surrounding the island, and the possibility of securing wealth: "And I was going to sea myself – to sea in a schooner, with a piping boatswain and pig-tailed singing seamen; to sea, bound for an unknown island, and to seek for buried treasures!" (47). The sense of mystery surrounding the island that lies "Offe Caraccas" (placing it in the Caribbean) comes from Jim's unfamiliarity with lands beyond the English shore, and from the stories that he has heard thus far from the seamen – including the rough drunken sailor, Billy Bones – who visit his father's inn (39). The treasure, furthermore, is buried, adding to the idea of the romantic quest, the anticipation of discovery and the uncertainty associated with its retrieval.[36] The promise of gold contributes to the commodification and the desirability of the Caribbean space.

At the same time, there is trepidation when Jim imagines the island before he actually sets sail with Squire Trelawney:

> I approached that island in my fancy from every possible direction; I explored every acre of its surface; I climbed a thousand times to that tall hill they called the Spy-glass, and from the top enjoyed the most wonderful and changing prospects. Sometimes the isle was thick with savages, with whom we fought; sometimes full of dangerous animals that hunted us; but in all my fancies nothing occurred to me so strange and tragic as our actual adventures. (43)

According to Lazú, "Islands offer a unique space within which to construct the most fantastic worlds imaginable – ones that offer limitless adventures for young travelers in children's books."[37] Islands were portrayed as "sites of encounters with strangeness and adventure" because they were "constructed in terms of a geography of isolation and self-sufficiency".[38] The fascination we see in Jim's description is also accompanied by a sense of danger. This ambivalence is also seen in Crusoe's attitude towards the island in Defoe's novel. It is first the "Island of Despair" (52) but as he begins to make it his home, it becomes his "beloved island" (104). At the same time, the fear of "savages" is never far from his mind, and he is careful to keep watch and to protect himself. Much of Jim's conception of the island he has never seen comes from assumptions about the Caribbean based on accounts he has heard. The Caribbean becomes another world away from the security and solidity of British reality.

Towards the end of the novel, there is another description that is worthy of attention because it provides another common nineteenth-century British view of the Caribbean that accords with the colonial fantasy. Before sailing back to England, the crew stops at the "nearest port in Spanish America":

> It was just at sundown when we cast anchor in a most beautiful land-locked gulf, and were immediately surrounded by shore boats full of negroes, and Mexican Indians, and half-bloods, selling fruits and vegetables, and offering to dive for bits of money. The sight of so many good-humoured faces (especially the blacks), the taste of the tropical fruits, and above all, the lights that began to shine in the town, made a most charming contrast to our dark and bloody sojourn on the island. (183)

Although this passage is quite different from the previous description of the Skeleton Island in Jim's imagination, the idealistic portrayal is consistent with the exoticization of the Caribbean landscape and people. The physical setting is "beautiful" and "charming", but the human landscape is equally important to the establishment of this idealized setting. The humans in the passage are not individuals; they are only identified in terms of racial markers, and are there simply for the viewing pleasure, entertainment and feeding (with their exotic "tropical fruits" and vegetables) of the crew. The contrast with Skeleton Island is necessary for plot purposes – the novel is nearing its close so there is no need to construct this space as menacing as well as beautiful – but the passage, nevertheless, betrays a fetishization of the Caribbean space that was based on ill-informed assumptions and on a fantasy.

In the novels examined thus far, the established perspective is British. Britain is the literal point of departure for the characters who embark on perilous journeys to the Caribbean, which is situated on the peripheries of normalcy and ordinary experience. As John Rowe Townsend points out, adventure for the British "was something you found overseas; increasingly it was connected with the building of that empire on which the sun has now set".[39] It is not surprising that a mutiny takes places aboard the *Hispaniola* because the schooner represents instability: it is situated on the unpredictable sea that becomes a liminal space between home (Britain) and an Other world (the New World); but it is also named after the first island rediscovered by Columbus and colonized by the Spanish, presented in Defoe's and Kingsley's novels as colonial competitor in the region. As C. Wee argues, "The emerging nation-empire is contrasted against the decline of an illiberal scion of the old tainted, obviously multiracial, Catholic Roman empire. . . . For Kingsley, . . . national culture and identity are bound to imperial destiny."[40] Diana C. Archibald also contends that the New World was presented as "a playground for the daring Britons, a place for them to prove their superior intelligence and courage of the English".[41] The Caribbean was a remote place that was Othered for its associations with adventure and lucrative possibility, but it also became a space in which ideals of Britishness could be explored and established.

Through these fictional and fantastic representations of the region, the construction of the Caribbean as virgin territory open for the penetration and exploration and plundering by the British colonizer or explorer became established in the imaginations of the British reading public. As Ymitri Mathison argues, "Adventure fiction . . . codified and mapped . . . the empire's exotic objects, lands and peoples so that they could be more readily consumed by a wide spectrum of the public."[42] The acquisitiveness of the explorers and the potential and wealth represented by the unexplored region became an established theme and the focus, more specifically, of *amusement* for boy readers, the next generation of imperialists. According to Green,

> the adventure tales that formed the light reading of Englishmen for two hundred years or more after *Robinson Crusoe* were, in fact, the energizing myth of English imperialism. They were, collectively, the story England told itself as it

went to sleep at night; and, in the form of its dreams, they charged England's will with the energy to go out into the world and explore, conquer, and rule.[43]

Politically, then, the adventure tale of imperialism was perhaps "more influential than the serious novel".[44]

PRIMITIVIST FANTASY AND THE BLACK CHILD

The political significance of Defoe's novel is also seen in its presentation of non-European peoples, particularly the Amerindian Friday, which was also influential on the construction of non-British, non-white/black characters in nineteenth-century writing. The colonial relationship between Crusoe and Friday has been widely examined by literary critics. Friday is exoticized as part of the colonial fantasy and is characterized as easy to manipulate and dominate. He is subservient, willing not only to please Crusoe, whose foot he places on his head, but also to have his entire culture replaced by British values. There is, however, another way in which Friday and Crusoe's relationship is characterized that is useful to an understanding of how colonized people were Othered in imperial literature. Crusoe describes the relationship between Friday and himself as that of "a child to a father" (157). The non-British, non-white adult is infantilized to reinforce the dominance of the British white adult. As Bill Ashcroft writes, "the colonized other was represented in terms of tropes which invariably justified imperial rule, no matter how benign it saw itself to be. In this process, no trope has been more tenacious and more far-reaching than that of the child."[45] This fantasy of the colonized as infantile and primitive, appearing in *Robinson Crusoe*, was influential on the construction of other black characters in nineteenth-century children's writing.

The development of philosophical conceptions of childhood made the infantilization of the colonized desirable and feasible. John Locke and Jean-Jacques Rousseau were the two philosophers who were responsible for the conception of childhood that consolidated in nineteenth-century writing and that still largely persists in the Western world. Locke saw the child as a *tabula rasa*, potentially good though inherently inclined to evil, so the civilization of children depended on (adult) parents and schoolmasters who could guide them to enlightenment.[46] A similar conception of colonized people emerged, and the connection between the two became consolidated in the thinking and writing of imperialism. Rousseau's noble savage associated childhood with nature and primitivism, and this too became crucial to imperial discourse and the construction of the colonized Other: "The noble savage is and ever will be a 'savage' for the noble savage is the barbarian as natural child with childlike innocence, and therefore capable of a better rapport with the natural world, but without the innately superior understanding and creative ability of the dominant Christian civilization."[47] Jo-Ann Wallace goes so far as to call the concept of "child" a *"necessary precondition* of imperialism – . . . the West had to invent for itself 'the child' before it could think a specifically colonialist imperialism".[48] It must be pointed out, though, that as far back as the fifteenth century, Columbus also significantly had described some of the natives he had met as "simple children of nature" (and others as "cannibals").[49] Ashcroft also points out that it was Montaigne, in his essay "On Cannibals" (1580), who first suggested that cannibals "live in an Edenic state of purity and simplicity",[50] although Rousseau is the "philosopher whose name has almost become synonymous with the idea of noble savagery".[51]

Ashcroft also establishes the connection between the emergence of the philosophical conception of the child and the concept of race as a category in the eighteenth century. These two concepts, he argues, became "virtually interchangeable in their importance for imperial discourse".[52] "Scientific" arguments popular at the time also "proved" that black people were lower on the evolutionary ladder and that they exhibited the biological and psychological characteristics of children. The trope of the child was important in the discourse of empire because it contained the contradictions and ambivalence inherent in imperial discourse: "Authority is held in balance with nurture; domination with enlightenment; debasement with idealization; negation with affirmation; exploitation with education; filiation with affiliation. This ability to absorb contradiction gives the binary parent/child an inordinately hegemonic potency."[53] The association with primitivism also helped to consolidate the view that colonized people, especially those who were racially different, needed to be governed by the superior colonizer. According to Michael Paul Rogin, primitivism "developed into a full-blown, racialist theory during the nineteenth century, deriving national identity from racial superiority and justifying on racialist grounds the right of one group to exploit, displace, and exterminate another".[54] Rogin refers to this as a "primitivist" or "cultural fantasy".[55]

The link between the child and print in Locke's comparison of the child to a blank slate is also important to an examination of how ideas about black characters were written or inscribed into texts. Colonized lands and people were seen to be empty of meaning, waiting for the colonizers to write them into being. Ashcroft expands:

> Neither the child nor the colonial subject can have access to meaning outside the processes of civilization and education which bring them into being.... Until they are "inscribed" by being brought into inscription, introduced to literacy and education, they cannot be "read" in any meaningful way. The child, then, signifying a blank slate, an innocent of nature, a subject of exotic possibility and moral instruction as well as a barbarous and unsettling primitive, suggests an endlessly protean capacity for inscription and meaning.[56]

Indeed, both philosophers, by conceiving of the child in their particular ways (Locke as the blank slate and Rousseau as a wild plant), were also inscribing the child into being or imbuing the child with meaning. By examining a selection of nineteenth-century texts, we can also begin to uncover the ways in which these philosophical inscriptions of the child and of the colonized influenced further inscriptions of black characters in British writing for British children. Because "the habitual tropes characteristic of a particular textual attitude come to stand, virtually, as received truth, as knowledge of the world",[57] these early constructions of black characters also led to the perpetuation of the primitivist fantasy of the Other.

"MUTE BUT PICTURESQUE": REPRESENTING THE PICCANINNY[58]

According to Gail Ching-Liang Low, "Primitivity, as reconstituted through the image of the noble savage and the imaginary bond between the white adventurer and the black man is central to the boy's story of heroic valour and moral fortitude."[59] *Robinson Crusoe*'s far-reaching influence is, therefore, unsurprising. By 1904, with the production of J.M. Barrie's *Peter Pan or The Boy Who Would Not Grow Up* at the Duke of York's Theatre, the influence of Defoe's novel was very well established. Although in the preface to the play, Barrie "confesses" that he has no recollection of writing the play, *Peter Pan* was, in fact, heavily influenced by his adventure story *The Boy Castaways of Black Lake Island, Being a Record of the Terrible Adventures of the Brothers*

Davies in the Summer of 1901 Faithfully Set Forth by Peter Llewelyn Davies (1901), which fit squarely in the tradition of the Robinsonade and was very much influenced by Stevenson's *Treasure Island* and *Kidnapped*, both of which Barrie had read and loved.[60] Barrie's story featured four boys (four of the five Llewelyn Davies children, who belonged to a friend of Barrie) who run away to sea and who find themselves shipwrecked on Black Lake Island, a tropical island, where they have adventures with a pirate, tiger and crocodile, all of which eventually made their way into *Peter Pan*, and none of which was associated with everyday life in Britain. Like *Robinson Crusoe*, the story is presented as if written by one of the characters to whom this adventure happened, Peter Llewelyn Davies – the same Peter who (along with his brothers) became the inspiration for Peter Pan.

Barrie's play (rewritten and published in 1911 as a novel entitled *Peter and Wendy*) combined the fantastic island setting with the pirates to create the enchanting yet menacing world of the Never Land, where the Lost Boys can romp freely with Peter Pan, catch mermaids and eat elaborate pretend dinners, but where they are constantly under threat of capture by pirates. The boys, all British, are allowed to live out the fantasy of explorers inhabiting a new world. And, significantly, this new and fantastic world features characteristics of Britain's colonized lands: "the flamingos, lagoons and wigwams have significant imperial implications, as do their subsequent relationship with pirates, Native American and Caribbean cultures, and African animals", as Christine Roth argues.[61] Also notable is that Peter Pan's nemesis, Captain Hook, was based on Captain Swarthy, a black pirate, of *The Boy Castaways*, which is consistent with Low's assessment of boys' adventure stories above – although in his later reincarnation as Captain Hook, this racial detail seems to have been abandoned.[62] The play, however, introduced another non-white character native to this Never Land in Princess Tiger Lily, "belle of the Piccaninny tribe" (*Peter Pan*).

The construction of Tiger Lily and her tribe of "redskins" reveals the primitivist fantasy of Other peoples. The generic appellation "redskins", which defines the group according to physiognomic alterity, marks them as Other to the normative white Self embodied by Peter Pan and the Lost Boys (who, despite their own tribal name, are introduced as individuals by the stage directions). As Karen Coats points out, "As a master signifier, Whiteness is the screen against which any 'other' culture is projected; it embodies the universal, making any other ethnicity the particular, the curious, the deviant."[63] Paul Fox defends the text, arguing for its subversiveness through its "emphasis upon roles being played", "shallow caricature[s]" and expectations about how white and non-white peoples supposedly behave.[64] Clay Kinchen Smith also argues that Barrie undermines racial stereotypes in the play.[65] Fox and Smith argue that stereotypes cannot hold in a story about fluid identities, a story in which characters shift from role to role. However, Peter is the character with the most agency in this regard – indeed, he even impersonates Tiger Lily herself at one point – and it is useful to examine the stereotype of Native Americans regardless of its potential subversive meaning, as it accords with the primitivist fantasy and *reveals* the very expectations that Fox and Smith argue are being challenged. According to Roth, "Like nineteenth-century travel narratives, the [story telescopes] readers into an imaginatively stimulating foreign setting in which [the narrator attempts] to mediate [his] own cultural presuppositions and desires between those [he] voyeuristically observe[s] in these foreign cultures."[66]

There are several ways in which Tiger Lily is marginalized and Othered. As Emily Clark contends, "Every aspect of [Tiger Lily's] presence points the reader toward an uninformed yet commonplace definition of indigenous populations in the colonies as animalistic, exotic, entertaining creatures."[67] She "seems to function as a spectacle for the reader and the male community of Neverland", reducing her effectively to an object – not least because she is also female.[68] Though she is a princess, proud and aloof, which gives her a certain degree of dignity and power, Tiger Lily defers to Peter, whom she calls the "Great White Father", and who stands in as a proxy to her real but *absent* father. It is unclear whether Tiger Lily is indeed a child (although she has been portrayed as such in some versions – the Disney film comes to mind), but the bestowal of this epithet on Peter conceptually casts her and the Piccaninnies as children – and casts Peter, who is *clearly* a child, as an adult simply because he is white and they are not. The appellation of "Piccaninnies" for the tribe also infantilizes and disempowers them, as the word "piccaninny", possibly derived from the Spanish *pequeño* for "little one", "was first employed by Europeans to refer to the children of different ethnic, usually colonized, peoples".[69] The usual paternalism of colonization is, therefore, apparent.

Tiger Lily's name, an amalgam of an animal and a flower, also objectifies her. Moreover, it directly associates her with Nature, and with primitivism.

She is characterized as the noble savage, on the fringes of civilization despite her royal status: "Her character represents a marriage of both independence and oppression that forces her to consistently remain on the farthest boundaries of Neverland. Her name . . . especially contributes to her liminality."[70] She is at once desirable (as a lovely rare flower), innocent and pure (as a lily), and dangerous (as a tiger): her tribe's "braves would all have her to wife, but she wards them off with a hatchet" (*Peter Pan*). Her first words are also menacing, although the threat is directed at the pirates: she asks her tribe members whether the pirates should be scalped. According to Roth, "she is most often illustrated as a little girl . . . , but she is also an erotic femme fatale".[71] This particular characterization of indigenous people as libidinous yet also menacing has been written about by Anne McClintock, who argues that colonizers came to see and to represent the Caribbean (and the Americas) as a "porno-tropics".[72] Furthermore, Tiger Lily is contrasted with Wendy, who serves as the white, British, civilized, stable mother figure to the Lost Boys. Both characters (along with Tinkerbell) vie for Peter's affections, but Peter is clearly partial to Wendy – a more "appropriate" attraction, as white British women were "typically constructed as the symbolic bearers of the nation".[73]

Clark also points out Tiger Lily's "linguistic silence and invisibility", as evident in the text's description of the Piccaninnies as "mute but picturesque" (*Peter Pan*).[74] Clark draws attention to the visual absence of Tiger Lily in the text, but the text itself makes a comment on how the Other should be visually represented through the use of the stage direction "picturesque". Ideally, the Piccaninnies contribute to the exotic landscape of the Never Land. One might recall Crusoe's description of Friday as well: he is described as pleasant to look at, "a comely, handsome fellow", with a "very good countenance", who had "all the sweetness and softness of an European" (154), but he is, nevertheless, a "poor savage" (157) or a "poor creature" (158) in need of English civilization. Homi Bhabha's concept of recognition and disavowal is at work here.[75]

Both Friday and Tiger Lily are also silenced in the texts, though in different ways. Although Friday has his own Kalinago culture and language, these are eradicated in favour of the "superior" English culture and language. Friday's native language is effectively silenced, and it is also noteworthy that his English utterances are mainly in response to Crusoe, and there is limited direct speech by Friday in the novel. Furthermore, Crusoe is usually in the subject position, and Friday in the object position:

> I . . . let him know I was very well pleased with him. In a little time I began to speak to him, and teach him to speak to me; and, first, I made him know his name should be Friday, which was the day I saved his life. I called him so for the memory of the time. I likewise taught him to say master, and then let him know that was to be my name. I likewise taught him to say Yes and No, and to know the meaning of them. (154–55)

This often makes Crusoe the active participant and Friday the passive participant in their interactions, resulting in a kind of metaphorical muting as well.

In *Peter Pan*, whereas the white characters are articulate and verbose, the Piccaninnies function, for most of the play, as spectacle, so they are silent. When the Piccaninnies do speak, their language once more marks them as Other. It is characterized by the use of expressions like "ugh" and the "-um" suffix, typically associated with linguistic stereotyping of Native Americans.[76] Tiger Lily speaks individually, albeit very little (she has four lines); Great Big Little Panther has two lines; but the rest of the Piccaninnies speak as a group (and only twice), mainly to register their agreement with her: "Ugh, ugh, wah!" (*Peter Pan*). Peter, on the other hand, is able to code-switch and character-switch, adopting identity after identity at will.

Tiger Lily's few lines also, significantly, have to do with speaking or not speaking. In her first line, she asks the opinion of the rest of her tribe on the decision to scalp the pirates: "What you say?" The second time she speaks is when she has been captured by Hook and the pirates. Her response to Smee's instructions not to mewl in the face of her impending death is a stoic "Enough said." However, the stage directions tell us that Smee is "chagrined because she does not mewl" because he "would have preferred a farewell palaver". The final time we hear her speak is to adopt Peter as authority and protector: "The Great White Father save me from pirates. Me his velly nice friend now; no let pirates hurt him." The orthographic representation of her speech further serves to alienate her from the English-speaking characters. Her accent is different and her grammar, like Friday's, is singled out as incomplete, imperfect. Her final line is: "Tiger Lily has spoken." The princess has made a pronouncement, but it is only when Peter says, "The Great White Father has spoken" (*Peter Pan*) that the exchange comes to an end. Tiger Lily's silence in the face of danger with the pirates demonstrates her courage, rebellion and dignity as a princess, but later her authority is undermined by Peter's last word that silences everyone.

In the German nineteenth-century verse story "The Inky Boys", appearing in Heinrich Hoffmann's picture-book *Struwwelpeter* (1844), there is another black character also marked by his silence and worth mentioning, even if briefly. This book was translated into English in 1848, as well as into several other languages, and became very popular throughout Europe. Michelle H. Martin argues that this early portrayal of a black child might be "one of the first – and maybe *the* first – European depiction of a black child in a children's text".[77] Because of its influence on subsequent portrayals of black children in children's literature, it therefore cannot be overlooked. The story, like the others in the collection, is a cautionary tale and seems anti-racist: the great supernatural adult authority figure, Agrippa, warns the white boys that they should not tease the black boy, and then metes out punishment when they do not heed his advice. However, the *punishment* comes in the form of being dipped in black ink, leading Martin to interpret the story as "explicitly anti-racist yet implicitly racist".[78] It reinforces the Otherness and the inferiority of the black child. Apart from not having a voice in the story at all while the white boys call him names through direct speech, he is nameless, only referred to as the "Black-a-moor", which identifies him, like the "redskins" of *Peter Pan*, only in terms of his physiognomic and national alterity. The black child is defined only by the white characters in the story. The racist epithets flung at him by the white boys serve to define him from their perspective. Although appearing to be sympathetic, the (implied white) narrator describes him as "woolly-headed", condescendingly calls him a "poor fellow", and refers to him at the end of the story as "the harmless Black-a-moor". Even Agrippa – in the black child's defence! – uses the argument that "if he tries with all his might, / He cannot change from black to white".[79]

The subtle racism in the story recalls William Blake's eighteenth-century poem "Little Black Boy", which similarly argues for the innocence of the black boy while also reinforcing his Otherness and inferiority. As Jan Susina writes, "Hoffman's [sic] attempt humorously to confront discrimination inadvertently results in paternalistic racism in that the black figure requires protection from the great white father."[80] Paternalistic racism, as defined by Donnarae MacCann, refers to "good intentions coupled with white standards, a white perspective, and an assumption of white superiority".[81] Blackness is ultimately seen as a punishment, and Hoffmann's story suggests that it is rude to be unkind to those unfortunate enough to be black. The silence of (and surrounding representations of) black characters in the nineteenth century highlights the fact that they were being defined by the perspective of the colonizers, who were constructing them according to their own desires and needs to preserve the primitivist fantasy of the colonized Other.

"A CURIOUS DREAM": WAKING UP, RETURNING HOME[82]

Part of the reason for the colonizers' conception of the Caribbean as a strange, exotic and Other geographical location, and of the native peoples as primitive, was the fear of difference. Naming and defining the unknown in the colonizers' own terms, transforming *terra incognita* into *terra cognita*, were ways in which they could control the Other and contain their own psychological destabilization, as I have argued in chapter 2. Indeed, the fantasy of the New World revealed a great deal about the British as well. As Peter Bishop argues,

> one can gain a powerful insight into a culture's sense of identity precisely through its fantasies of "Otherness".... Identities of place are formed through a constant process of negotiation between fantasies of Self and Other, of Home and Away, of Here and There. Who we think we are is inextricably connected to who we think we are not. How we imagine where we are is directly related to how we imagine other places.[83]

The presence of the Caribbean in the British literary imagination, therefore, allowed for the establishment of "cultural ... dichotomies".[84]

Abroad was often contrasted with home in terms of the unfamiliar versus the familiar. Home is constructed as a stable place, whereas abroad is often represented as menacing, shifting, in need of definition and domination. According to Archibald:

> In its [the Victorian novel's] most basic form, a virtuous, moral, noble, respectable, comfortable, pretty, and/or trustworthy, old England is contrasted with a savage, rough, wicked, vulgar, indecent, violent, and/or hypocritical New World. More rarely, a paradisiacal New World appears to advantage against the corrupt Old World, but even in such cases, the New World usually functions primarily as a mirror in which the Old World can see itself more clearly in order to reform and thus be restored to greater glory. The New World, in these cases, is not ultimately destined to become the new center, either ideologically or geographically. Again, however, texts that tap into the vast network of New World

images become enmeshed in a tangled web of socioideologically constructed relationships. Once one leaves "home", for whatever reason, one journeys to a dangerous land whose very existence inevitably challenges the center, calling its centrality into question.[85]

This is quite evident in *Robinson Crusoe*, which "records the traumatic dislocations inherent in creating a transnational social imaginary".[86] This "traumatic dislocation" is apparent in several subsequent children's texts that took as their subject different kinds of confrontations with the unfamiliar, and was often manifested in attempts to create a sense of home in foreign landscapes, and a longing for, or return to, home.

Crusoe, faced with an alien landscape in which he is terrified of being attacked and eaten by animals and humans alike, cultivates a sense of home on the island by planting a bower after he satisfies the more immediate need of providing himself with food. His use of terms and names consistent with the English landscape to describe the parts of the island that he cultivates reveals his longing for home and also his dominion over it: "this was all my own; . . . I was king and lord of all this country . . . and had a right of possession. . . . I came home (so I must now call my tent and cave). . . . I fancied now I had my country house and my sea-coast house. . . . I was lord of the whole manor; or, if I pleased, I might call myself king or emperor over the whole country which I had possession of" (74–75, 76, 96). As John R. Gillis argues, "Importing old world landscapes had a similar effect of domesticating a world that initially defied description. At every step of the way, exploration and colonization depended on fictions, or an illusory familiarity."[87] Crusoe's "obsession with ordering and civilizing the world, that is, the island around him becomes emblematic of the British colonial project abroad".[88]

Lewis Carroll's *Alice's Adventures in Wonderland* (1897), one of the most popular and influential children's books of the nineteenth century, might not directly deal with the Caribbean, but the imperial project does influence the ways in which Wonderland and Alice's experiences there are constructed. Caroline Webb argues that Alice is "a child immersed in Victorian cultural perceptions of race in contemporary English attitudes to the Other".[89] She goes further to show that Alice can be read as an imperialist herself in the way she negotiates her (constantly shifting and unstable) position in the unfamiliar, curious world of Wonderland. Alice, too, suffers the "traumatic dislocation" of being away from her familiar and "civilized" Victorian society in the waking world, and having to confront a "curious" and "strange" place that completely destabilizes her.

When she first enters Wonderland, Alice tries to enter the beautiful garden, a literal rendering of the conception of the New World as utopic and Edenic that colonizers sometimes had, as Archibald mentions above. But, as Fiona McCulloch points out, "The quest romance is parodied – the garden that Alice so desperately wants to enter is artificial and scary, even intimidating."[90] Her expectations are not met any more than the European conception of the New World as a paradise was. Wonderland challenges her epistemological and ontological security in the same way that the New World shook the foundations of what the British knew (or thought they knew). In Wonderland, Alice, too, no longer knows what she knows – and whatever she knows turns out to be useless – but she also no longer knows who she is. She is repeatedly asked by the hookah-smoking caterpillar about her identity – "Who are *you*?" – and she realizes that her experiences in this new world make that question impossible to answer: she wonders to herself, "Who in the world am I?" (35, 15). The animals and people are predatory and savage and Alice, not understanding the rules that govern this land (indeed, there are no rules!), constantly feels threatened. Moreover, there are many references to cannibalism in the story, reflecting the fear of being consumed, literally and metaphorically, by the Other.[91] Even language, the system through which we construct and understand our world, Alice realizes, is "prone to numerous slippages and instabilities" and cannot help her to make sense of Wonderland.[92] As Webb puts it, "Like the English in their colonies, Alice shows herself unable to deal with those she meets on other than her own culture-bound terms."[93] The search for certainty and meaning – but the sort of meaning that can only come from her own ideological framework – in an absurd world is the journey Alice undergoes in the story. It is the psychological journey of the colonizer.

Robinson Crusoe, Treasure Island, Peter Pan and *Alice's Adventures in Wonderland* all end with a return to the normalcy, stability and familiarity of home. According to Karen Coats:

> [The Never Land of *Peter Pan* is a] treacherous place, a place where [the children's] lives are endangered on a regular basis and thrills are always linked to violence. This sort of excitement is exhilarating at first, but it induces a careless forgetfulness and irresponsibility to others that Wendy finds disturbing.

Her sense of values, even her sense of humanity, is strongly linked to home and family, and if that means going home and accepting the responsibility of growing up, then so be it.[94]

To choose to go back to Britain is to do the "adult" thing; it is to choose not to remain in a state of childishness, but to embrace the maturity and the stability that come with adulthood. The return home to England is, therefore, necessary for development because the Other world is constructed as in a state of incompleteness, even of backwardness. Perhaps this is related to the popular concept of colonized places being ever in a state of childhood, a point Ashcroft has recognized in tropes of development in relation to colonized spaces.[95] Peter Pan, who chooses to remain in the Never Land, the place associated with perpetual childhood, will never grow up. There is no resolution for him – no *future* for him.

Returning home can be the only resolution to these strange adventures and curious fantasies, which is how Other worlds are constructed – as having a sense of *unreality* to them, as places hovering about the margins of reality. This draws attention to the idea of the New World as fantasy, as it was, in fact, being represented and constructed by these texts that created and perpetuated certain ideas about what these places were like and, in so doing, contributed to the idealization of Britain and British people. Writing for children in the nineteenth century, therefore, was not a culturally innocent pursuit; it had a crucial role to play in the valorization of British ideals of civilization and in the furtherance of the colonial project.

NOTES

1. Peter Hunt and Karen Sands, "The View from the Center: British Empire and Post-Empire Children's Literature", in *Voices of the Other: Children's Literature and the Postcolonial Context*, ed. Roderick McGillis (New York: Routledge, 2000), 48, 40.
2. Mary Louise Pratt, *Imperial Eyes: Travel Writing and Transculturation* (London: Routledge, 2007), 3.
3. Karen Sands-O'Connor, *Soon Come Home to This Island: West Indians in British Children's Literature* (New York: Routledge, 2007).

4. Jacqueline Lazú, "National Identity. Where the Wild, Strange and Exotic Things Are: In Search of the Caribbean in Contemporary Children's Literature", in *Children's Literature: New Approaches*, ed. Karín Lesnik-Oberstein (New York: Palgrave Macmillan, 2004), 190.
5. Patrick Brantlinger, *Rule of Darkness: British Literature and Imperialism, 1830–1914* (Ithaca: Cornell University Press, 1988), 11.
6. Lazú, "National Identity", 190.
7. Martin Green, *Dreams of Adventure, Deeds of Empire* (New York: Basic Books, 1979), 5. See also Brantlinger, 11.
8. M. Daphne Kutzer, *Empire's Children: Empire and Imperialism in Classic British Children's Books* (New York: Garland, 2000), 10.
9. Ibid., 13.
10. Ibid., 10.
11. John Rowe Townsend, *Written for Children: An Outline of English-Language Children's Literature* (Philadelphia: J.B. Lippincott, 1974), 27.
12. Examples of "Robinsonade" novels include *Coral Island* and *The Swiss Family Robinson*, neither of which were set in the Caribbean, but which were influenced by Defoe's novel nevertheless.
13. Martin Green, "The Robinson Crusoe Story", in *Imperialism and Juvenile Literature*, ed. Jeffrey Richards (Manchester: Manchester University Press, 1989), 37.
14. John Locke's *Some Thoughts Concerning Education*, published in 1693, was another influential treatise on education, which characterized the child as a *tabula rasa*.
15. Jeffrey Richards, introduction to *Imperialism and Juvenile Literature*, 8.
16. Richard Phillips, *Mapping Men and Empire: A Geography of Adventure* (London: Routledge, 1997), 24–25.
17. Green, "Robinson Crusoe Story", 35.
18. Barish Ali, "The Postcolonial Gothic: Haunting and Historicity in the Literature After Empire" (PhD diss., State University of New York at Buffalo, 2005); Rashna B. Singh, *Goodly Is Our Heritage: Children's Literature, Empire, and the Certitude of Character* (Oxford: Scarecrow Press, 2004), 151.
19. Peter Hulme, *Colonial Encounters: Europe and the Native Caribbean, 1492–1797* (London: Methuen, 1986), 176.
20. Pratt, *Imperial Eyes*, 3.
21. Green, *Dreams of Adventure*, 41.
22. Townsend, *Written for Children*, 28.
23. Daniel Defoe, *Robinson Crusoe* (Ware: Wordsworth Editions, 1994), 161. Subsequent references are taken from this edition and appear parenthetically in

the text. Based on the position of the island, some have argued that it might be Tobago, but there is no sound evidence to support this claim. See Ian Watt, *The Rise of the Novel: Studies in Defoe, Richardson and Fielding* (London: Chatto and Windus, 1957).
24. Kutzer, *Empire's Children*, 2.
25. Hulme, *Colonial Encounters*, 208, 206, 213.
26. Peter Redfield, *Space in the Tropics: From Convicts to Rockets in French Guiana* (Berkeley: University of California Press, 2000), 1; Ann Marie Fallon, *Global Crusoe: Comparative Literature, Postcolonial Theory and Transnational Aesthetics* (Farnham: Ashgate, 2011), 1.
27. Hulme, *Colonial Encounters*, 186.
28. V.S. Naipaul, "Columbus and Crusoe", in *The Overcrowded Barracoon* by V.S. Naipaul (London: André Deutsch, 1972), 206.
29. Kutzer, *Empire's Children*, 1.
30. Maria Nikolajeva, "Fairy Tale and Fantasy: From Archaic to Postmodern", *Marvels and Tales* 7, no. 1 (2003): 140.
31. Hulme, *Colonial Encounters*, 182.
32. Robert Louis Stevenson, *Treasure Island* (London: Dean and Sons, n.d.), 43. Subsequent references are taken from this edition and appear parenthetically in the text.
33. Andrew Bundy argues that the search for El Dorado is a "fragment" of the Holy Grail legend. This also contributes to the construction of the Caribbean as romantic myth. "El Dorado and the Grail Legend: Memorandum on Twinship in Wilson Harris's Body of Civilization", *Journal of Caribbean Literatures* 2, nos. 1–3 (Spring 2000): 31.
34. D. Graham Burnett, *Masters of All They Surveyed: Exploration, Geography, and a British El Dorado* (Chicago: University of Chicago Press, 2000), 25.
35. Ibid., 13.
36. William Blackburn traces the connection between the boys' adventure story and medieval romance in "Mirror in the Sea: *Treasure Island* and the Internalization of Juvenile Romance", *Children's Literature Association Quarterly* 8, no. 3 (Fall 1983): 7–12.
37. Lazú, "National Identity", 189.
38. Ibid., 190.
39. Townsend, *Written for Children*, 69.
40. C.J.W.L. Wee, *Culture, Empire, and the Question of Being Modern* (Oxford: Lexington Books, 2003), 8.
41. Diana C. Archibald, *Domesticity, Imperialism and Emigration in the Victorian Novel* (Columbia: University of Missouri Press, 2002), 16.

42. Ymitri Mathison, "Maps, Pirates and Treasure: The Commodification of Imperialism in Nineteenth-Century Boys' Adventure Fiction", in *The Nineteenth-Century Child and Consumer Culture*, ed. Dennis Denisoff (Aldershot: Ashgate, 2008), 173–74.
43. Green, *Dreams of Adventure*, 3.
44. Ibid., 49.
45. Bill Ashcroft, "'Primitive and Wingless': The Colonial Subject as Child", in *On Post-Colonial Futures: Transformations of a Colonial Culture* (New York: Continuum, 2001), 36.
46. Ibid., 39.
47. Ziauddin Sardar, *Postmodernism and the Other: The New Imperialism of Western Culture* (London: Pluto, 1998), 111.
48. Jo-Ann Wallace, "De-scribing *The Water Babies*: 'The Child' in Post-Colonial Theory", in *De-scribing Empire: Post-Colonialism and Textuality*, Chris Tiffin and Alan Lawson, eds. (London: Routledge, 1994), 176.
49. Stephen Spencer, *Race and Ethnicity: Culture, Identity and Representation* (Abingdon: Routledge, 2006), 61.
50. Ashcroft, "Primitive and Wingless", 40.
51. Gaile McGregor, *The Noble Savage in the New World Garden: Notes Toward a Syntactics of Place* (Bowling Green: Bowling Green State University Popular Press, 1988), 19.
52. Ashcroft, "Primitive and Wingless", 3.
53. Ibid., 36–37.
54. Michael Paul Rogin, *Fathers and Children: Andrew Jackson and the Subjugation of the American Indian* (New Brunswick, NJ: Transaction, 1991), xv.
55. Ibid., xxi, xxii.
56. Ashcroft, "Primitive and Wingless", 41.
57. Ibid., 36.
58. J.M. Barrie, *Peter Pan or The Boy Who Would Not Grow Up* (1904; Project Gutenberg, 2003), http://gutenberg.net.au/ebooks03/0300081h.html. Subsequent references are taken from this edition and appear parenthetically in the text.
59. Gail Ching-Liang Low, *White Skins/Black Masks: Representation and Colonialism* (London: Routledge, 1996), 62.
60. Jill P. May, "James Barrie's Pirates: *Peter Pan*'s Place in Pirate History and Lore", in *J.M. Barrie's* Peter Pan *In and Out of Time: A Children's Classic at 100*, ed. Donna R. White, C. Anita Tarr (Oxford: Scarecrow, 2006), 72. This influence is seen in the characterization of Jukes, one of the pirates "who got six dozen on the *Walrus* from FLINT" (Barrie, *Peter Pan*).

61. Christine Roth, "Looking through the Spyglass: Lewis Carroll, James Barrie, and the Empire of Childhood", in *Alice Beyond Wonderland: Essays for the Twenty-first Century*, ed. Cristopher Hollingsworth (Iowa City: University of Iowa Press, 2009), 31.
62. As Singh points out, although "black and dark are used so persistently in conjunction with Captain Hook that it is hard to avoid the racial connotations ... Captain Hook is not black, nor a redskin; he is a white man". *Goodly Is Our Heritage*, 79.
63. Karen Coats, "Blinded by the White: The Responsibilities of Race", in *Looking Glasses and Neverlands: Lacan, Desire, and Subjectivity in Children's Literature* (Iowa City: University of Iowa Press, 2004), 125.
64. Paul Fox, "The Time of His Life: Peter Pan and the Decadent Nineties", in White and Tarr, *J.M. Barrie's* Peter Pan, 39. See also Paul Fox, "Other Maps Showing Through: The Liminal Identities of Neverland", *Children's Literature Association Quarterly* 33, no. 3 (Fall 2007): 252–68.
65. Clay Kinchen Smith, "Problematizing Piccaninnies, or How J.M. Barrie Uses Graphemes to Counter Racism in *Peter Pan*", in White and Tarr, *J.M. Barrie's* Peter Pan, 107–26.
66. Roth, "Looking through the Spyglass", 32.
67. Emily Clark, "The Female Figure in J.M. Barrie's *Peter Pan*: The Small and the Mighty", in White and Tarr, *J.M. Barrie's* Peter Pan, 313.
68. Ibid., 311.
69. Carolyn Dean, "Boys and Girls and 'Boys': Popular Depictions of African-American Children and Childlike Adults in the United States, 1850–1930", *Journal of American and Comparative Cultures* 23, no. 3 (2000): 19.
70. Clark, "Female Figure", 311.
71. Christine Roth, "Babes in Boy-Land: J.M. Barrie and the Edwardian Girl", in White and Tarr, *J.M. Barrie's* Peter Pan, 57–58.
72. Anne McClintock, *Imperial Leather: Race, Gender and Sexuality in the Colonial Contest* (New York: Routledge, 1995), 21.
73. Ibid., 354.
74. Clark, "Female Figure", 308.
75. Homi K. Bhabha, *The Location of Culture* (Abingdon: Routledge, 1994).
76. Jane H. Hill, *The Everyday Language of White Racism* (Oxford: Wiley-Blackwell, 2008), 164.
77. Michelle H. Martin, "'Hey, Who's the Kid with the Green Umbrella?' Re-evaluating the Black-a-Moor and Little Black Sambo", *Lion and the Unicorn* 22, no. 2 (1998): 147.

78. Ibid., 152.
79. Heinrich Hoffmann, *Struwwelpeter* (New York: Dover, 1995), 10–13.
80. Jan Susina, "Reviving or Revising Helen Bannerman's *The Story of Little Black Sambo*: Postcolonial Hero or Signifying Monkey?", in *Voices of the Other*, 240.
81. Donnarae MacCann, *White Supremacy in Children's Literature: Characterizations of African Americans, 1830–1900* (London: Routledge, 1998), xxvi–xxvii.
82. Lewis Carroll, *Alice's Adventures in Wonderland: A Norton Critical Edition*, ed. Donald J. Gray (New York: W.W. Norton, 1992), 98. Subsequent references are taken from this edition and appear parenthetically in the text.
83. Peter Bishop, "Shangri-La Revisited: Imperialism, Landscape and Identity", in *Landscape and Identity: Perspectives from Australia: Proceedings of the 1994 Conference of the Centre for Children's Literature, University of South Australia* (Adelaide: AusLib, 1994), 21.
84. Lazú, "National Identity", 190.
85. Archibald, *Domesticity, Imperialism and Emigration*, 4–5.
86. Fallon, *Global Crusoe*, 2.
87. John R. Gillis, *Islands of the Mind: How the Human Imagination Created the Atlantic World* (New York: Palgrave Macmillan, 2004), 46, 61.
88. Archibald, *Domesticity, Imperialism and Emigration*, 28.
89. Caroline Webb, " 'I'll Be Judge, I'll Be Jury': 'Tail'-Telling, Imperialism and the Other in *Alice in Wonderland*", *Papers* 20, no. 2 (2010), 1.
90. Fiona McCulloch, *Children's Literature in Context* (London: Continuum, 2011), 50.
91. See Rose Lovell-Smith, "The Animals of Wonderland: Tenniel as Carroll's Reader", *Criticism* 45, no. 4 (2003); and Margaret Boe Birns, "Solving the Mad Hatter's Riddle", *Massachusetts Review* 25, no. 3 (1984).
92. McCulloch, *Children's Literature*, 51.
93. Webb, "I'll Be Judge", 8.
94. Karen Coats, "Child-Hating: *Peter Pan* in the Context of Victorian Hatred", in White and Tarr, *J.M. Barrie's* Peter Pan, 3–4.
95. Ashcroft, "Primitive and Wingless".

CONTRIBUTORS

GISELLE RAMPAUL is Lecturer in Literatures in English, University of the West Indies, St Augustine, Trinidad and Tobago. She is co-editor (with Geraldine Elizabeth Skeete) of *The Child and the Caribbean Imagination* and editor and producer of the podcast series *The Spaces between Words: Conversations with Writers*.

BARBARA LALLA is Professor Emerita, Language and Literature, University of the West Indies, St Augustine, Trinidad and Tobago. Her publications include *Postcolonialisms: Caribbean Rereading of Medieval English Discourse*, *Defining Jamaican Fiction: Marronage and the Discourse of Survival*, the companion volumes *Language in Exile: Three Hundred Years of Jamaican Creole* and *Voices in Exile: Jamaican Texts of the Eighteenth and Nineteenth Centuries* (co-authored with Jean D'Costa), and the novels *Cascade* and *Arch of Fire*.

RHONDA KAREEN HARRISON is a tutor in Literatures in English, University of the West Indies, St Augustine, Trinidad and Tobago.

J. VIJAY MAHARAJ is Lecturer in Literatures in English, University of the West Indies, St Augustine, Trinidad and Tobago.

JAK PEAKE is Lecturer in American Literature, University of Essex, United Kingdom.

GENEVIEVE RUTH PHAGOO is Lecturer with the English Language Foundation Programme, University of the West Indies (Evening University), St Augustine, Trinidad and Tobago.

www.ingramcontent.com/pod-product-compliance
Lightning Source LLC
Chambersburg PA
CBHW021356300426
44114CB00012B/1253